Tales of an Animal Communicator

Master Teachers

Tales of an Animal Communicator

Master Teachers

Nancy A. Kaiser

Tales of an Animal Communicator
Master Teachers
©2011 Nancy A Kaiser

Cover and text design by Janet Aiossa/Adam Hill Design

The poem "The Dash" appears in chapter 11.
Copyright 1996, Linda Ellis, Linda's Lyrics, www.lindaellis.net

Published by:
Aronya Publishing
494 Timber Lakes Dr.
Todd, NC 28684
828-265-4220
nancy@nancykaiseranimalcommunicator.com
www.aronyapublishing.com

ISBN: 978-1-61364-586-4

Printed in the United States of America

Tales of an Animal Communicator

Master Teachers

To the animals who shared their
lives & lessons & love with me.
I'm honored to share our wonderful tales.
Thank you for choosing me to be your voice!

Canine Masters

Gentle Ben
My Little Shadow (Shadow The Perfect)
Sweet Licorice (Licorice)
Heavenly Hana (Hana Banana)
Simply Saba (Saba Baby)

Equine Masters

Jolly Man (Jolly)
Mr. Watch It (Watch It)
Just Like Pop (Junior)
Truffles (Squiggles The Special)
Because Of Love (Love)
Truly Inspired (Dash)
Fashionably Late (Randy)
Follow Your Heart (Stormy)

Feline Masters

Rainbow
Bandit Hope (Bandit)
Butch Cassidy (Butchie)
Lucky
Petal
Merlin
Crystal

Contents

Introduction

I'm soon turning 60, which I find astonishing. The years have flown by so fast, creating an amazing journey that has brought me to this point in my life. Everything up until now needed to occur before I could begin writing the book I've always intended to write. Everything in the Universe always happens for a reason and in its perfect timing, and this book's timing is now.

I cannot remember a time in my life when I haven't been fascinated with animals – all types of animals. When I was very young, my folks took my brother and me to see "Patty the Porpoise" on a Florida vacation. I fell in love with the bottlenose dolphin and I begged my parents to go every night. It was as though I'd reconnected with an old friend. Eventually, the attraction owner took pity on them and waived the entrance fee.

I came out of the womb with an innate love of horses, which no one in my family understood, since there were no horse people in our family. My love for dogs was no surprise, because both my parents loved dogs: we had Collies for many years and then Labradors.

My folks were willing to give me riding lessons, but our local park system's stable had a minimum age requirement of eight years old. It seemed an eternity until I turned eight. From the age of six, my mom would take me to gaze longingly at these magnificent creatures. I imagined one day riding into the sunset like Roy Rogers & Trigger. Happy trails to me….

Five years into my riding lessons, my dream of a horse of my own was realized for my 13th birthday. I've had one or more horses ever since, and each has contributed immensely to the person I am today. The sense of responsibility I learned from caring for my own horses has served me well throughout my life. I wish more kids could have a horse to teach them, but horses have become very expensive. I'm extremely grateful that I grew up when I did.

From childhood through college, I successfully showed my jumpers and hunters, as well as others' horses. Training and jumping horses was my passion from the start. It is the one constant in my life that always brings me great joy no matter what else is confronting me. There is no better therapy for me than being on the back of a horse.

After high school, I choose to follow my father and grandfather into pharmacy. This was a mental decision based on my belief that as a pharmacist I'd always be able to support my horse. I thought I'd made a very mature decision that would chart the course for the rest of my life. I decided against a career training horses because I never wanted to jeopardize my one joy in life. I never wanted to resent going to the barn.

My pharmacy career robbed me of spending every day at the barn. Luckily, my heart knew I was meant to work with horses and put me back on target when I fell in love and married an equine veterinarian. I left pharmacy to manage our vet practice, equine hospital, and horse farm in central New Jersey. I was back where I needed to be, whether I knew it or not.

For the next 27 years I worked alongside my husband to care for our practice, hospital, and farm; our horses, dogs and cats; and our clients' horses. Working with horses is an all-consuming occupation, a lifestyle. Even during the most stressful of times, I was happier than I'd ever been working as a pharmacist. My heart was so right about where I belonged.

In the early '90s, I was shown my true path by one of my husband's patients, a Quarter Horse filly foal named *Because Of Love*. Love helped me uncover my abilities in animal communication and healing, which changed the course of my life forever.

All my life I'd carried on conversations with animals, which I thought were imaginary chit-chats. Animals were my friends, and I talked with them about everything. It never occurred to me that these dialogues were anything more than fantasies. A perfect example is recorded in my poem, "Lacey," composed for a school assignment 45 years ago. The poem resurfaced when both my parents died on our farm in 2000. I'd totally forgotten about it, but Mom had saved it in a scrapbook of memories for me. The subject was picking out our new Collie puppy.

Lacey

The snow was deep,
The wind was fierce,
But neither kept me away.
With frozen hands and frozen feet,
I hurried to the cage.

There she was so small and meek,
But I knew no other like her
I would meet.
I watched and stared
And laughed and sighed.

As we walked on,
My mom, my dad and I,
I knew no other dog would do.
No other but my little friend,
Who waited for me 'round the bend.

I quick ran back.
And there she was,
Sitting,
Saying,
Won't you take me home today?

At last, my mom and dad agreed.
No other dog like her had they seen.
So, now my little Lacey
Was coming home with me.

What I believed was born of my imagination, Love taught me was reality. I had truly heard Lacey's plea to come home with us. I'd received a telepathic communication whether I knew it or not, or believed it or not. As a 15-year-old with Lacey, I didn't realize telepathically communicating with animals was possible. As a 42-year-old, a generous soul came to teach me what's truly possible and altered my beliefs dramatically.

I began working with many of my husband's patients, who were instrumental to my development. Countless times over the years we'd commented, "If we could only ask them what happened, where they hurt, etc." Now, we could. Various animals started appearing to teach me about each new healing modality I was learning. My learning curve was quite rapid, because it was in perfect timing for me. Not only would I know what the animals were saying, thinking, and feeling, but I could offer solutions to my clients for the challenges they faced.

Seven years ago, my husband retired. We sold our farm and moved to the Blue Ridge Mountains of North Carolina. Six weeks after our arrival, my husband walked out – and I began the most painful, yet transformative, chapter of my life to date. My journey through the darkness is retold in my book, *Letting Go: An Ordinary Woman's Extraordinary Journey of Healing & Transformation*, which was published in June '08. While not the book I'd always intended to write, *Letting Go* needed to be written first to allow me to heal from my "dark night of the soul."

Looking back, I can honestly say there isn't anything I'd change – not even the pain of my divorce, which resulted in amazing personal growth that has freed me to focus on my animal communication and healing work. My journey of healing also unearthed my gift for writing (which I was totally unaware of), making the time perfect to begin my series of books of animal tales.

In 1904, the Pawnee Chief Letakota-Lesa stated, "In the beginning of all things, wisdom and knowledge were with the animals; for Tirawa, the One Above, did not speak directly to man. He sent certain animals to tell men that he showed himself through the beasts, and that from them, and from the stars and the sun and the moon, man should learn. Tirawa spoke to man through his works."

Master Teachers is the first book of a series and contains the tales of those "certain animals" that shared incredible lives and lessons with me. All but one lived with me, and all willingly gave their love, support, and guidance to this lucky human. In an effort to provide continuity and flow, their tales will follow mostly chronologically, yet intermingling just as their lives did. They are my "master teachers." I'm humbled that they chose me, and honored to share their tales and teachings with you.

The wealth of knowledge that I've acquired through my work with animals is far too much for one book, hence the series. My third book, *Tales of an Animal Communicator ~ Being A Clear Voice*, will focus on all I've learned from my clients' animals. I believe that the animals and people I'm meant to help find their way to me. I also believe part of my mission is to share their teachings so all may benefit from their wisdom. For now, let's saddle-up and meet my *Master Teachers*. Hang on; it's been quite a ride!

Chapter 1

∞

My Epiphany

In April of 1993, my husband ran into an old friend at our local feed store. Boots was a local Quarter Horse trainer and asked Bob for a second opinion on a week-old filly foal that had been born with scoliosis – curvature of the spine. Little did I know that this friend's innocent request for help would introduce me to one of the most influential animals in my life.

Bob examined the filly and really couldn't recommend euthanasia, although several other veterinarians had. Bob didn't feel the foal was suffering inhumanely, even though her condition prevented her from getting up on her own or walking once helped up. Boots was willing to give the foal a chance and try whatever Bob suggested.

The horse's attitude is instrumental in making these types of decisions. Is it willing to try? Is it allowing us to help them? Does it want our help? Our conclusions are based on intuition and years of experience. Although we'd never seen a foal with this rare condition, she was answering "yes" to all our questions. The filly displayed a remarkably strong will and incredible determination.

My role in this tale started out quite innocuously. I accompanied my husband to assist in any way I could. Mostly I lent moral support, peppered with expertise from raising numerous foals on our own farm. It was heart-breaking to watch the filly struggle to stand, and once up, not be able to move around and play.

Young foals often nurse every half-hour. Two hours would be the longest one would let a foal go between meals, for both the foal's and the mare's sake. The filly had to be helped up in order to suckle, which meant someone needed to be available at least 12 times day and night. Having cared for numerous critically ill foals at our hospital, I knew just how exhausting this was. Nevertheless, Boots was willing as long as the filly was.

It was intriguing to see the filly attract specific people to her. A team gathered, each with skills to contribute. The team was anchored by Boots and her husband, who were willing to give her a chance, despite having no guarantees. My husband contributed his medical expertise and became the guiding, positive force through it all. A veterinary chiropractor performed spinal adjustments, while another friend and client, Kathy, offered TTouch treatments, an innovative method of energetic healing.

Boots called the filly *Wild Woman*, due to the antics she'd go through trying to play in a less-than-perfect body. I have to admit that I couldn't see how this was ever going to be a normal, useful horse. I felt so sorry for her, but everyone wanted to try, including the filly. Everyone donated their time and services. We all were involved for one reason: to help the filly. This was so refreshing in a society of "What's in it for me?" Our love of horses provided our guiding light.

The filly was otherwise very healthy and growing just like any other Quarter Horse foal would, which made it even more difficult for her and those helping her. I knew everyone was hoping that time and Nature would correct her spine so she could begin to live a normal life. She tried so hard, but I could feel how frustrated she was with her uncooperative body.

Around two months old, the filly grew depressed and uncooperative. Bob examined her and found her physically healthy, except for her scoliosis. Without telling my husband and me, Kathy had an animal communicator working with the filly as well. The things she reported the filly had told her were truly remarkable, such as: she had come to teach, she was starting to wonder whether all the suffering was worth it, and she didn't like people feeling sorry for her. The filly's last comment shook me. I was guilty of that, and I felt awful. The communicator said that the filly had decided to try awhile longer, but we had to be more positive around her.

In early June, the communicator was coming to the area to teach a workshop with the filly's chiropractor at Kathy's farm. The communicator was going to Boots' farm the day before the workshop to work with the foal. As luck or fate would have it, we were called out on a colic emergency and couldn't meet her. We went to Kathy's the next day for the workshop. Bob was becoming interested in chiropractic and wanted to observe the chiropractor in action. I went along for the ride, my curiosity piqued about the communicator.

After watching the workshop, I knew this was what I was meant to do. It was as though a cosmic two-by-four hit me in my consciousness – *I'd communicate for the filly*! I'd communicate for *all* animals; their thoughts, desires, needs, feelings, everything. This would become my life's work.

Driving home from Kathy's, I was overcome with the first true knowing I'd experienced in my 42 years. Communicating with animals was a learnable skill. I knew it was what I was meant to do with my life. To finally be rid of the barrier that had always separated me from the animals would be phenomenal. I was third in my class in pharmacy school, so I was confident I'd be able to learn this. No matter what was needed, I *had* to learn to talk to animals. Step one was finding a teacher and finding one *now*.

The only person I knew who was psychic was a gal I'd met seven months earlier in New York City. We'd sat next to one another at a meeting and developed an immediate connection, which I thought odd since we were so different – or at least that's what I thought. She was a psychologist and clairvoyant counselor.

I called her the next day and explained about my epiphany and my need for a teacher. She laughed, telling me that she'd been getting a message that a surprise was coming her way. She figured I was it. She was not an animal communicator, but was the ideal person to help me awaken these talents that were buried until the timing was right.

Thus began my weekly forays into Manhattan that lasted over a year. I had neither the time nor money to do this, but somehow I found both. When the student is ready, the teacher(s) appear. I must have been over-ready because the Universe began showering me with incredible teachers and experiences.

Wild Woman was two months old when I began my trips to the city. I couldn't wait to become a more active member of her team. I had no idea how long it would take for that to happen. I had homework from the start. Devouring the books I was asked to read was the easy part. The first thing necessary for anything psychic is a quiet mind. Learning to quiet my left brain was excruciatingly difficult for me. Meditation is the doorway to a quiet mind; twice daily was my prescription.

I held the responsibilities of three people on our farm. Finding the time to meditate once a day (let alone twice) was a challenge, but my desire to talk to the filly motivated me. The exercise I was taught, using colors, really helped me. I'd go into the bedroom, close the door, and try to meditate. When I think back to those days, I smile. Practice definitely makes perfect. Today, I can communicate while driving if need be.

One early morning between my first and second sessions in the city, we got a phone call from the local police. Bob was their go-to vet for any large-animal crisis. Someone called them regarding a doe deer roaming around their yard with a fawn hanging out of her hind end. This was a rare event for us, working with a wild one.

As we rushed to her, I wished I could communicate to her that we were coming to help. We found the doe lying down covered by a blanket to keep her calm. Two cops were standing guard over her. I went to her head and sat stroking her neck while my husband removed the already decaying fawn. She had obviously been in trouble for quite a while. She somehow knew to come out of the woods to "ask" the humans for help.

Bob gave her injections of antibiotics to combat infection, cortisone to help with shock, and a rabies vaccine. She never moved a muscle the entire time. She knew we'd come to help her. I joked that she'd be the healthiest doe in New Jersey. One of the cops had a friend who kept deer in an enclosure, but Bob and I wanted to give her time to recover and remain wild. We agreed to return in a couple of hours to check on her.

Before we left her, I cautiously pulled the blanket from her face. I just had to meet her. Those amazing doe eyes were filled with sadness, but also gratitude. I thanked her for allowing us to help her while I continued to stroke her lovingly. Our souls touched. This was one of the most rewarding things I'd ever done. There was no material gain, yet I felt spiritually wealthy from the experience.

I was filled with bad feelings about the cop with the friend. I didn't want this doe to lose her wild life, albeit in New Jersey. I decided to attempt to communicate with her, although I had no idea how. I went into the bedroom, quieted my mind as best I could, and "told" her that if she felt well enough she needed to go into the woods, otherwise the other people would take her to live in an enclosure. We'd come back soon to check on her, and if she wasn't well enough, we'd bring her to our hospital until she recovered. I promised I wouldn't let her end up caged for the rest of her life.

While I had tons of things to do on the farm, the wait to return to the doe seemed like an eternity. Bob had to make some vet calls first. About two hours later, we returned to find the doe and the blanket missing. I was very worried that the cop had come back earlier and taken her. Why else was the blanket missing? Bob called the police and was told they hadn't been back yet. The missing blanket had me doubting their information. I hoped I'd get to the truth the following day in my second session in the city.

I shared my experiences of the preceding week with my teacher. She couldn't believe how much support I was getting from the Universe. I voiced my concern about the disappearance of the doe and the missing blanket. I wondered if the doe had heard my message. My teacher asked her and she replied, Yes. Then, my teacher told me to communicate with the deer. I thought she was kidding. I had only been studying with her for one week. But she wasn't laughing.

Despite not having a clue about what I was doing, I quieted my mind and started a dialogue just like I'd done all my life. What I hadn't expected was to "hear" a response. The doe said, *I'm fine and am forever grateful to you and the kind man. By the way, the blanket stayed on for two miles before it fell off.* Wow! I felt another of those knowings. I knew that I'd done this before. I didn't know where or when, but it was very familiar. There was a buzz of energy throughout my body.

We discussed the other happenings during the week and then I told my teacher about a dear friend's horse that was having surgery the next day for an ankle injury. Unknown to my teacher, the horse also had an unusual heart condition. Immediately, she was concerned about the anesthesia because his heart was not normal. I was astonished.

My teacher started to say she'd talk with the horse, but quickly backed off. Her Guides told her that I had to counsel him, because I would know exactly what to tell him. Whatever I did would make all the difference.

Were they for real? This was a life-or-death deal with a dear friend's extremely valuable show jumper. My teacher told me not to argue with destiny.

For the rest of the day I felt a heavy burden of responsibility. I already had plans to drive with my friend to the university hospital the next morning. How coincidental that I'd be there after the surgery. I worried that the Universe was making a terrible mistake asking a novice to assume such an important role.

After dinner, I went into the bedroom, followed my color meditation exercise, quieted my mind, and started a conversation with my friend's horse. At least, I hoped I was. It was a one-way conversation: me talking but hearing nothing in return. I described everything that would be done with him the next day. I wanted him to know exactly what to expect – no surprises.

I spent a lot of time on the anesthesia portion, especially how to wake up from it. Coming out of anesthesia is extremely dangerous for horses. Having a 1,000- to 1,200-pound animal flailing around can be hazardous to everyone. With his heart condition, it was crucial that he accept the loss of mobility. Horses' sense of safety resides in their ability to get up and run – their fright-flight response. Anesthesia robs that from them and can create panic. I told him not to try to get up until he felt really awake; there was no hurry. He should simply stay down until he knew he could stand, then just get up easily. Then I asked my Guides for a sign or something to help me know whether I'd actually communicated with the horse.

Afterward, I realized that the Universe was absolutely correct in its assessment – big surprise! Given my years of assisting with the surgeries that Bob had performed, I was knowledgeable about equine surgery. My teacher was not. She wouldn't have known any of the specifics that would help him cope with the next day's events, whereas I'd helped recover numerous horses from anesthesia without any injuries. My life had prepared me for just this moment.

I couldn't sleep the whole night. I couldn't wait to get to the hospital to see how the surgery went. I felt like I had before my first few horse shows as a kid: happy, anxious to go, confident. I had no worries. I thought about another of my friend's wonderful jumpers that had received joint injections years earlier. I had had a strong foreboding beforehand, which I didn't share with my friend. The mare developed a joint infection and died, despite a very long and expensive fight to save her. I never forgave myself for not speaking up about my feelings. I felt none of those feelings this night.

About 5 am, I heard my horse, Junior, running around the front pasture near our house. I looked out the window and saw that he was genuinely frightened – but of what? I walked outside to try to calm him before he hurt himself. As I climbed the fence, I saw the threat. I was staring into the eyes of a doe deer! I just smiled and thanked my Guides for the sign.

No, I don't believe it was the same doe, but I do believe this doe offered to be my sign as a thank-you for helping one of their own. I didn't have much longer to wait until my friend and I began the two-hour trip to the university hospital. I really couldn't wait to get there now.

I could sense the worry in my friend as we drove. Given that she was such a close friend, I opened up to her about my recent epiphany and my communication with her horse. I wasn't sure what she thought of my confession, but she listened intently. She was the first person besides my husband who knew what I was up to.

Like a good movie script that intensifies the drama, nothing flowed smoothly that day. We had unusually heavy traffic that delayed our arrival (which really didn't matter since the surgery started late and took much longer than expected). The staff at the hospital didn't seem to know anything. They couldn't answer any of my friend's questions about her horse. All of these things compounded her worry and concern. The tension was alarming. I was so glad I was there for her.

Unlike her, I was feeling great. None of these things had an effect on the positive feelings I was having. It was as though I knew everything was fine no matter what happened – which for me was not the norm. Back in the day, Bob said I worried enough for the entire nation, and he was right. So, this was a big change for me.

Eventually, the surgeon found us and put an end to my friend's suffering. The surgery was more involved than he anticipated, but he successfully repaired the ankle. I couldn't wait, so I asked how the horse handled the anesthesia. He quickly replied, "Like a champ! He got up so easy." My friend and I exchanged glances and smiles, acknowledging the success of the secret she and I shared.

The surgeon took us to the horse. The minute I saw him, I knew he'd been out of surgery for quite a while. He was way too stable for a horse that had just come out of anesthesia. It was apparent that the staff had really blown this one and caused my friend unnecessary anguish. It provided a wonderful contrast for me to learn from – her intense worry and my knowing that all was well. The longer we visited with him, the better my friend and her beloved horse seemed.

As for me, I was flying high with the realization that I could talk with Wild Woman without further delay. The Universe was right after all; it knew that it wasn't sending a novice to do an experienced communicator's job. The occurrences of the past week were staggering for me. Obviously, there was a place outside my conscious mind that knew exactly how to communicate telepathically with animals. My job was to bring that buried knowledge out from its hiding place into my conscious mind. I wondered what else might be hiding along with it. I couldn't wait to find out. I now understood that the rest of my life would be forever altered by the events of this astounding week.

Chapter 2

∞

Because Of Love

My experience with my friend's jumper showed me that I was indeed communicating with an animal. But while the horse had no problem hearing me, I wasn't hearing anything back. I decided just to be grateful that I was sending the message properly. Receiving was obviously going to take a little longer than a week to learn. I'd give myself whatever time was necessary to learn how to receive a telepathic communication. Knowing the animals understood the information I sent was inspiring.

I communicated with the filly as much as possible, but a one-way conversation makes it hard to know if there's actually been an exchange. I went to Boots' farm as often as my obligations would allow. Even though I wanted to be there daily, I had a vet office, hospital, and farm that required my attention, too. But other situations came up with some of Bob's patients that allowed me to practice my newly discovered talent.

One afternoon, I tried hands-on energy work that I'd been reading about. My intuition guided my hands as I "applied" the energy to the filly while she was lying down. She began nuzzling me, seemingly enjoying it. I asked her if it was helping, but again I couldn't hear her reply. I didn't have a clue what I was doing, but the foal's positive reaction was good enough for me. I couldn't be frustrated; it had only been a few weeks since my epiphany.

The next day during our third session, I asked my teacher if the filly had felt anything from my hands-on energy work. She assured me that she had received great benefit. Her Guides informed her that we were to expect the unexpected. Okay. The filly confided to her that she wanted to get out of her "bad body." I certainly understood it, but I hoped she didn't give up yet. My teacher also told me that I had saved the jumper's life at the university hospital – good to know.

When I got back to our farm, Bob told me the filly was much improved, especially her attitude. That night I asked her about the energy work. I still didn't hear her reply, but I sensed her answers, which was new. The foal was standing the next day while I flowed energy, making it very difficult for this novice healer. At night, I requested that she stay down while I worked on her.

The next day, Boots shared that the filly had gotten up by herself a couple of times. This was monumental! My intuition guided my hands to areas in need of healing energy. The filly stayed down and was almost asleep when I finished. I communicated a thank you and a hope that I'd helped. She let out a huge sigh that I interpreted as "yes." At night, I asked my Guides to show me a sign to let me know that I was actually doing something.

Boots called first thing to tell us that the filly had gotten up twice already on her own. I was elated and thanked my Guides for my sign. When I got to Boots', the filly nickered and struggled to stand, showing me what she could do. I knew she was extremely proud, so I made a big fuss. I did the energy work while she stood perfectly still the entire time. It was the longest I'd seen her stay standing. She was very affectionate, giving me equine kisses as I was leaving. Boots reported later that the filly got up five or six times throughout the day. Needless to say, she and her husband were thrilled.

I decided after doing the energy work the following day that I'd ask some questions while I was with the filly. This time I heard rapid answers. Is my touch helping you? *Yes, it relaxes me and the pain lessens. Please don't stop.* Are you happy that you can nurse whenever you want now? *Yes, and so is my mother.* Do you have much pain? *Pretty much all the time, but everyone is helping me, so it's okay.* You aren't planning on leaving, are you? *Not yet. I've got too much to teach.* You've taught me so much already. I don't want you to stay just for me. *You're not my only student.* I figured as much.

I wasn't sure if it was truly the filly speaking or just my imagination creating the responses since her answers were what I wanted to hear. As I got up to leave, she stretched her nose towards me as if to say "Thank you." I gave her a hug and kiss, thanking her for all she'd taught me already.

The next day, the filly was up when I arrived but not standing well. The combination of her growing, muscular Quarter Horse body and being up more often and for longer periods was taking a toll on her. She didn't care that I had come. When I tried to reposition her weaker hind leg she got angry and bit at me. I apologized. Once she lay down, I did some energy work and then left. Bob had been having concerns about her right hind leg, and today I saw what he meant. It was worrisome.

Boots had decided to register the filly with the name *Because Of Love*. How appropriate since everyone was drawn to her just for that reason. I'd always disliked the name Wild Woman, because I knew her antics stemmed from her frustrating life in a less-than-perfect body. From now on, she'd be known as Love. How perfect!

Given the positive results I was seeing, I worked daily with the filly despite all my other responsibilities. During our next session, my teacher suggested applying the energy long-distance. Do what? She explained that I didn't need to be with the filly to help her energetically. It was called long-distance healing. This would be a huge help since Boots' farm was a half-hour drive each way. Time was always my enemy on our farm.

My teacher also said that I'd made all the difference with the foal, which encouraged me. But there were others sharing their skills with Love as well. She was receiving spinal adjustments by the chiropractor. Kathy was contributing her TTouch sessions, and Kathy's communicator was occasionally talking with her. Bob lent his medical expertise whenever necessary along with his undying positive outlook. Sadly, Bob was going to get infinitely more involved given the increasing weakness in her right hind leg.

Being the most inexperienced member of Love's team – at least as far as my communication and healing skills were concerned – I was worried about making mistakes with her. My teacher reassured me that I wouldn't make any mistakes with Love. She said, "We make the right mistakes at the right time with the right people and animals." I hoped so. My teacher wanted to meet Love, so our next session would be at Boots'. I'd have to be her chauffeur since she was a true city-dweller, with no vehicle.

Doing Love's energy work via long-distance techniques saved so much time. I only hoped it was as effective. Bob felt Love's right hind leg needed support before something tragic happened. Her ever-increasing weight was compromising it. If she damaged her hind leg, it would mean the end for her. I asked if she would allow us to put a splint on her leg. *If you think it will help.* She was very cooperative while we worked on her, but the following day she told me she felt crummy all over.

Splinting only the lower portion of Love's leg wasn't helping. Bob added a removable cast that fit over her hock, reinforcing her entire leg. Once again, Love was very cooperative. I knew the up-front explanation of the cast helped her understand and accept the cumbersome support apparatus she was now carrying around.

It was time for our session at Boots'. My teacher met Love and gave us a lot of information from her Guides. She told us we needed to do something to support Love's weight so her leg could heal. She said, "Love needs one of those gizmos (carts) used to support the rear end of a paralyzed dog." Well, we all started with a million reasons why it wouldn't work with a horse, but she wouldn't listen. My teacher was adamant. Love needed a gizmo; end of discussion.

Bob and I left for four days in the Adirondacks. I was exhausted from the double round-trips into Manhattan the day before, but I felt it had been a very worthwhile day. We took a mini-vacation hiking in Nature that renewed me. I didn't talk to Love until we got home, apologizing for my silence. I asked how she was feeling. *My shoulders bother me and I feel over-all crummy.* Are you in pain? *I just ache all over.* Is the brace helping? *Yes.*

Boots relayed that Kathy's communicator told the filly that if she decided to leave, it wouldn't be fair. This really upset me. I told Love that I disagreed with the other one who talks to her. What she told her was wrong. I told Love not to worry about us. If she were ready to move on, then she should. We loved her and would miss her, but we'd understand. Do you want me to explain this to the others? *No, not now.*

Bob and I caught up with Kathy at Boots'. We stopped obsessing about the right hind leg and looked at the whole filly. Love needed assistance with the ever-increasing weight of her growing Quarter Horse body. We finally accepted that she'd never get outside on her own. The cart's time had come. I don't think any of us wanted to admit that the cart might be the best we could give her. We wanted more for this wonderful horse that had come to teach us, but it was time to get realistic. Our job was to give her the best life experience possible. She deserved no less. Slings have been made for horses, but a cart was another animal altogether.

Before bed, I talked with Love about the cart, asking if she would tolerate it. *I don't know if it's worth trying anymore.* I reminded her that she'd come to teach and asked if her lessons were taught. *No. I really want to go outside.* I asked if she would keep trying if we could get her outside. *I'll try if I can go out soon.* I could feel how desperate she was to leave the confines of her stall. I'd been so focused on her condition that I hadn't given much thought to the fact that all she knew of life was her stall. None of us really knew what was possible, but I promised Love I'd do whatever was necessary to get her outside. *Really? I promise!* Love taught us that possibilities are unlimited with an open mind.

Besides being a terrific horse vet, Bob was extremely handy. He started building the cart, because he wanted me to be able to keep my promise to Love. See, everything because of love. Having no model to work from, and other clients' horses to take care of, made its construction even more difficult. I told Love that Bob was building something that would help her go outside, but it might take some adjustments to get it right. Would she cooperate when we were ready? *Yes, hurry!* I explained she needed to act sensible, so she didn't get injured. *Yes, just hurry, hurry.*

I'm sure it seemed like eons to her even though animals have no sense of time, but four days later Bob finished the cart. It was late in the day and Love didn't seem interested when we arrived with the cart. Eventually, she got up. We attached the cart, but it bent. So, it went back to our farm for some further work.

Bob repaired Love's gizmo and returned the next day. I had other commitments, so I couldn't help. It worked this time. Bob was so excited as he painted a picture for me. Love galloped out and started eating grass. In her excitement, she moved around too quickly and broke a wheel. Bob said she loved it! I wished I could have been there to see her, but Bob deserved to share this special event with Love. He was always positive no matter what. He never gave up, just like Love.

I talked with Love that night. *It was wonderful. I'm so sorry I broke it, but I got so excited.* I told her it was okay and that I was so happy for her. I explained how hard Bob had worked on it and asked what she thought of him. *He is the only one who has been positive throughout. He always has an answer for each new problem.* Throughout all of this, we continued with a collection of splints, casts, and braces, trying to strengthen Love's right hind leg. I applied hands-on healing energy when I was with her and long-distance healing energy as often as possible when I couldn't be with her.

Love's foray outside had everyone energized, including the filly. Boots located someone who could build a cart in heavier metal. I explained to Love that someone was building a stronger cart for her and she had to be patient and not get disheartened. *I want to go out.* Bob worked on repairing his while we waited. I could tell Love was getting discouraged. Animals have no sense of time. All they know is now. I kept encouraging her to be patient. *I need to go out. I don't know how much longer I can wait.* Love felt really down.

After hearing how depressed Love was, Bob brought his cart back while I was in the city with my teacher. Apparently, he pressed her; Love got angry, and then he got angry. For the first time, I sensed frustration in Bob. He said, "She laid down in the barn and wouldn't try." I went upstairs to get Love's version. What happened? *I have to go out!* Bob tried today, and he said you wouldn't try. *It hurt my stifles. It was humiliating.* Bob wants to know how he can help you. *I don't care about the leg braces. I just want to go out.*

The stifle joint is in the horse's hind leg and is comparable to the knee of the front leg. The stifle is unique in that it contains a locking apparatus that allows the horse to relax all its muscles and sleep while standing; a definite advantage in the wild. For whatever reason, Love's stifles were bothering her that day.

I asked Bob what happened. What did they do to Love? Bob confessed they'd kind of forced and manhandled her, i.e., disrespected her. They'd tried to carry her. "Well, no wonder! Love needs to do it herself," I declared. The breadth of her emotions continually amazed me. Love wanted so desperately to be independent. It broke my heart to know she never would be, but I couldn't let her sense that from me. I'd learned early on how much she picked up from those around her. I wasn't going to make that mistake again.

I continued to encourage Love to be patient while I applied healing energy and waited for the stronger cart to arrive. *Again, I don't think I can stay much longer.* Is your mission done? *No, not really.* Didn't you come to teach me? *Yes.* Have I learned all I should? *No.* Did you come to teach others? *Yes. Boots, Bob, Kathy, the other communicator, and my chiropractor.* Have they learned everything? *No.* Could you please be patient with people and stay to help us? *I'm trying, but I'm so sad and tired. I don't know if I can make it. If I can't get outside, I don't want to live within four walls, no matter what.* I spent longer than usual, flooding Love with healing energy, trying to heal her emotional state as well as her imperfect body.

Boots called to say the filly seemed really alert, happy, and energized – very different from the last week or so. She said Love was lying down just like a normal foal would, with all four legs tucked underneath her. This was a momentous first. I asked Love what had changed. Excitedly, she confessed, *I can feel things in both my hind legs that I've never felt before. My bad leg doesn't bother me, because I know where it is now. Is it painful? No, it's just sensations.*

The new cart still wasn't ready, so we went over with Bob's cart. I sensed Love's excitement. Bob wanted me to handle her head, because he knew I'd let Love do whatever she wanted to. This was her deal. We're just there to support her. My promise had been kept as I helped her outside. She was amazing – flying as fast as she could to the grass to graze. I was ecstatic to finally see her out of her stall.

We headed back in when Bob felt she'd done enough. Love cantered back in, breaking another wheel and bending the cart. She did it on her own. She had an amazingly strong will and endless determination. I was so proud of her, and of us. Bob said she was the most alert he'd seen her, with a very normal head and neck carriage; all were encouraging observations. She stayed up for quite a while – meaning she wasn't too tired. I, on the other hand, was exhausted from her Herculean effort.

Her short time out had her sweating and breathing like she'd run five miles. I told her I was appalled at how hard she had to work. *I don't mind. It's my turn to work. You've been doing all the work 'til now.* As I talked with her, I felt a buzz down both of my legs that I interpreted as the new sensations Love was feeling. I thought I'd be happier seeing her outside, but knowing how many people she had to rely on was disheartening. She'd never be truly independent, which I knew was so crucial to her. We were so much alike, this remarkable filly and I.

The next day, Love was exhilarated when I asked how her muscles felt after all her exertion. *They're a little stiff, but that's okay. Being outside makes my lungs expand, which feels good.* I told her the new cart was finally ready. *I know it's outside my stall.* I told her we'd be out the next afternoon.

I'm sure it will take some adjustments. Please be patient. *Hurry.*

The stronger cart was donated by the generous builder. Love attracted the most wonderful people to her and brought out the best in everyone. The cart supported her weight and had wheels that swiveled. She galloped out, calling to the other horses. She seemed so proud of herself.

Later, I asked what she was screaming at the other horses. *When I told them you were going to fix me so I could go out, they told me people wouldn't if it was too hard. I wanted to show them they were wrong about people.* The older horses' low opinion of people broke my heart, but I certainly understood it. I asked how she felt. Did anything hurt? *I don't really know how I feel. I'm enjoying it so much. I don't focus on anything negative.* Smart gal. Do you feel your hind legs? *Not much, just a little. I use my hips to move them when I'm going fast enough. That's why I go fast.*

We got Love out again the following day. She was elated, moving fast and attempting to buck and play just like any four-month-old foal. She almost got away from me. I was leaving for a weekend workshop at the Omega Institute in Rhinebeck, New York, the next morning. She'd be without my help the next few days. I'm not sure who was happier about her adventures outside, Love or me. No doubt Love, because I knew this was the best we could give her, while she had no expectation for her future. Animals know nothing of future. For Love, *now* was all she knew – an important lesson we humans could learn from our animal brothers and sisters.

Chapter 3

∞

Unearthing Buried Treasure

*A*s I drove towards the Omega Institute for my weekend work shop, *Mother Earth Spirituality*, I thought about the joy of seeing Love so happy for the first time in her life. It was a tempered joy, because I knew this was the best we were ever going to be able to give her, and it was so much less than this remarkable soul deserved. I was so grateful that animals only focus on the present, because her future was disheartening, in my opinion.

I pondered my decision to take this course taught by Lakota Sioux lawyer and author, Ed McGaa, also known as Eagle Man. A friend had mentioned the Omega Institute when I told her about my newly discovered skill of communicating with animals. She thought I might be interested in what Omega offered. When the catalog came, there were hundreds of workshops to choose from; some were fairly mainstream, others quite unusual.

After looking through the catalog, Ed's course was the only one that really attracted me. My left brain got involved and began trying to figure out which I *should* take rather than which I *wanted* to take. I went back and forth between courses on meditation and others that I thought might speed my progress in learning telepathic communication.

I'd already given up trying to take an animal communication course with America's leading communicator, Penelope Smith. After four unsuccessful attempts to take her course, I received the Universe's message that I didn't need to *learn* to communicate. I just needed to reawaken the knowledge and *remember*.

Luckily, my heart wrested the decision away from my left brain, so I was about to meet a culture that believed what I'd always felt deep within. Ed required all participants to read one of his books beforehand. Reading *Rainbow Tribe* was like reading about me. Maybe I wasn't so odd after all. There were others who believed what I did. After 42 years, I finally vanquished my feelings of isolation thanks to Eagle Man's book. I couldn't wait to meet Eagle Man and learn all he'd come to share.

I called Bob after I got settled in at Omega. He informed me that Love was down most of the day and didn't use her hind legs at all when she was in her cart. I connected with her next. What's wrong? *I pulled all the muscles in my back bucking yesterday. It was foolish, but so much fun. I just wanted to play.* Her desire to play like a normal foal was encouraging to see, but at the same time sad. I applied lots of long-distance healing energy all along Love's back before turning in.

By the end of the first day, I was reeling with all that I discovered I had in common with Native American Indians. It was surreal. Ed's assistant, Catherine, and I had a real connection. She was an ex-Wall Streeter, who'd moved to Arizona. When I shared with her about my recent epiphany, Catherine asked if I could speak with her dog, Haley, who disappeared in Mexico not long ago. I told her I'd be happy to try, but reminded her I was just a novice.

The big news for the day was that Eagle Man was leading a Sweat Lodge Ceremony after dark. I'd learned about this purification ceremony in *Rainbow Tribe*, but I never expected to experience one. As we gathered for the ceremony, multiple large bolts of lightning struck with no accompanying thunder or rain. Normally I'm afraid of lightning, but surprisingly I continued walking to the lodge with no apprehension whatsoever.

It was a huge lodge, accommodating 30 to 35 people. Ed had to perform two ceremonies to handle all who wanted to take part. Suddenly, a bat circled clockwise around the lodge. Eagle Man remarked that the earlier lightning and the clockwise-circling bat were signs from Mother Nature validating the importance of our ceremony. Bats represent rebirth to the Native American, which fit perfectly. The Sweat Lodge Ceremony purifies mind, body, and spirit. Exiting the lodge represents being reborn from the womb of Mother Earth.

I entered early in the first group and sat along the back edge of the lodge, which was circular and covered with tarps to prevent any light from entering. In this first ceremony, there would be two circles of people in order to fit as many as possible inside. As I sat waiting for the lodge to fill, I became uneasy and extremely nauseous. It was tight, confined, and already very warm. I looked right, left, and behind trying to figure out where I could barf if need be.

My nausea was so intense I almost asked to leave, but I sensed this ceremony was crucial to unearthing buried knowledge I'd come to Omega for. I meditated, asking for help with my ever-increasing queasiness. I told my soul and whoever else was listening that I needed to stay put. Despite the total darkness, sweltering heat, and feelings of claustrophobia, my physical symptoms disappeared as quickly as they came. This was my first lesson about emotions, i.e., energy being able to create physical symptoms – and it wouldn't be my last. Wow!

By entering the lodge with no expectations, I couldn't be disappointed. The Sweat Lodge Ceremony was profound, sacred, and beyond anything I might have imagined. The darkness was unlike anything I'd ever experienced before. Just after Eagle Man invited all Spirits into his lodge to join his ceremony, I saw with my own eyes (not with my third eye that sees psychically), many purple orbs flying around the lodge. They were fast, mesmerizing, and quite discernible in this complete absence of light. One purple orb slowed right in front of me, growing larger as the rest of it caught up with itself. It stayed briefly hovering as if watching me, before zooming off again. I was overwhelmed by the direct connection I sensed with this tiny amoeba-like glob of purple energy. It was astonishing.

For those who were seeking a natural name, Ed would ask Great Spirit for one. This ability was a gift from Spirit that Ed had received years earlier. When my turn came, Ed declared, "This is a very powerful name! It will give you the strength to stand on your own. It will help you in your work with the animals – Igemu Winam, which was Sioux for *Mountain Lion Woman*."

Judging from the reactions of the other participants, it was apparent that this was an important name, although I had no idea what Mountain

Lion represented to the Native Americans. I just knew I'd always been attracted to cougars – but I was attracted to most animals. Once our ceremony was complete, I needed to uncover the significance of this name and what it held for my future.

I was struck by the sharp contrast of not wanting to leave the lodge verses my earlier nausea upon first entering it. Now I felt safe within its circular walls, just as I'm sure I must have as a fetus within my mother's womb. Exiting from the intense heat of the lodge into the cold of the night air felt very much like a rebirth. First thing I needed was a shower, and then I wanted to try to reach Catherine's lost dog Haley.

I'd called Bob twice before the ceremony and again just after my shower, but he wasn't home. I asked for help reaching Haley. Catherine had helped me so much; I wanted to repay her somehow. I didn't actually speak with Haley, but what I heard was, *Haley was called away because it was time for Catherine to be alone. Haley is fine. She is with someone who needs her more now.*

I sat outside the lodge waiting for Catherine to emerge from the second ceremony, so I could tell her what I'd discovered. I was mesmerized by the night sky. There were as many stars as I'd seen on our trip to Kenya. While staring at the stars, I observed *five* shooting stars – a first for me. I wasn't sure, but it appeared that several stars were wiggling, sort of dancing. I assumed I was imagining it until the next morning several others described the same phenomena.

I grabbed Catherine as she exited the lodge. I told her what I'd found out about Haley. She was so grateful and happy, hugging me for a long time. "I'll never forget you." I sensed the peace she gained from the information. Helping her really made me feel great. I headed back to my little room to reflect on this absolutely unforgettable day.

I finally reached Bob, who'd been out on a colic emergency. Next, I quickly checked with Love, who was still feeling stiff. I explained that I'd be home late tomorrow and would see her the following day. Images swirled through my mind as I tried to sleep. I felt so grateful that I'd followed my heart and chosen what was undeniably the best workshop for me. Finally, I drifted off to sleep.

The morning session consisted of reviewing everyone's natural name and sharing our Sweat Lodge Ceremony impressions. I learned that mountain lion represents leadership, which was a little scary for a woman who was very much like a cougar, living a solitary life on her farm with her animals. Catherine found me and exclaimed, "What a name! Wow!" Even she was impressed with my natural name. Ed drew the symbol for my name, Mountain Lion Woman, and spelled it in Sioux when he signed his book for me.

As I headed off to lunch, Catherine called out, "Mountain Lion Woman!" I spun around as though I'd been hearing that name all my life, which really surprised me. My weekend workshop had been filled with treasured information and experiences. I was reluctant to leave Omega with its amazingly peaceful energy, but I was anxious to get home to my husband, my animals, my farm, and of course, to Love.

Chapter 4

∞

Expect the Unexpected

I was exhausted from my magical weekend at Omega. Fortunately, the traffic was light, making the drive much easier. I arrived home to my two Lab brothers, Shadow and Licorice, but no husband. Bob returned a little while later. He'd been at Boots' treating Love. She'd suddenly spiked a 104.5° fever combined with severe diarrhea. A horse's normal tempera-ture ranges from 99.5 ° to 101.5 °. Love's temperature was worrisome, but nothing like a person with 104.5. I was crushed with his news since the filly had been very healthy, except for the spinal problem that brought us all together. I was too drained to talk with Love. It'd have to wait 'til morning.

Boots called early. Love was bad. Bob rushed over while I fed and turned out our horses. I drove to Love in tears. I just knew she was leaving. I wasn't prepared yet to say good-bye. Bob was heading back to run a blood count when I arrived. I could tell by his eyes he wasn't optimistic.

I rushed into Love's stall. She was in so much physical distress, yet her eye radiated peace and acceptance; seeing that made my tears flow more. I got control and started asking questions. Are you leaving? *Yes.* Is your work done? *Yes, almost.* Have I learned everything you wanted to teach me? *Almost.* I don't know how to help you leave. I'm new at this, but I'll try. *You have to. It's your job.* When I asked for verification, I heard, *Yes. Let her go,* and sensed her running over grassy fields. *This is what you wanted for her. Let her go!* But I couldn't just yet, as tears of mixed joy and sorrow fell uncontrollably.

I told Boots we needed to reach Kathy's communicator and my teacher to verify my information; neither answered, so we left messages.

As much as I wanted to be wrong, I knew in my heart that the information was accurate. I returned to Love and sat stroking her while I called on the strength of Mountain Lion Woman to stop my tears and help me flood this kind, selfless, and special friend with all the love and healing energy I could muster. Love confessed, *I waited for you to come back.* I thanked her and continued stroking her beautiful Quarter Horse neck.

Kathy's gal called saying Love hadn't decided yet, and that Love would tell Boots when she was ready. She also said Love thanked me for staying with her. It made her feel better. I wondered about my information, but only for a moment, due to my strong knowing.

Love's blood wasn't too bad, so Bob returned with IV fluids and Salmonella antiserum. Fluids have to be given slowly, especially with a horse as stressed as Love was. At first, as the fluids and antiserum flowed into her catheter, her gums were gray and she felt cold – indications of her terribly compromised circulation. I whispered that it was okay for her to go if it was time, as my tears started again. Love's escalating stress forced us to stop the fluids after only 75 percent had been given. Now she felt warmer and her gums were a healthy pink; both encouraging signs. Maybe I was wrong? I dearly hoped so!

Bob and I headed back to our farm for lunch and to give Love time to improve, we hoped. I still had all my farm chores to do. My teacher called back, stating that Love hadn't made a choice yet. I was devastated. The two experts agreed that she hadn't decided. My teacher said I needed to go back immediately. Love needed my touch desperately. I called Boots and asked her to sit with Love and stroke her until I could get there. It was very important!

Bob headed back, but I had to bring in all our horses first, due to an approaching storm. As I was leaving, Bob called. Love was terrible, and Boots was ready to euthanize her. They'd wait if I wanted. Yes! I'm supposed to help her. I hated to make her wait the 20 minutes it would take me to get there. I *flew*, hoping no cop was hiding around a corner. Bob had given her two different painkillers while she waited.

Love was alone when I got there. I rushed in and stroked her with a trembling hand while fighting back my tears. I'll miss you. Thank you for showing me what my life is supposed to be about and for everything you've taught me. I'll help you now as best I can. Both Bob and I were crying. What was taking so long? Boots' husband was on his way back from somewhere.

I kept stroking Love's head and neck while looking into those peaceful brown eyes. You'll be freed soon from your prison. You can run and play. Love made a few attempts to get up, but was too weak. Several times her legs moved in a very strange way, like she was trying to shake off her useless body.

Everyone was finally present. At 4:35 PM on August 16, four months and one day from when she entered this life experience, *Because Of Love* was set free. I wanted to stay connected as she released from her imperfect body, but I was way too emotional to hold the connection. I wanted to feel her freedom, but I just couldn't. I knew her decision had been made hours earlier, despite what others thought. Love's parting lesson for me was to believe what my heart tells me. *Believe in yourself!*

Bob confessed that he'd sat at our kitchen table crying after the blood work, despite its normal results. He just had an overwhelming sense that Love was dying. After he put her down, he did something he's never done before or since. Bob went back to Love's body to remove her spine. He felt there was something he could learn from it. "Expect the unexpected" echoed in my head as he opened her body. The first thing we saw was a totally healthy digestive system. How was this possible given the severe diarrhea she'd been experiencing? Her entire intestinal system was pink and healthy looking. Bob had no explanation. Oddly enough, dissecting Love's body wasn't nearly as hard as we'd expected. We knew it wasn't Love. She was gone.

Upon removal of her skeleton, which was a monumental task, there was no evidence of any deformity in it. Where was her scoliosis? Her spine should have been curved somewhere, yet it was perfectly normal looking. We looked at one another, totally baffled. How could this be?

Next, I did something I've never done before or since. I asked Bob for a piece of Love's hide, to serve as a reminder of this most incredible friend who'd changed my life forever. Eighteen years later, I'm stroking her hair as I type this. It still feels like it did the day she left this earth, and it elicits so many memories, both happy and tragic.

I left a message for my teacher after I got home, explaining that Love had returned Home. I was completely spent, emotionally and physically. It had all happened so fast, making it incomprehensible. I tried to contact Love, but felt and heard nothing. I talked with Love's mother, Dinah, who was very sad. I sent her some healing energy with the last bit of strength I had.

The next day, my teacher called – very upset that she'd been wrong, and I'd been right. I explained it wasn't a matter of right or wrong, but one of interpretation and asking the proper questions. I told her my connection to the animals was very strong. They were always truthful with me. It was my gift. I told her Love had taught me to trust my knowing – big time. My teacher couldn't reach Love either, which wasn't a surprise.

Several days later, I met Boots for lunch and asked if I could write Love's story. I wanted everyone to write down what they'd learned from Love. Boots thought it sounded like a great idea. She said Kathy's communicator had talked with Love, who'd sent messages. Love knew Bob had done all he could, and she loved him. She loved me and thanked me for being with her when she left. She will be coming back, and we'll know her by her eye.

Later, when I was freed from my intense emotions, I struggled with the contradictions resulting from Love's postmortem. Her life had been dictated by her scoliosis, an obvious spinal deformity; yet at postmortem her physical spine appeared normal. In addition, Love succumbed to what appeared to be an infection resulting in severe diarrhea, yet her entire intestinal system was pink and healthy. Being a pharmacist with extensive medical training, this was inconceivable.

I was hungry for understanding – an explanation of why there was no physical evidence of Love's scoliosis and intestinal infection in the body that she'd left behind. Love showed me that there was much more to our world than just what can be seen, heard, and felt by our five senses. Many years and many teachers later, I would finally accept the lesson begun by my nausea in the sweat lodge, and continuing with the mystery of Love's physical illnesses and her seemingly healthy body postmortem. The teaching I struggled so long with – unbalanced energy and/or emotions are the root cause of "dis-ease" within the physical body.

Our physical illnesses originate from disharmony in the energy bodies that surround our physical body. When the imbalances, negativity, and disharmony persist for too long, symptoms appear in the physical body. The key is to correct these things before they affect the body, because healing the physical body is a much slower process than healing an energy body.

Love came to teach people. In order to do this, she needed physical limitations to attract us to her. When her mission was nearing completion, Love's soul created severe conditions that would allow her to return to Spirit. Once her soul released from her body, the energies causing her scoliosis and severe diarrhea departed, *leaving the physical form undamaged.* It would take many more teachers creating sudden and unexpected life-threatening illness to allow them to return Home, before I totally embraced their powerful lesson.

Five nights after Love's transition, I felt an incredible, buzzing energy as I began to meditate, more than ever before. Love, is that you? Are you with me? *Yes.* How are you feeling? *Rested now, much better.* I told her how much everyone missed her and loved her. *I know.* Love, I want to write a story about you; would that be okay? *Yes, you're supposed to, so many more people will learn.* What's the single most important lesson you want them to learn? *Take action through Love. If they keep love as the basis for their decisions in life, everything in life will work for them. People need to let their hearts guide them for the good of all creatures, both human and non-human.*

The other communicator said you'd be coming back. *Yes.* Will you be a horse or something else? *A horse.* Why? *It's my choice.* How long 'til you come back? *About six months.* What will you look like? *When you see my eye, then you will know.* We're sorry we couldn't help you more, especially Bob. *It was how it had to be. You did the most that you could. No more could have been done. Tell Bob any more was out of his control.*

I told Love we'd kept her skeleton and hoped she didn't mind. *No. It was what you were supposed to do. When people see the spine and learn what I was able to do with your help, they will truly learn the power that love has. Love allowed me to do what I shouldn't have been able to do.* I told her I had a piece of her hide and felt she'd left it for me. *Yes. You're supposed to have it. It will give you power and always remind you of my lessons as you travel to help the animals.*

I told Love I wanted to feel the freedom she now enjoyed if I could. I *needed* to run and play with her like I had hoped we could've done on earth. All of a sudden, I felt her racing around, bucking, rearing, and calling. It was so truly joyful and real for me that it created tears. I felt her moving away and knew we had talked for the last time. *I won't talk to you again until I come back.* I cried harder, shouting, Good-bye 'til then!

It was apparent from our discussion that even Love didn't understand that her deformity was one of convenience. It was a necessary component to achieving her purpose and then returning to Spirit as a more evolved soul. I truly believe the lack of evidence of the scoliosis and severe diarrhea is a more powerful teacher than if we'd found proof of both.

The effect that Love's presence had on my life was nothing short of remarkable. Because of Love, I discovered my life's purpose, acknowledging that communicating with animals was absolutely what I was meant to do. So many people never know their life's purpose. This was perhaps Love's greatest gift, one that I'll treasure always. I'm forever grateful to Love for coming exactly when her student was ready. My only regret is that she couldn't stay longer.

Embracing my destiny released the creative powers of the Universe. Animals and experiences flew to me, ensuring that I'd continue uncovering buried skills necessary for my work to help heal the human-animal bond. I remembered an agreement I'd made long ago to help bridge the chasm that had developed between animals and humans. I had no idea where, when, or with whom I made the pledge, but I felt it very deep within. I was thankful to Love for awakening me from my slumber. I will tell you now that Love does return, in an almost perfect body and with another powerful teaching for me. However, that tale has to wait for my next book.

Master Teachers tells the tales of the animals who provided the lessons, love, guidance, and support that helped unlock hidden gems lost within me – treasured assets that were crucial to developing a successful animal communicator, healer, and author. All but Love are my personal animals; brothers and sisters, sons and daughters, and grandsons, as it were. I am honored that they chose to share their lives with me. These are their tales and teachings that I'm proud to share with you. Without these unique and special souls, I wouldn't be who I am. They are my Master Teachers.

I apologize, dear friends, for taking so long to tell your tales, but everything has its perfect timing!

Chapter 5

∞

Hindsight

Love's teaching not only transformed my future, but also enlightened my past. Having my belief system turned upside down and backwards made me wonder what I'd missed in the past, due to living within an illusion. Working with Love cracked open my much-closed, left-brained mind, enabling me to see events with a totally new perspective.

My days became more complicated as a result of Love's appearance. Not only did I have all my previous obligations of farm, hospital, vet office, husband, and animals, but added to them were all the experiences the Universe was bringing to me to keep me on my new path. I was grateful for all the support, but overwhelmed by it as well.

In the few quiet moments I had, I contemplated my past – yearning for lessons I'd missed in the moment. My first thoughts were about my Yellow Lab, Gentle Ben, who'd joined me after I married and moved onto the farm. My husband sensed how much I missed having a dog and suggested I get one. I found a Lab breeder through our local small animal vet. Ben was the last available pup, so choice wasn't an issue. He was a wonderful yet exasperating Lab. My husband's allergies forced Ben to sleep in the barn, which was tough for me. But I figured a dog in the barn was better than none at all.

Ben possessed the mellow attitude of a Labrador. All our barn cats loved him. He knew whenever a critically ill horse or foal was in his barn. He'd hover outside their stall worrying and wanting to help, not unlike me. Ben helped bring many foals into this world. Once I knew all was well with both mare and foal, I'd let Ben in the stall. In every case, the mare allowed Ben to lick and clean her foal. The mares read his non-threatening energy. It was astonishing. Obviously, in the wild he'd be considered a predator, especially by a new mother.

Ben had one frustrating habit – wandering off the farm, mostly at night. He'd wait until we were preoccupied with the horse we were treating, and then bam, he'd escape. I'd think about him, look up, and find no one outside the stall assisting us. I'd get so angry and worried. He always made it back safely, except once.

One morning, I looked out my bedroom window and saw Ben across the street. I was furious and yelled to him to come home. As soon as his name left my mouth, a car flew around the sharp curve we lived on. It was as though everything morphed into slow motion. I screamed for Ben to stay, but it was too late. I saw the car hit Ben, and my heart stopped. *I'd killed my beloved Ben!*

Bob had heard the whole thing. I was hysterical as we ran to the road expecting to find a lifeless, yellow body. Instead, we found nothing. I *heard* the hit. He couldn't have survived it, yet he was gone. We had to find him in case there was a chance we could save him. He could bleed to death if we didn't hurry. Not only was I crying uncontrollably, but I was riddled with guilt – if I hadn't called him at just that moment . . .

We started looking on foot, but he was nowhere in sight. Bob left on our tractor, and I got on my retired jumper, Jolly Man. We searched all the fields surrounding the farm. I returned empty-handed and defeated. A long while later, I heard the tractor and ran down the drive. I saw Ben's limp body draped over Bob's lap. I ran towards them crying. Ben had run *five* fields over on the opposite side of the road before stopping near some bushes. I don't know how Bob ever found him. Five hours had passed since the accident; five of the most excruciating hours of my life.

Ben was dazed but alive, with no outward signs of injury. We rushed to our small-animal vet's clinic. Concern about concussion, shock, and internal injuries made Ben's vet keep him overnight for observation. We returned to visit just before closing. It was as though Ben didn't know who we were, which was eerie and worrisome.

Ben was cleared to come home the next morning. He recognized me, which was a relief, but he was moving guardedly. I was so thankful to have Ben home. I wish I could tell you that Ben learned a lesson about wandering, but I can't. However, *I* learned a huge lesson. Never again would I call any dog unless I knew it wasn't going to cause an injury. I'd dodged a bullet this time, but I couldn't go through that agony again. Ben continued to be a roamer, albeit less of one as he aged. He always made it home safely, except that one time.

When Ben was 13½ years old, he got sick with a bad diarrhea. Our wonderful small-animal vet-friend treated him accordingly, and he appeared to be improving. Ben had moved into the house a few years earlier, so I slept downstairs with him in case he needed to go out quickly. I'd been encouraged with his progress the day before and hoped to see him eat his breakfast.

While standing over his bowl, Ben's rear-end sank to the floor, our eyes locked, and I heard, *I can't do this anymore.* At the time, I'd thought it was my imagination, but I heard it loud and clear, in my head in English. My heart broke as I climbed the stairs in floods of tears telling my husband, "I think I'm being selfish. I think Ben wants to go." I almost couldn't get the words out; verbalizing them bored so deep a hole into my heart.

While we waited for our vet-friend to come to our farm to euthanize Ben, I fed him everything I couldn't over the past few years due to a previous gastric bleed. I almost fed him a leftover pork roast but thought wiser of it. I waited outside with Ben, who followed me everywhere just like always. We sent Ben Home, burying him on his bed underneath a favorite tree with his rawhide bone that he always carried around.

I was horribly despondent. Ben was the closest friend I'd ever lost. Following my conversation with Love after she'd died, I decided to see if I could speak with Ben. I had no idea if it would be possible so long after his death. *I'm here with you all the time.* I love you and miss you so much. *I know.* I look at your picture first thing each morning and last thing each night. *I know. It is what keeps me with you; the strength of your love for me.* I hope you're not angry that the new dogs are in the house a lot. I love them too. *No, I understand it all.*

About six months after Love died, I had to euthanize one of our barn cats, Speckles, who'd become leukemia positive. I'd asked her to just leave the farm, so she wouldn't infect the other cats, but she didn't. I hated the choice she made, forcing me to put her down a week before my birthday. The day before my birthday I tried contacting her, but heard nothing.

I couldn't fall asleep that evening, so I tried again, reaching her this time. I smiled; just like in her life – always on Speckles' terms. *I'm fine. I was ready to leave. I didn't want a diseased body. I understand your responsibility to the other cats. I'm with Ben.* I sensed Ben's energy surrounding me; warm, soothing, pleasant, while he confided, *I'm still always with you. It's me fooling with the new dogs making them bark at the ceiling in the barn.* I wondered if that was you. Still the devil-catcher – a term of my dad's for someone who causes trouble.

Thanks to Love, I knew those agonizing words of Ben's that I heard so clearly almost two years earlier were real. Ben tried to show me what I was capable of, but I'd missed his lesson. Gentle Ben was an outstanding teacher, but the timing for this lesson was off. There are many more concepts that Ben teaches me, such as reincarnation, when he returns three more times over the next 20 years. Obviously, this special soul and I have much to teach one another.

There is no doubt that this was the correct Yellow Lab pup waiting for me to claim him 34 years ago. Ben's plea to return Home was the first telepathic communication I'd received, despite not recognizing it that fateful morning. Love's appearance in my life was in perfect timing. She became a catalyst of profound change in me, but Gentle Ben was my first Master Teacher, even though it took some time for me to become aware of that fact.

Chapter 6

∞

Answering My Cries

Sometimes during communication consultations, I need to access understanding from a higher source. Most animals don't know what's causing their behavioral issues or illnesses. The information comes through as automatic writing, a form of channeling. During one session, I was told that companion animals came into being to answer our souls' cries for help. Companion animals form a support staff, so to speak, helping us survive our time on Earth, a challenging place to reside. The message resonated deeply within me, since I'd always felt like my animals took more care of me than I did of them.

After losing Ben, I couldn't think about another dog. Ben's vet and our dear friend, Gary, called to check on me when we returned from our previously planned two-week vacation – and to tell me that he had a client with a litter of ten Lab pups. I thanked him for calling, but I simply couldn't consider another dog. I was still grieving for Ben. I cried for weeks and felt sorry for Bob, who'd come into a room or the barn and find me wailing away, totally inconsolable. I called Gary back after a month of no improvement. I asked Gary when the puppies were born. The day before Ben died was all I needed to hear. I called his client and inquired about a yellow male. She had three yellow, but only one male. This was spooky, because Ben was the only yellow male with two yellow sisters. Even before Love, I had considered the question of fate versus coincidence often. Post Love, I knew nothing was a coincidence.

I went to look at the pup, telling Bob that I was just going to see what he looked like, nothing more. After all, Ben was an exceptional Lab, and

I wouldn't settle for anything less. Who was I kidding? What puppy isn't adorable? I was met by the lady, the pups' mother and grandmother, and ten fat and happy tail-wagging Labrador puppies. It was joy-filled chaos.

Sitting on the floor, I was covered in little Labs. My broken heart began to melt. I picked up the yellow male, who fit in the palm of my hand at four weeks old. We stared into each other's eyes, and I asked, would you like to come home and love me? I need someone to love me. His eyes said, *Yes*, as our souls touched. That was all she wrote. I hugged Shadow for the first time that day. I'd chosen the name years earlier because Ben followed me everywhere. I'd always joked that the next one probably wouldn't shadow me, but I needn't have worried.

I went from being unable to consider a new dog to being incredibly anxious for Shadow to come home. I made a date to visit again two weeks later, splitting up the 4-week waiting period. My folks were leaving on a road trip, as I was leaving for my puppy fix. I teased them that their Lab was getting old – maybe they'd be interested in a pup. There were six black pups still available. Shockingly, my mom, who normally had to think forever before making a decision, said, "Let's do it. You pick out a male." I asked if she cared if he had some white markings, since a couple of the pups did. "No white," she replied, so I choose the largest solid black male pup. Mom named him Licorice, after one of her favorite candies.

The pups came home at nine weeks old. I recommended that we keep them together initially while they recovered from the loss of their family. My mom smiled and informed me that they'd bought the black pup so mine wouldn't be lonely. This was totally unexpected. I never would've chosen two males, had I known. But they'd be neutered at the appropriate age, so I wasn't too concerned. I registered the pups with the AKC as My Little Shadow after my favorite childhood poem by Robert Louis Stevenson, and Sweet Licorice due to the sweet nature that was evident as soon as Licorice arrived on the farm.

While reviewing their pedigree papers, I was astonished to find that Ben's full brother was their paternal grandfather. I'd inquired about Ben's breeders before looking at Gary's client's pups. I'd hoped to get a relative of Ben, but they'd stopped breeding. Seeing Ben's family in the pups' bloodlines warmed my shattered heart. Even before I had any inkling of universal orchestration, it was hard at work in my life, stepping in to assure that I brought home the souls that were waiting for me, whether I was aware of it or not.

As my awareness grew from working with Love, my recognition of Shadow and Licorice as Master Teachers developed. I decided to ask if we'd been in other lifetimes together. It turned out that Licorice had been in one with my husband, but never with me. I asked Shadow. *Yes.* When? How? All I heard was, *Tina.* Confused, I kept asking and hearing back *Tina. Tina.* Are you telling me that you were my best friend, Tina, who died when we were six? *Yes!* Have we been in other lifetimes together? *Yes, many; too many to discuss.* I'd read in many books that souls evolved from mineral to plant to animal to human, never going backward. I verified the information with my Guides. This revelation just shot a hole in that theory, but I remembered Love's last lesson for me; *trust and believe in yourself.*

Tina's dad worked for Esso, and the family had been relocated to Holland. Tina walked up to the front of her Dutch classroom to work at the chalkboard, coughed, and dropped dead. Apparently, she had an unknown heart ailment. The family returned home and stayed with us, since their house had been rented. I remember Tina's funeral as though it were yesterday. My parents sat with Tina's parents, and a neighbor sat with my brother and me. The neighbor took us up to the open coffin as is the custom; a bizarre custom, but a custom nonetheless.

I can see Tina in her coffin to this day, 54 years later. She looked pale and asleep in a lacey pink party dress. It was surreal and traumatic for a six-year-old looking at her dead best friend. Since then, I simply cannot and will not go near an open coffin. I never shed a tear over Tina's death when it happened. Recognizing that my friend chose to reenter my life resurrected my sadness, grief, and sense of loss from deep within, enabling me to finally cry and let them go.

Shadow and Licorice turned two the week after Love returned to Spirit in 1993. They lived with me for almost 15 years, showering me with unconditional love every moment of every day. Their tales will weave throughout this book according to when they occurred. Not to worry; you'll be reading much more about these two remarkable Teachers.

Chapter 7

∞

Nothing's By Chance

The more I read and learned about the workings of the Universe, the more I was amazed by the wonder of it. Prior to being awakened by Love, I never thought much about such things. Having been raised by parents who were basically atheists, I really didn't know what I believed. I definitely wasn't an atheist. I'd always felt there was something out there; I just wasn't sure what. Following the path that Love laid before me, I began learning about life beyond my five senses.

The most significant lesson was about the continuation of Spirit. Talking with animals that had died taught me that death wasn't the big final Nothing that most people feared. Though the body was gone, the consciousness continued. I'd never thought much about death, but after communicating with Love, Ben, and several other animals that had died, I released any fears that I may have had regarding death.

I prefer the term *transition*, which better describes what actually happens. Transition/death is nothing more than a change in form. The energy that comprises our soul vibrates very slowly while in the physical body. When the body dies and the soul releases, the energy returns to a rapidly vibrating spiritual state. The purple orbs that had entered the Sweat Lodge Ceremony at Omega were proof positive of this for me. Talking with deceased animals was the icing on the cake, so to speak. For me, knowing that Love was returning, transformed the ambiguous concept of reincarnation into reality.

I started thinking about new kittens for the barn, since we were down to one older cat, Rexall. I'd never had kittens before. Most of our barn cats just wandered in as adult cats and stayed. Rexall had come from my family's drugstore when it closed. The idea of reincarnation piqued my curiosity about whether or not new kittens might actually be old friends.

I tried taking two feral kittens that a client had trapped on her farm. After failing to socialize them, I sadly returned them. Obviously, these weren't the "right" kittens. I alerted our small-animal vet-friend, Gary, to my search for new kittens. He was hunting for kittens, too, for another friend.

My teacher and I discussed the new kittens in one of our sessions. She informed me that one was an old dog-friend, which added to the pressure of finding them. Could it be Ben? My curiosity was killing me, so I meditated, asking which dog? *Velvet.* Velvet was my tricolor collie that stayed behind with my folks when I married and moved to my new farm. I couldn't wait!

A few days later, Gary reported back that he'd located some kittens. There were three available. I'd only been considering two, but I didn't want to risk leaving Velvet behind. I decided to see what happened – something new for me. Normally, I'd be the one directing the circumstances. My newfound perspective handed control over to the wonder of universal orchestration, whose existence I was just starting to acknowledge.

My teacher thought three sounded right to her during our session prior to picking up the kittens. My confusion had me seeking advice from my Guides, who told me, *You have already agreed to help these souls.* How many? *Two.* Do I know the second one? *Watch It.* No, I don't think so. If you knew what I . . . The second the words left my mind, I stopped. These were my Guides; of course they knew what I did. *You made an extraordinarily hard decision, but since you made it based on love, the decision was right. He wants to come back.*

Mr. Watch It was the last soul I thought would ever return to me. He was my first personal foal. The second horse I'd ever started. I don't use the term break or broken, which arose from the old-time method of training horses by "breaking" a horse's spirit into submission. My goal is to create a willing and cooperative partner. Watch It taught me not to play with foals in the pasture. Playing with him as a foal made me a pasture mate in his eyes. Watch It matured into a big, beautiful Thoroughbred who used to gallop full-speed straight at me, always stopping just short of touching me.

It always frightened Bob, but I trusted Watch It. Eventually, as much as I loved to play with the babies, Watch It taught me it was safer not to.

Four years before my revelation about communicating with animals, I made the most agonizing decision of my life when Watch It was eight years old. He'd been in training since he was two. I'd even shown him several times. An extremely knowledgeable Olympic-level trainer with whom I'd shown horses since childhood was helping me with Watch It – who was becoming more and more challenging to ride. She suggested sending him to another trainer who worked with eventing horses. Three-day eventing is an arduous discipline for horses, consisting of day one, dressage; day two, cross-country jumping; and day three, stadium jumping. She felt Watch It would make a great event horse because of his boldness and confidence.

I followed her advice and sent my first-born "son" off to learn something more suited to him. I've always felt the real job of a horse trainer is to recognize what a horse is best at and let him do it – even if it's not what you're interested in. I hoped we could find what Watch It enjoyed doing.

My friend called a few weeks later. The eventing trainer had given up. She was sending Watch It back because he'd given her lots of trouble. She thought it might be pain-related but wasn't really sure. She categorized Watch It as *dangerous*.

I was shocked and confused. I'd never felt danger from Watch It, but then I was his "mother." There's a saying in the horse world – one plus one equals one. It typifies the goal all horse trainers are seeking: for horse and rider to work as one being. I'd attained that with Watch It, my first in many years of training horses. It is an incredible feeling.

So, Watch It came home from event training. Now what?

I kept riding him, but was at a loss about what to do. I'd had him with expert trainers in two different disciplines with little success. My old jumper was already retired. I couldn't justify the cost of retiring an eight-year-old with behavioral issues. One afternoon while riding him, Watch It turned nasty for no apparent reason. He reared, spun, and ran off. He'd never done anything like that with me before. I was so angry and scared that I got off and never rode him again. I couldn't afford to get hurt.

I told Bob what had happened when he got back from vet calls. For days, I agonized over what to do. Financially, this was a disaster. We had nine years of expenses tied up in him. I knew I could sell him because he was a big, handsome, sound Thoroughbred. Emotionally, I was distraught. This was my first child. I didn't want him going from trainer to trainer, being mishandled due to whatever his behavioral issues were. If two Olympic veterans didn't have the answer, I doubted anyone did.

My trainer friend helped make the decision for me. Bob was at her farm working on a horse, and he shared my anguish with her. She told him she understood completely. She'd had to make the same decision about a foal out of one of her greatest show jumpers. Hearing her story helped me choose to euthanize Watch It rather than subject him to an abusive life. The next morning, we put Watch It down. I lugged guilt and sadness around for years. While I knew it was the best decision for Watch It, I felt guilty that I couldn't help him, fix him. Now you understand my hesitation about who one of the kittens was.

Three days before Christmas, as we headed out the door to get the kittens, a hawk flew close over our heads. I'd been receiving messages from hawks ever since my epiphany. I asked if it had a message for me. *Love everything and it will come back to you. Love is a bond for eternity.*

Two kittens were waiting for us when we arrived; a calico and an orange and white male. I asked the Universe what names would be appropriate. *Hope and Butch.* Those certainly weren't names I'd have chosen. I appended the calico's name to Bandit Hope due to a perfect mask on her face that I couldn't ignore. The little male became Butch Cassidy. Which is which, I asked? It turned out that Butch was Velvet, and Bandit was Watch It.

Over the years as I learned new methods of healing and honed my communication skills, I often thought about what Watch It's life might have been like if it hadn't taken me so long to awaken. I probably could have helped heal him. Eventually I let that go, because I could see the great life he was enjoying with me as Bandit Hope. She stayed for 16 long years until congestive heart failure necessitated that she be sent Home, five years after moving to the mountains.

It was interesting that these two particular souls incarnated together. While they didn't know each other in their previous lives with me, they had similar tragic endings. Velvet, the collie, became deaf in her old age. Several months after her demise, my dad shared with me that he'd hit Velvet while moving the car in the drive. He rushed her to the vet hospital, but she couldn't be saved. I hadn't been able to visit due to all my responsibilities on the farm. The fact that it took him so long to tell me reflected the pain and guilt he still harbored over the accident. His eyes glistened with tears as he finally told me.

After my parent's last Lab died, Butchie and another barn cat, Lucky, spent the days in my folks' house, which I found puzzling since neither were cat people. I'd come in finding Lucky in my mom's lap and Butch sitting next to my dad. Velvet had dearly loved my dad – all dogs did – even though she was my dog. Seeing Butch with Dad was further proof for me that Butch had indeed been Velvet. I wanted to tell Dad, so he could find the same peace I did when I learned that Watch It had returned. But it took a long time before I had enough confidence to tell my parents about my new skills.

Eventually, one of Bob's clients wrote a book about animal communicators, and she included me in it. Being included in a book felt like validation, so I left a copy at my folks' house, with pages turned down. As expected, my mother thought it completely ridiculous. I could tell my dad had mixed feelings. It went against everything he knew to be true, but this was his daughter, and he was always so proud of me. They were both dying of cancer, which forced the issue for me. I wanted to be truthful with them before I lost the opportunity. I did tell Dad about Butch and Velvet. I'm just not sure whether he believed it or not. I wanted so much for him to let go of the guilt he still carried over Velvet's death, while he still had the chance.

Experiencing the universal orchestration surrounding the arrival of these two little kittens into my life opened my mind even further to the wondrous truths that rule the workings of our world, both physical and – even more importantly – spiritual. I would no longer look at life in the same way. Butch and Bandit helped me learn to look far beyond my five senses to where the real miracles are created. I was just beginning to grasp that there is a method to the madness, whether we see it or not.

Chapter 8

∞

Animal Messengers

*L*ove's life and transition opened the floodgates of the Universe for me. I was inundated by experiences that hastened my awakening. Support came in many forms to keep me on course. I read any book that I felt attracted to, no matter how bizarre it looked. I embraced that which resonated with me and set aside that which didn't until I was ready to accept the information. I began experiencing what Deepak Chopra terms synchrodestiny, in his book *The Spontaneous Fulfillment of Desire – Harnessing the Infinite Power of Coincidence.*

My nightly meditations were filled with questions for my Guides. The ability to access such incredible information, combined with my unending curiosity, moved me rapidly along my learning path. Not only could I telepathically communicate with animals, but I also had the ability to access information regarding them, i.e., illnesses, injuries, behavioral challenges. The more I practiced, the more my self-confidence grew. My once-closed mind was thrown open by the results I was seeing and hearing in the animals I talked with.

Each animal represents something in Native American culture. Much of my early reading was focused on these traditions. Unusual appearances by an animal sent me to *Medicine Cards* by Sams and Carson. I began to learn what different animals' messages were. For example, hawk represents messenger, which certainly fit with my experiences. Deer represents gentleness, reminding me to be gentle with myself. Animals offer messages whether we realize it or not. You don't have to be able to communicate telepathically in order to receive their messages. All you need is to be aware and alert.

Most of my days were spent running the farm and hospital and caring for all the animals. It was a physically demanding lifestyle that didn't allow for much else. The appearance of these animal messengers always coincided with my missing out on crucial information due to my preoccupation with chores. It was as though my soul and/or my Guides knew that they could get my attention through an animal, and they were right. The messenger animals' appearances reaffirmed my newly embraced belief about the interconnectedness of all life. How else could an animal carry a message from my soul or my Guides that I'd been missing?

Often while spreading manure in the fields, I'd see hawks flying high. I'd close my eyes, meditate, and ask if it had a message. Sometimes it was just a red-tail soaring effortlessly on the gentle currents, but many times the hawk conveyed a message. After hearing the message, I'd open my eyes and the sky would be empty. The messenger hawk had disappeared as quickly as it had appeared. I intuited them to be spiritual hawks – or owls, or deer, or whatever appeared in my line of sight. Many brought me needed encouragement in the early days of my awakening. I'd like to share some of my messages to open your awareness, so you don't miss out on your own. Their messages were sometimes delivered just by their appearance and other times as direct telepathic communications that I heard.

Three months after Love left, an owl flew overhead late one afternoon. This was the first owl I'd seen on our farm in 16 years. I'd heard plenty of them hooting at night, but had never seen one. Owl spoke to me: *I see you work hard all day long taking care of your animals. You have to work just as hard to take care of yourself!* I thanked the owl for my message. It was so true, but I failed to follow its sage advice. It wasn't until many years later that this message came again, but with much pain attached to it. Perhaps if I'd listened more astutely to owl's message, I could have saved myself much sorrow. Perhaps . . .

Two weeks after the owl's message, a hawk told me, *Stay on course. Be Mountain Lion Woman.* How can I be sure I'm on course? *Keep seeking guidance like today from the creature-beings.* Thank you. Is there anything I can do for you? *Just keep helping the creatures. Stay on course.* Several weeks later, after losing a client's horse to a severe colic, a hawk flew 15 feet above me, calling. It was magical. *You don't control the results, the Universe does. You are not responsible. As long as you act from love, caring, and with compassion, that's all that is asked of you. Creature-beings thank you and appreciate all you do regardless of the consequences when you treat them with such respect and compassion. They know the results are not in your power. They accept this; you must too. Just continue to use your knowledge and experience, for it is the will of the Universe. The creature-beings are grateful.*

This message was for both Bob and me. We were committed to saving all the animals in our care, which was unrealistic and took a heavy toll. Opening my awareness to the forces within the Universe helped me release my over-burdened heart from all the losses over the years. The more I studied, the more I came to understand my place within the web of life. It was exactly as the hawk stated, and I was forever grateful to whoever sent her, for it allowed me to do my work from an entirely different perspective. I still grieved terribly over our losses, but I no longer felt responsible for them.

These are just a couple of examples of my messages. Many animal messengers are discussed in my first book, *Letting Go*, which recounts my painful, but transformative, recovery from divorce after moving to the mountains of North Carolina. While I navigated through my Abyss and Tunnel, I felt completely disconnected. I was cut off from the web of life that I'd once felt so safe within. Animal messengers had disappeared from my life. Seeing my first hawk from my house in Todd sent a shiver of recognition through me. Could it be? Had I finally found the connectedness that had been missing for so long? More and more messengers began appearing, heralding my return to being Mountain Lion Woman once again.

As my abilities and my connectedness with all around me developed, I needed fewer messengers, because my intuition was keener. Eighteen years later, there are still times when they come to let me know I'm missing something very important. Many times their appearance alone is enough, such as deer crossing my path, offering the message *be gentle with self.* Several deer means the message ends with an exclamation point!

While I don't include animal messengers among my Master Teachers, the information that I received from each was of great import in that moment. Don't miss out on yours. Keep alert, quiet your mind, ask if there's a message. Then listen, and thank your animal messenger for coming to you. I guarantee it will be of significant value to your life.

Chapter 9

∞

Deeper Understanding

Communicating with my animals allowed me to better understand them. Two of my Master Teachers, Squiggles and Junior, were eight- and nine-year-old horses, respectively, when I uncovered my skills. They were Mr. Watch It's full sister and brother. Although they came from the same gene pool, all three were as different as night and day personality-wise. I believe this is because animals do indeed have individual souls.

Junior was a beautiful mover who was a real challenge to train as a youngster. He was so afraid of stepping over a pole on the ground that I needed Bob to lead Jolly Man in front to show Junior the pole wasn't going to get him. With patience and time, Junior gladly trotted over the poles and eventually began jumping, albeit cautiously.

As Junior turned five years old, I told Bob that I was considering selling him if he didn't start to like jumping. I couldn't enjoy jumping Junior if he remained reticent. He was a gorgeous mover who'd make a wonderful dressage prospect for someone else. Dressage concentrates on intricate, complex movements on the flat – a horseman's term meaning not over jumps. My passion is jumping, although I can appreciate the level of training that dressage requires.

Junior had no trouble understanding what I was contemplating, because he returned to training with a new zest for jumping. No longer was he unsure of himself; he jumped anything I sent him towards and jumped it happily. Junior turned into the easiest horse to jump that I'd ever trained. I joked with my husband about how Junior must have heard what I was thinking.

The thought of losing his comfy home made jumping not such a bad idea. I wouldn't know until four years later that this was exactly what happened.

Junior always gave me fits trying to keep blankets on him in the cold weather. Back then, we used something called Wonderwear that went underneath the blanket to keep the blanket from rubbing the hair off their shoulders. It fit snugly using Velcro attachments in two different areas. Most mornings, I'd come in the barn and find Junior's blanket on, but the Wonderwear was on the ground stomped into the bedding. How? It was simply astonishing. I almost put him in the stall with the closed-circuit TV that we used for foaling mares and critically ill horses, so I could see how in the world he managed this without hands, but I never did.

Now, I could just ask Junior why he tore his blankets off. I asked him if he was just bored at night or did he really want to be naked? *I don't want to be blanketed!* I thought I was helping by keeping you warmer. *It's not our way.* Squiggles doesn't take them off. *She's more tolerant.* No kidding. This was a mild understatement. I then asked Junior why he had come to me. *To remind you of why you have horses. We need to be equals. You need to not control us all the time.* I was quite surprised by his response.

Junior's remarks brought greater understanding regarding the previous year's occurrences. Due to my financial fear at the time, I'd decided to market Junior. I felt selling him would help ease money pressures we were experiencing. I moved him to a local farm with an indoor ring for a friend to begin working, because I didn't have the time. Truth was, I really didn't have the heart. Deciding to sell him was killing me. I'd already lost his brother, Watch It, a few years earlier. As I was getting him ready for her to ride the first time, he kicked me. I'd been kicked *at* as a warning, but never actually kicked by a horse – and certainly not by one of my own.

In retrospect, Junior knew what I was thinking and feeling, which resulted in his hard kick. What he didn't understand was that I was angry with the circumstances that had brought me to the decision I'd made about marketing him. I wasn't angry with him, but he sure let me know he was angry with me. Junior continued to express his displeasure by being difficult for my friend.

My friend and I agreed I'd take over until Junior settled down; at least, that was the plan. I started jumping him, and he was great for me. During a trail ride we took to give him a break from the monotony of the indoor ring, we ventured upon a huge herd of deer, which should have sent him flying in the opposite direction. Instead, Junior stood there staring at them with his heart pounding. Then, a rabbit jumped across his path, but he never spooked.

My heart took back control from my mind. This was a wonderful horse that I loved. How could I sell him? *I couldn't.* I brought Junior back home. This had all been my idea. Bob never did understand why I was selling Junior. Even though I was still asleep to my communicating skills, the information came through. Junior guaranteed it by being difficult for my friend, necessitating that I get involved.

Deer and rabbit were also conveying messages to me, but I was still asleep. As I've already said, deer represent gentleness. Their message is a reminder to be gentle with myself, which fit perfectly with my fear-based choice. A large number of deer is like someone shouting the message. You guessed it, rabbit represents fear. Back in the day, I harbored many fears, mostly of the financial variety. Luckily, my heart knew that Junior had other amazing lessons to teach me, which required that he stay right where he was. Junior taught me that my horses weren't possessions. They were relatives – equals. They were about *love.*

I no longer live in fear of anything – a result of believing that everything I need will always be provided by the Universe. It's an incredibly freeing place to live, and it changes everything. Junior provided a huge lesson for me about fear-based decisions. Ironically, even before I embraced my belief about being provided for, we always had enough money to take care of ourselves, our farm, and our animals.

A couple of months after Junior's understatement about his sister being more tolerant, Squiggles stopped eating. This terrified me because we had almost lost her to colic. Two years earlier, Squiggles, my big, gorgeous Thoroughbred mare, had developed a ten-foot impaction in her large colon. I'd told Bob if we couldn't correct it, I wasn't going to take her elsewhere for surgery. Colic surgery required a team, which we didn't have. Our past losses were the reason that I wasn't opting for an expensive surgery with no guarantee for success.

We treated Squiggles for two days with no real sign of improvement. I knew how stoic she was, which can be a double-edged sword with a horse.

While being stoic is helpful with painful conditions in horses, it also works against them. By the time they let you know they're feeling bad, they're in dire condition. I'd learned about her gene for stoicism from Squiggles' mother, May Ban.

Late during the second night, the injections of analgesics only lasted a few minutes instead of hours. I didn't need Bob to tell me what that meant. I'd been doing this for long enough to know; we were at the decision point. I stood beside Squiggles in tears. My "daughter" had fought so hard for so long. Through my agony, I heard Bob say, "I think we should consider surgery," which opened the floodgates of emotions.

My deep love for Squiggles wouldn't let me give up on her. My financially-based decision to put Squiggles down was suddenly replaced by my heart-based one that required we get her to a referral clinic as quickly as possible. I knew better than most that the sooner you do colic surgery, the better your chances. Thanks to my mind-based decision, we had erased that advantage.

As we drove Squiggles to the other clinic about ninety minutes away, Bob explained about the surgeon we were headed towards who specialized in colic surgery. He felt he was an excellent surgeon and that Squiggles deserved a chance. The surgeon and his team were waiting when we arrived. They examined, prepped, and had Squiggles on the operating table very rapidly. The surgeon wanted us to wait until he determined what Squiggles' situation was – if she had a chance of survival.

We watched from an observation room. I'd regained control on the long drive and was non-emotional and acting professionally. Squiggles was covered with surgical drapes, so I couldn't see her face, which helped with my detachment. When the surgeon's scalpel opened her midline, her gas-filled bowel burst through his incision. I was shocked but fascinated as he used some gizmo to quickly deflate her distended bowel, allowing it to recede back into place. He examined her abdomen, then gave us a head nod meaning she had a good chance for recovery. We told him to do everything he could for her. Bob said, "Treat her like she's your own," as we headed back to take care of the other horses at home.

My mind was reeling on the drive home. I was exhausted from our two days of intensive care, which included very little sleep. This wasn't unusual for us. Running an equine hospital creates many sleepless nights, but usually it's with a client's horse. I was emotionally drained over possibly losing a dear friend, a "daughter." I knew it'd be a while before we heard anything, but the surgeon called much sooner than expected with a very positive outlook. I couldn't wait to get back to Squiggles.

The surgeon took us to Squiggles. She looked dreadful after multiple days of pain followed by abdominal surgery, but she was alive. I flew to her, hugging her neck while crying tears of joy and relief. My powerful emotions stemmed from believing that I'd never see her alive again. I heard the surgeon say, "Wow! I had no idea." I had handed over my vet tech's hat when I handed Squiggles over to the hospital staff. I smiled through my tears, telling him I was her "mother" now, not her nurse. "I'm glad I didn't know that before surgery," he teased.

We were so grateful to the surgeon and his terrific staff for all they'd done for Squiggles. I hated to leave her, but I had other horses depending on me at home. The surgeon felt she'd be ready to travel home the next day. I remember telling him, "Let's wait and see. She's *our* horse," insinuating that things didn't always proceed as anticipated for us.

We were almost to the clinic the next day when Bob's beeper went off. It was the surgeon saying that he might have to go back in. I couldn't say that I was completely surprised, based on past experiences with our own horses. The biggest difference with Squiggles was that she'd survived the first surgery. While I comforted her, we discussed the options and decided to hold off on another surgery, to give Squiggles' bowel a chance to start working on its own. We stayed for as long as we could, then returned home, leaving the surgeon again with the instructions to treat her like she was his own.

Squiggles' bowel went from complete stasis to diarrhea a few hours later, so further surgery wasn't necessary. I visited her every day and stayed as long as I could. The clinic was terrific about giving me unlimited access. There were definitely perks to being a vet's wife. I'd walk Squiggles and let her graze, hoping to raise her spirits (and mine). The surgeon thought she was ready to leave and I wanted her home, but it didn't feel like she was ready to me. Bob asked me each time I got home, and I'd report that she wasn't ready yet. Bob had learned over the years the uncanny ability I had of knowing when a horse or foal was sick or well. Years later, I understood what I was feeling and sensing from her. I was picking up her communication to me even though I didn't realize it.

It was Easter Sunday, three days post-surgery, when I returned from my time with Squiggles and told Bob, I'm picking up Squiggles tomorrow. "She's ready!" I couldn't put it into words back then, but I just *knew*. She once again felt like the mare I'd raised from a foal and loved so much. It was the best Easter ever.

For the next couple of months we dealt with a salmonella infection in her bowel, which required that she be apart from the other horses due to its highly contagious nature. Luckily, it was one of the least pathogenic strains of salmonella. I spent several hours each day over the next two months hand-grazing Squiggles away from the other horses. I knew how important grass was to her recovery. Grass is what horses are born to eat.

I learned a lot from Squiggles by merely watching her graze. Not all understanding and lessons require direct communication. Keen observation can be just as revealing. I tried to choose what grass Squiggles ate. (Talk about control issues!) I showed her what I believed was best for her; the young, rich grasses. Squiggles passed right by them and tugged at the old, thick, tough grass. Time and time again this happened until I gave up on "helping" her.

As Squiggles' intestinal system healed, her choice of grass changed. I watched her start with the least rich, older, thicker grass and over time end up with the rich, young grass that I knew was most nutritious. She knew exactly what was best for her and followed her own intuition. I thought about how much wiser she was than I.

Thanks to Squiggles, I let my intuition guide what I ate as I recovered from my hysterectomy several years later. After my surgery, I didn't eat much of anything for ten days. I started eating only small amounts of fruit, gradually returning to my normal diet as I recovered. I learned that the body wants to focus its energy on healing itself, not on hard-to-digest foods.

Given this history, you can see why I panicked when Squiggles stopped eating two years after her surgery. Now, however, I had the advantage of being able to communicate with her and gather information from my Guides, who shared that Squiggles had a rotavirus, a pathogenic organism that causes intestinal disturbances. I asked my Guides why she kept getting sick. *It's part of her reason for being – for you to learn.* I've already learned so much. Isn't that enough? *You have to learn to allow her to be sick. She is working through karma this way. She will achieve large soul growth in this lifetime.*

While I didn't like what I heard, it certainly brought me a deeper understanding of the reason behind her illnesses. I talked with Squiggles next. *I don't feel so bad.* I love you and I hate that you're sick again. *I know, but it's all right.* I don't want you to leave. I enjoy having you here with me. *Don't worry. If I leave, I can always come back. We've been in many, many lifetimes together.* This last information wasn't a surprise to me. I'd always felt a very deep connection to Squiggles, who became known to everyone as Squiggles The Special.

By the time this illness was resolved, Squiggles had gone without eating or drinking for 18 days. We supported her with appropriate medications, an herbal tonic that we took ourselves, and tube feedings twice daily. Her feedings consisted of a bucket full of milk, eggs, honey, and a fiber supplement. Our two Labs, Shadow and Licorice, loved Squiggles' milkshakes. They'd wait outside her stall to lick whatever was left in the bucket; Bob always made a little extra for them.

We ran blood work frequently to monitor her progress. Bob kept saying he didn't know what else to do. I told Bob we were giving her everything she needed to heal herself. We needed to give her time. I treated her with the same healing energy I'd used for Love. With Squiggles, it was always applied hands-on, since she was just across the barnyard from my home. Squiggles patiently cooperated throughout her ordeal, allowing Bob to pass the stomach tube – which isn't comfortable – to feed her. Just another example of the tolerance that her brother spoke of.

Squiggles never acted painful, but then she was the queen of stoicism. After 18 days of intense observation and supportive care, she ate some hay. I was ecstatic, even though I'd have preferred that she'd started drinking first. We had to continue tubing her with fluids until she started drinking two days later. Whatever it truly was that was wrong with Squiggles, she fought it off and healed herself – with some support from us. Thankfully, this was the last serious sickness she had until it was time for her to leave me years later. But her greatest lessons for me lay ahead. I didn't know at the time just how remarkable this mare was, my Master Teacher extraordinaire.

Chapter 10

∞

Lessons Are Never Lost

C ommunicating with my animals not only enhanced our understanding of one another, but it enriched our relationships. The lessons I was learning from my studies and my communication consultations brought clarity about past events as well. Every life experience is significant and contains lessons even if we don't recognize them in the moment. The lessons are never lost; they are merely locked in our memory vault until the proper time.

Unrealized lessons from my past moved from the deepest caverns of my brain to be seen in a new light. Seeing with new eyes, so to speak, allowed me to retrieve many hidden lessons. One of the most painful for me involved my indecision and the circumstances surrounding the euthanasia of my dear jumper Jolly Man.

Resurrecting these lessons led to the immediate resolution and release of corrosive guilt and regrets that I'd hidden deep within me since Jolly's transition four months prior to Love's birth.

Jolly and I joined forces one Easter Sunday when he was 6 years old, and I was 20. Little did I know then that we'd be together for the next 22 years. We had a great partnership and showed until I graduated from Pharmacy School in '75. Jolly was the best jumper I ever had. I continued to ride him as much as I could while practicing pharmacy. After I married, the obligations of our vet office, hospital, and farm left little time to ride. Jolly was relegated to being herd leader for whoever was out in the pasture with him, even though he was only 12 years old and still at his peak as a show jumper.

Believing Jolly would be healthier if exercised, I found him a wonderful home when he turned 16 years old. I told them if anything changed, I needed to be the first to know. Loading Jolly on the trailer for the long trip to northern New York state was extremely difficult for me. I struggled to keep my tears in check, failing miserably. I believed I was doing what was best for Jolly. I was crying because I thought I'd never see my friend again.

Jolly went to a young girl whose folks couldn't afford to buy her a horse. I couldn't think of a better situation. I just knew this girl would love Jolly and look after him. Given his age, he didn't need someone who wanted to jump and show a lot. It was a win-win, except for my broken heart. Three-plus years later, when the farm owner called, I thought it was to tell me that Jolly Man had died. He hadn't, but the little girl was moving and no one else wanted Jolly.

Jolly arrived back on our farm looking great for a 20-year-old, so I knew my decision had been a good one for him. My situation really hadn't changed, so I agreed to let a client's son – who trained hunter/ jumpers – use Jolly. The young man didn't get along with him at all, so Jolly came home after a couple of months. I hadn't realized that Jolly was a hard horse to ride and jump. He'd been the easiest horse I'd ever ridden. As I brought Jolly home for the second time, I acknowledged the special partnership we had. I tried one more time with another client who operated a boarding and showing facility. She wanted Jolly for one of her students. He stayed about six weeks until I brought him home due to extreme weight loss. The older a horse is, the harder it is to get weight back on them if they lose it.

Jolly was like an equine boomerang; he just kept coming back. Three strikes and you're out! Jolly wasn't going anywhere else. For whatever reason, he was meant to stay on Fair Chance Farm. Jolly possessed a wonderfully cooperative nature, so what better babysitter for the young horses we were raising? I couldn't think of a more dependable teacher for our yearlings and weanlings. Jolly appeared quite satisfied with his new mission of keeping everyone in line.

About six months before I met Love and had my epiphany, Jolly began losing weight despite eating well. One of the downsides of helping our horses live longer is that they out-live their teeth. I'd been struggling with the decision to euthanize Jolly for four months. We had another vet who specialized in geriatric dentistry help us with Jolly's aging teeth. They were very worn, creating inefficient chewing. Bob and the other vet removed one tooth and filed others that were causing irritations on his gums.

The upper arcade of the horse's jaw is wider than the bottom. Horses chew in a circular grinding motion. Because of this, over time the outside of the upper teeth and the inside of the lower teeth develop sharp edges. These sharp edges cause scratches and sores on the horse's gums, which limits his willingness to chew. A technique called *floating* files the sharp edges down allowing the horse to chew efficiently, thereby digesting his feed better. Most horses need to be floated yearly, but it really depends on the hardness of each horse's teeth.

Jolly wasn't bothered by the floating, but the tooth removal was excruciatingly painful. When I checked on him later that evening, I felt his severe discomfort. I wouldn't learn for another year that I was an empathetic healer and truly was feeling his pain. Watching someone I loved in great pain and believing that I caused it was agonizing. I felt totally responsible and I was consumed with guilt.

We did everything we could to make Jolly more comfortable. It took four agonizing days before he ate and drank normally. We kept him hydrated via a stomach tube until he began drinking again on his own. I admonished myself constantly for allowing this to happen to my dear friend. Jolly never treated me any differently and appeared to enjoy the time I spent trying to soothe and console him (and me).

I kept trying to justify the decision to remove his tooth in an effort to assuage my guilt. We did what we thought was best for Jolly – that which would allow him to stay longer. Eventually, I accepted that all one can do is make the best decision at the time with the information available. I agreed with Bob and the vet dentist that these procedures were in Jolly's best interest. Sadly, the dental work only improved his chewing for two weeks. It just wasn't fair that such a wonderful soul suffered so much pain for so little benefit, but then, "Who said life is fair?" I thought I was helping, but it failed – leaving me feeling disheartened and defeated.

I continued to agonize over what was best for Jolly. My confidence was shaken to the core. The hardest decision is that of euthanasia, especially if the animal isn't sick. Jolly would graze for a while, but spend most of the day standing with his head lowered, seeming to have lost interest in life. He looked sad and pathetic, which was not the Jolly Man I'd known for 22 years. I suffered over what to do for months. One evening, the student was ready. A portrait of Jolly in his prime hung over my bed – a Christmas gift from my folks. I studied the painting that night comparing its handsome subject at six years of age to the thin, pitiful-looking horse in the pasture. I knew with absolute certainty what to do.

I made arrangements with a neighbor, who could help us bury Jolly. While I knew it was the best thing for Jolly, I was consumed with guilt and regret over the situation with his painful dental work. Not wanting to upset Jolly, I walked towards the hole that awaited him holding back my tears. His body would spend eternity in the corner of our big pasture next to the pear trees he loved, while his Spirit returned Home. Images filled my mind: that Easter Sunday 22 years earlier when I first jumped him, all the shows, trail rides, training – everything.

Jolly's unsettling transition was a first for us. After injecting the proper amount of drug for Jolly's weight, he slowly collapsed while I lovingly guided his head to the ground. I couldn't hold back the tears any longer. Grief consumed me. At this point, horses are unconscious and near death and within moments the heart stops; the deed is done. Except, Jolly's heart didn't stop. He was moving as though slowly running. I knew he was unconscious and felt no pain, but it was excruciating to watch. While Bob ran to the drug room for more solution, I sat with Jolly flooded in tears. In my heart, I knew my decision was right, but agonizing doubt crept in. Bob returned with more euthanasia solution, and Jolly was finally set free.

I gained some clarity about Jolly's transition after talking with a wonderful old horse who'd been trying to tell his person that he wanted to go Home for over a year. My client explained how she'd been making and breaking appointments to euthanize her horse for just that long. As soon as they shared this with me, I knew that Jolly had been doing precisely the same thing. For those four agonizing months, Jolly had been telling me he was ready to go Home. Thoughts that I'd interpreted as my own were actually coming from Jolly Man. Who knew?

When I began working as an animal communicator, I'd often feel torn between roles: the vet's wife and the communicator. As the vet's wife, I was all about saving lives. As the animal communicator, I soon learned that it's not always about healing the physical body. Healing the soul/spirit is far more essential – the soul continues on long after the body has been left behind.

The heartrending memory of Jolly's euthanasia plagued me for a year, until a dying broodmare came to my rescue. We were working with a client's broodmare with very unusual and serious medical issues. While my husband was doing everything humanly possible to save this mare's life, the mare shared with me her wish to return to Spirit. I felt her increasing sadness and since my allegiance is always with the animal, I advised her to create something that couldn't be healed if she truly needed to transition. Late the next night, a violent seizure broke the mare's shoulder – an injury that was impossible to heal. Secretly, I was happy for her, because I'd felt her intense desire to return to Spirit.

Astonishingly, the mare required additional solution to stop her heart and free her soul. As I felt her soul release, I thanked her for her gift – the knowledge that I'd made the correct decision for Jolly Man. Instantly, the enormous burden that I'd been carrying since that sad day lifted from my heart. This need for additional solution only happened on these two occasions in almost 30 years of euthanizing horses. This was no coincidence. Through this broodmare, the Universe provided me with the ultimate gift of understanding.

My new perspective allowed me to let go of all my self-imposed blame, guilt, and regret. So much of the end of Jolly's time with me could have been different had I known about my abilities at the time. I could have asked if he wanted his teeth worked on. I could have asked if he wanted to stay. While I felt bad about keeping him here four months longer than he wanted, I accept that everything happens for a reason. It was no wonder Jolly was my equine boomerang. How else would I learn his lessons? Thank goodness the Universe kept returning Jolly Man to the place he needed to be, to the person he was trying to teach.

Chapter 11

∞

When Least Expected

A year after Love entered our lives, I found myself back at Boots' farm. Bob was doing reproductive work on some of the broodmares. I didn't join him often on calls because of all the responsibilities on our own farm. I hadn't seen Boots much since Love died, so I decided to come to help with the mares. With horses, the goal is to breed the least number of times possible. The vet determines the optimum time to breed, which is within 24 hours prior to ovulation, by palpating the mare's ovaries. Six to eight hours is ideal.

Between mares, I noticed a tiny kitten watching me. It was a tiger, my favorite color. I picked up the kitten, fooled with it a little, and put it back down as we headed to the next mare. One of Boots' barn cats had obviously had a litter a couple of months earlier, but I really didn't think much more about it.

We returned a few days later to breed the mare that Bob felt would be ovulating soon. When we finished, I nearly stepped on the little tiger kitten. I picked him/her up apologizing for almost squishing it. Boots' husband noticed and asked, "Do you want that kitten?" I quickly answered, "No! Don't you want it?" He said they had too many cats already. They'd never miss it. I looked at Bob, confessing that, while I didn't understand it, I *loved* this kitten. I was feeling a deep love, which was totally out of character for me. I'm really not a cat person, but there was something special about this kitten.

I found Boots and told her that her husband had offered me the kitten.

I could tell she wasn't keen on giving me the kitten; hesitantly she said, "Sure, take it home. If you change your mind, just bring it back." As Bob and I headed back to our farm, I asked if this kitten was someone I knew. A huge smile spread across my face and throughout my entire being as I heard, *He's Ben!* It was a little less than three years since that fateful morning when Ben said he couldn't do this anymore. I'd been hoping that one day he might return, but hadn't considered his appearance as a cat. But it made sense. I was much more likely to take on an extra barn cat or two rather than another dog or a horse.

I was thrilled to have my old friend back, regardless of species. The next morning, I headed to our vet-friend Gary's clinic to have the kitten examined. As I started my car, the CD player came to life with Mandy Patinkin singing "Somewhere Over the Rainbow." I thought, what a great name for the kitten. Rainbow it is! Ben/Rainbow taught me that the power of love will prevail if we follow our heart. I could have very easily ignored Rainbow and left him at Boots'. What a loss that would have been for me and a lot of wasted reincarnating for him. When you least expect them, miracles happen.

While I believed the information I was receiving about who the different animals had been in my life, I still was skeptical. I required lots of physical proof, back in the day, and the Universe provided more than enough over the years. I began to see personality traits of Ben's in Rainbow, despite the difference in species. Prior to this, I wouldn't have thought it possible, but Ben/Rainbow taught me it was. And it wasn't just me. Bob commented numerous times about how much certain behaviors of Rainbow reminded him of Ben. It was heartwarming to know Ben had come home, bringing a powerful lesson about reincarnation with him.

I fell victim to the Universe's devices a few months later when I found Butch outside our house late one night – not purring. Butch *always* purred loudly like an engine, so I knew something was wrong. I took his temperature, which was 105°. I called Gary, who asked me to meet him at his clinic, so he could x-ray Butch. While Gary and I were working on Butch, I heard lots of meowing from a back room. I looked at Gary, and he just shook his head.

Gary explained that a few nights earlier someone had tossed kittens from a car, like trash, in front of his farm. He already had more cats than he needed, so he brought them to his clinic to find a home for them. If he couldn't find a home over the next three days, as much as he hated to, he'd have to put them down. After we finished with Butch, I followed my heart and the meowing and found two black kittens. Apparently, there'd been three, but the car ran over the third one, killing it.

Two days later, I inquired about the kittens. Gary had been unsuccessful so far, so I told him I'd take them if nobody else would. He said he didn't realize I wanted any more cats. I told him I didn't, but. . . I brought the unwanted kittens home the next day. I asked if I knew either, but I didn't. I asked about names and heard, *Petal and Lucky*. Once again, names I would never have chosen. So, the male became Lucky and the female Petal.

Butch recovered very quickly with no complications. Was it coincidence that Butch, who'd never been sick before, spiked a high fever just when these kittens were about to be returned to Spirit? Hardly. This was just another example of the interconnectedness of the web of life that we're all tangled up with, whether we recognize it or not.

Sadly, Petal fractured her pelvis about six months later. Being stepped on by a horse seemed the logical explanation. We kept her confined for more than three months, hoping her pelvis would heal. My heart broke as I watched her take several good steps, but then start limping badly as she left the crate that had been her home for more than enough time to heal her pelvis. There was nothing else we could do. So, Petal returned to Spirit while Lucky worked mouse patrol in our barn alongside Butch, Bandit, and Rainbow.

Four years later, the Universe stepped in once again. I guess It didn't think four barn cats were sufficient for Fair Chance Farm. Again, I was helping my husband palpate mares during breeding season, but at another client's farm. As we waited for the mares to be brought in from the pasture, I noticed a tiny kitten hiding among a pile of hay bales. The farm owner told me that they had a feral cat that kept having litters. These were her current ones.

I approached the kitten hiding in the hay, taking a closer look. When I got right in front, it hissed quietly at me. I laughed at the display of bravery from this itty-bitty baby. I picked up the month-old kitten, who was the most interesting color I'd ever seen – a filmy sort of charcoal gray. It had a basic black coat covered with a blanket of white hairs. It was really special. I huddled the tiny baby against my chest, then returned the kitten to its hiding place deep between the bales, so I could assist Bob with the mares needing to be palpated.

As we packed up to go, I looked towards the hay bales and saw not only the charcoal kitten peeking out, but also one that appeared to be calico with the same white "topcoat." I walked over to get a closer look. I'd just never seen cats with this coloring. They were unique. I asked our clients if they'd like to get rid of two kittens. They said they'd be happy to catch them when they were old enough to be weaned, which we figured was another month. Bob just walked towards the car shaking his head. He wasn't used to this from me – and neither was I. Later, when I asked about names for the kittens, I was told, *Merlin and Crystal.* Now, these were two names I really liked. I knew the grayish calico was female; they always are. She was Crystal. The name Merlin meant that the charcoal kitten was male.

Our clients trapped the kittens and had them waiting for me four weeks later. I drove straight to Gary's clinic so he could examine them. I asked if kittens ever change color as they mature like some breeds of horses do. He'd never seen that happen, so I felt confident that these strikingly distinctive kittens would stay that way. Well, you know that saying, *there's always a first time.* Sure enough, the kittens lost their white overcoats as they aged, ending up calico and black with a white smudge on its chest. We knew they'd been born in early April, so I decided it was April 1st, April Fool's Day. Despite losing their unique coloring, they were a wonderful addition to our growing legion of barn cats.

Crystal was sweet and quite shy. She emitted a very healing energy that I found quite interesting, given my newfound association with healing energies. Merlin grew into a pistol. He'd entertain me by hiding in a pile of clean straw we usually saved in the front corner of each stall. All of a sudden, he'd shoot out from under the straw pile and "attack" my rake or pitchfork. Merlin kept me laughing most mornings. Had I not been told what to name him, I'd have called him Robin after another incredibly funny guy, Robin Williams.

One morning when Merlin was about nine months old, he wasn't acting right. I ran to Gary's clinic with him. Gary wasn't sure what was wrong, so we ended up at a referral hospital. Merlin was admitted and underwent a barrage of tests, none of which resulted in a diagnosis. We decided they should keep him overnight, since they were better equipped to treat a cat. Everything we routinely used in our horse practice was too large.

Bob and I went back late in the day to visit him. I applied hands-on healing energy to Merlin, who was very depressed and just lay there. I hated leaving him, but I didn't have a choice. He made it through the night, but took a turn for the worse the following morning. I told them to hold off on euthanizing him until I arrived. I needed to be with him. I feel it is my responsibility to be with my animals when they transition. We rushed to the hospital, but Merlin couldn't wait, leaving shortly before we arrived. I felt terrible that he'd been alone. I'd been on my spiritual path long enough to know that it was Merlin's choice. It wasn't about me. Still, I was incredibly upset over losing this youngster, who'd brought me so much joy in his short time on Earth.

We brought Merlin back to the farm to be buried with all the other animals that we'd lost over the years. Having a farm enabled us to choose special resting places for each of our dear souls who transitioned. Later in the day, I found an unbelievably synchronistic email waiting for me. A friend, who knew nothing about my tragedy that morning, sent me a poem entitled, "The Dash."

The Dash

I read of a man who stood to speak
At the funeral of a friend
He referred to the dates on her tombstone
From the beginning – to the end.
He noted that first came the date of her birth
And spoke of the following date with tears.
But he said what mattered most of all
Was the dash between those years.

For that dash represents all the time
That she had spent on Earth...
And now only those that loved her
Know what that little line is worth.
For it matters not, how much we own:
The cars... the house... the cash...
What matters is how we live and love
And how we spend our dash.
So think about this long and hard...
Are there things you'd like to change?
For you never know how much time is left
(You could be at "dash mid-range")
If we could just slow down enough
To consider what's true and real,
And always try to understand
The way others feel.
And be less quick to anger
And show appreciation more
And love the people in our lives
Like we've never loved before.
If we treat each other with respect,
And more often wear a smile...
Remembering that this special dash
Might only last a little while.
So, when your eulogy's being read
With your life's actions to rehash...
Would you be proud of the things they say
About how you spent your dash?

As I read the poem by Linda Ellis, all my grief over losing Merlin erupted in a flood of tears. I was crushed to lose this special soul, who'd made me laugh so freely in the ultra-short dash he'd been given. When Merlin chose to go Home, I'd been consciously on my spiritual path and communicating with animals for more than five years. I'd learned from the year with my teacher in Manhattan, all my reading, and several workshops, that everything happens for a reason and always for our highest good. Losing Merlin at such a young age challenged this belief. I couldn't see what good reason there could be for Merlin's transition, or how it could be for anyone's highest good. I was bewildered and missed my little comedian terribly.

Chapter 12

∞

A Spiritual Sponge

The first couple of years after Love transitioned were packed with incredible experiences that opened my mind further and further to the unlimited possibilities that reside outside our five senses. Many animals flocked to me to help me hone my communicating skills and gain much-needed confidence. Due to my complete trust in animals, I never questioned what I heard or felt during my communications with them. I loved being able to help people better understand their animals, and vice versa. My challenge was finding enough time in my day.

I spent most nights reading books that found their way to me. I was fascinated with all sorts of topics. I was not unlike a spiritual sponge absorbing everything that interested me. I traveled back to the Omega Institute twice over the next two years for workshops with Michael Roads, "Talking with Nature," and Michael Harner, "The Way of the Shaman." I had brought their books home from Omega's bookstore when I attended the weekend with Eagle Man. All three of my forays to Omega were in perfect timing and profound for me. The experiences each offered were unique, and coerced my left-brained pharmacist's mind to consider a greater reality – a multidimensional reality.

Michael Roads led me on my first-ever guided meditation. His workshop contained numerous guided meditations that felt so real to me. During several, I was overcome with intense emotions. There was no doubt that what I was experiencing was real. There was no other explanation for the depth of feeling.

The shaman workshop built upon my experiences. Michael Harner taught me in one workshop how to journey to the "non-ordinary" reality. The upper and lower worlds are home to teachers who generously share information, guidance, and healing, if we seek it.

Being a spiritual sponge, I attracted exactly what the Universe wanted, experiences that challenged the illusion that I'd been living within for my entire life – the illusion that life consists of the five senses, where the only reality is that of the physical world. My time at Omega, my communicating, and my work with healing energies, had begun to erode my belief in a one-dimensional world. I was experiencing reality beyond our physical world, beyond my five senses, beyond anything I'd have thought possible. I had definitely entered this expanded reality – and continued to do so at will. All I had wished for was to talk to animals, but once I committed to that goal, my entire existence was forever changed, expanded, enriched.

In 1996, an acquaintance, who later became a friend and teacher, introduced me to a healing modality called Spiritual Response Therapy (SRT). Apparently, the Universe felt this student was now ready to reawaken healing skills buried even deeper than my communicating skills. Incorporating a healing modality into my skills would allow me to offer my clients unique solutions to the challenges and issues they brought to me.

SRT is a unique form of healing, occurring at the soul level. Using SRT in agreement with the soul, I identify emotional programs running at the cellular level. Many of these are past life influences. A spiritual education process occurs, releasing the negative emotions and replacing them with harmonious energy. The SRT information comes from the highest levels of the Universal Hierarchy and never interferes with the soul's present life purpose or its free will. SRT was developed for people, but I had no trouble using it with animals. Interestingly enough, many clients ask me to clear them after they've seen the positive changes with their animals. I always tell them to thank their animals for the healing work they just sought for themselves. Animals contribute to the quality of our lives in ways that, like this, are often not apparent.

Around the same time that SRT entered my life, my work with healing energies led me to explore vibrational healing. Physical bodies contain an electrical system that underlies all function. When imbalances within this electrical system happen, emotional and/or physical illnesses occur. Any modality that brings the pattern of vibration back into balance creates improved harmony and promotes healing. Vibrational forms of healing occur on a more subtle plane and results can take slightly longer to notice. Animals seem to respond much faster to vibrational healing than people.

Vibrational remedies – flower essences and gem elixirs – all work to bring the body and subtle energy bodies into alignment. This allows the needed flow of life-force energy through the electrical and circulatory systems, resulting in perfect health. I purchased my first set of flower essences from Machaelle Small Wrights' Perelandra in Virginia and started using them daily. While their effects were quite subtle, I did notice emotional benefits. I worked with them personally for several months before I began to offer them to my clients, who gave me very positive feedback.

After reading several books channeled by Gurudas about flower essences and gem elixirs, I purchased my first gem elixirs from Pegasus in Colorado. Over time, I've added to my collection of essences and elixirs, which now numbers 150-plus. I determine which remedy is appropriate by connecting to the animal's or person's High Self. I'm told the exact remedies that the soul requires – totally eliminating the need to study, learn, or memorize lists of flower and gem characteristics and their uses. If only I had known about this in pharmacy school! The resultant solutions are very specific to the challenges the animal or person is facing.

About a year after I incorporated flower essences and gem elixirs into my bag of tools, I attended a workshop on color therapy. Color therapy uses the same principle of healing: returning the vibrational pattern within the body to a state of perfect balance. Following the same technique, I connect with the animal or person and "hear" the appropriate colors needed to heal specific issues. Color therapy affects both the physical body and all of the individual's energy bodies, thus healing both physical and emotional conditions. I apply the colors using long-distance healing techniques normally twice daily for five to seven days, depending on the needs of the individual.

Animals were drawn to me with challenges whose solutions were found within the ever-expanding base of knowledge that I'd been acquiring. Many were horses within our vet practice; some animals were referrals from satisfied clients; and the rest were my own animals. My experiences during the two-year period of awakening to my talents as an empathetic healer were truly remarkable. I am forever grateful to all the animals that agreed to teach this sometimes slow student. I was honored and humbled by their dedication to my awakening and education. Each one's tale has stayed fresh in my mind over the years. Through my development as a communicator and healer, the animals have taught much that they've asked me to share with the human world. I am so proud to offer these amazing tales of my animal family that contributed to making me the woman and healer that I am today. I wouldn't be who I am today without them. Now that I've introduced most of them, I'd like to share more of the truly astonishing occurrences that filled our lives.

Chapter 13

∞

A Different Kind of Crystal

One morning, a red-tailed hawk almost hit my car. *Things are unfolding for you now. Keep alert! Don't miss the signs.* I saw three more hawks soaring later in the day. Well, I had no clue what all the excitement was about. Given the circumstances of the past several years, I was open to pretty much anything. I never expected what was about to transpire. Soon after my hawk messenger appeared, a gal pal called, asking me to join her at another's house about half an hour from the farm. Apparently, her friend knew someone who mined quartz crystals in Arkansas. It sounded interesting, so I agreed. Little did I know what the Universe and my soul had planned for me.

We ended up at her friend's yoga studio where many quartz crystals of varying sizes and shapes were displayed. There were so many crystals that it was somewhat overwhelming. I'd always been attracted to rocks, but I'd never really met crystals before. We were invited to a presentation three days later given by the miner. At that time, we could purchase crystals. Michael Harner's shaman workshop had given me a broader perspective on many elements within Nature. I knew crystals were among many shamans' healing tools.

Eventually, one smaller crystal caught my eye. Its appearance wasn't that impressive, but there was just something that kept me coming back to it. It was as though it was calling to me. Was it my imagination, or was it an old friend waiting for recognition? Remember, Shadow used to be my best friend Tina. I was open to all kinds of scenarios by now. The longer I stayed, the more I marveled at this one crystal. There wasn't another in the room that "spoke" to me. I had no idea how much anything was, but I decided to purchase the crystal after the gal's presentation.

I read whatever I could find on crystals. I couldn't stop thinking about this crystal. Every time I closed my eyes I saw it. It was as though I'd been possessed by it. I'd felt energized ever since meeting the crystal. I'd never experienced anything like it before, at least nothing in this lifetime. I simply couldn't wait, so I called the miner's friend who'd already mentioned my interest in the crystal to the miner. I was stunned to find out the crystal was very valuable, $2500, and really not for sale. How could this be? I had such a strong knowing that this crystal was meant to be with me. I was confused and *really* sad.

I wasn't sure if I could, but I decided to communicate with the crystal. As my teacher always told me, "Just ask." I explained to the crystal that if it was supposed to be with me, it needed to tell the miner. I also requested help from my Guides and Teachers. I used SRT to clear anything that was negatively contributing to both the sale and purchase of the crystal. The miner gave a very informative talk and agreed to meet with me a few days later to talk about *the* crystal. I continued to be obsessed with the crystal, to the extent that I drove right past the street I lived on – and I'd lived there for 20 years. Talk about preoccupied.

The yoga instructor called to say the miner was too tired from her trip into Manhattan to meet with me. I was shocked and very disappointed. I did SRT clearings for anything and everything affecting this situation. When I asked for assistance from the higher realms I heard, *free will on Earth*. Great, I realize this is a planet of free will, but help! I did all I could and was proud of how I'd accepted the circumstances. While I was still bewildered and unhappy, I had definitely come a long way.

Another hawk arrived with more insight. *You have responded to every turn in an enlightened way. There is nothing more for you to do. Have patience. Keep faith – you have done very well. Be proud no matter what!* While I still didn't understand, the hawk's message bolstered my sagging spirits. I asked the miner to choose a crystal for me, so I'd at least have something. She chose a smoky quartz wand with a beautiful rainbow in it. I had no idea what to do with it, but I figured I would in time.

Intuitively, I received information regarding a life in Atlantis when I worked with crystals. Several nights later, I asked Spirit to bring me any crystals that I'd programmed in previous lifetimes. A tiny voice cried, *You programmed me too!* It had to be my smoky wand. I felt immediate joy. Why didn't I sense you? *The first crystal is very powerful. It holds much wisdom. You were called by it and you were overwhelmed by its presence. You would not be ready to deal with its contents and power now. You programmed me to help bring you back. You have much yet to remember. We have much work to do.* I don't even know how to start. *Don't worry. Just trust in the process and trust in yourself. Let your inner self guide you and be patient! Everything will happen at the proper timing.*

Why am I compelled to touch you, like petting an animal friend? *I am a friend to be sure. You have tremendous abilities involved with your touch. You will become more familiar with these as your remembering continues. All will come in due time. It is pleasant for us because you transmit much love through your touch.* I questioned the crystal about the inclusions (shapes and scenes that form within it during the crystal's growth process) visible within its body, such as the rainbow. *What you see within me is the information to help you open the doorway to the wisdom you have hidden within. It is not the wisdom itself, for that is within you. What I hold are the truths to help you unlock the wisdom. This is my purpose. I am as excited as you are. Just stay open to love and the flow will come easily. Don't force anything. Just follow your feelings.*

To say I was blown away by this information would be an enormous understatement. The level of consciousness contained within this crystal was astonishing. It dramatically changed my belief about my ability to communicate with all of Nature's elements. My smoky wand was more than I ever expected – but I still felt there was another crystal waiting for me. I sent a request, prayer, message, meditation (whatever you want to call it), to Spirit each day, asking for the crystal that I needed to please find this miner. She was the only person I knew who "heard" the crystals' voices.

Almost three months to the day I began pleading with the Universe, I received a call from the yoga instructor. The miner didn't know what I'd been doing, but a crystal she dug up was screaming my name. I just smiled and thanked Spirit. This crystal was far less expensive, but still a considerable investment. To me, it wouldn't have mattered how much. This had to be the crystal I'd been dreaming about. I rushed to the yoga gals' house to meet my new old friend. The spectacular crystal was sitting on a table in the middle of a dimly lit room, making it quite mystical. As I approached it, tears welled up in my eyes. I couldn't believe how emotional I was.

Previously, the miner had shared with me that the first crystal's purpose was to awaken individuals to forgotten memories of working with crystals. I admitted that it was very effective at its job. The crystal that was coming home with me was larger, more complex, and much more beautiful than I ever expected. The arrival of this remarkable crystal was my first conscious experience with the power of manifestation that I possessed – and we all possess. For months I was blown away by the crystal and how it had found me. I ascertained that this magnificent quartz, dubbed my "big crystal," was one of immense information storage. Intuitively, I knew I wasn't ready to fully work with it. It's been sitting next to me since 1997, and I'm still not ready. However, I know the time is fast approaching for us to begin our work together.

I've acquired two other quartz healing crystals since. About six months later, a slightly opaque quartz crystal that looked like a rocket lying on its side, found me quite innocently one night. I'd joined some friends for a spiritual gathering and sat in front of several crystals displayed on a table. By night's end, I was bringing the rocket home with me. I wasn't sure why, but I felt drawn to it. My crystal purchases ceased until I journeyed to Mt. Shasta with friends in 2005. I've shared this experience in my book *Letting Go*. For those who haven't read my first book, don't despair. It's a tale that warrants inclusion here as well.

As I drove to the airport in 2005 leaving on my spiritual adventure to Sedona and Mt. Shasta, an owl flew over my car. *There is magic all around. Stay alert. Be aware. Don't miss the hidden magic!* Well, Owl had me curious and alert for sure. Toward the end of our astounding trip to Sedona and Mt. Shasta, my friends and I visited a store in Mt. Shasta called The Crystal Room. The shop was fairly large with an extensive collection of stones and crystals. While I have a great affinity for rocks and crystals, this shop was oddly uncomfortable for me. There were just too many crystals, which bombarded me with very chaotic energy.

We were invited back for a channeling session later that evening. None of my friends seemed interested, and even though I was tired too, I didn't want to pass on the opportunity. Owl's message compelled me to go. The channeling was in a room I hadn't seen earlier in the day. I was overwhelmed by the energy in this room – this time very positively. Instantly, I was calm and serene, which was a sharp contrast to my previous visit to the store.

I looked around at many, many large quartz crystals and thought to myself, okay, here's where the *real* crystals live. I'd never seen so many healing crystals in one place before. The energy I was bathed in was phenomenal. My intuition told me that these were powerful crystals used for information storage, communication, healing, etc. These weren't ornaments; they were tools, each with their own distinct purposes. I was extremely grateful that I'd decided to come.

One very odd-looking crystal on the bottom shelf caught my eye. A long, thin, clear crystal attached to an opaque base, its shape reminded me of a comet's tail. It looked like an antennae or a wand rising out of this very strange, unique base. It was in total contrast to all of the others and captured my attention. I was so glad I already had all the crystals I needed. . .

Bev, the shop owner, announced that after the channeling session, she'd been instructed to do a 13-bowl healing session for us. Each bowl vibrates at a different frequency, affecting the energy centers (chakras) in our bodies. Their sounds would align our energies horizontally, vertically, and diagonally. I'd experienced a crystal bowl healing meditation before, but not with 13 bowls. Several times during the channeling, I turned to look at the odd crystal sitting behind me. I couldn't believe myself. What was up with this crystal? I didn't want any more crystals. Leave me alone.

Bev's alignment session lasted more than an hour and was exceptional. Despite the tranquilizing effect of the singing bowls, I was distracted several times by the crystal behind me. Halfway through the bowl meditation, I had to lie back from my sitting position due to the mellowing effects of the bowls – which placed my head even closer to the crystal. I opened my eyes several times, turning to look at it. This crystal was screaming at me, but I wasn't looking for another crystal. This pesky little being was telling me that I did indeed need another crystal – I needed it! I was puzzled, but I finally gave in and asked Bev to hold the odd fellow for me until the next afternoon. *There is magic all around. Stay alert. Be aware. Don't miss the hidden magic!*

Bev was busy when I arrived the next day. I located where Bev had set aside the maddening, yet strikingly beautiful, crystal for me. A sales gal saw me pointing it out to one of my friends and asked if I'd held the crystal. Not yet, but I'd love to. I'd learned years ago not to touch quartz crystals without permission. It's a definite no-no. "Do you know it's Atlantean?" I knew, but not because anyone told me. All my crystals were Atlantean.

All my curiosity surrounding this crystal and its command of my attention reached a climax as she handed it to me. It calmed me instantly. It felt familiar, which made no sense. I perceived its happiness when we touched. Smiling, the sales gal proclaimed, "Ah, it *is* yours." She said many, many people had considered this unique crystal. I thought to myself, that's me: odd, unique, and different. Obviously, it had been waiting for a kindred spirit.

At that point, Bev was free and gave me a big hug when she saw me caressing my new partner. She examined the crystal thoroughly, gathering information about the crystal personalities contained in my odd fellow. Personalities are the characteristics and functions that a crystal possesses. Bev was deeply attuned to rocks and crystals. I'm always humbled in the presence of someone adept at their craft. Bev's expertise was as extraordinary as her collection. I asked her where the crystal had been mined. She informed me that all of her inventory came from one woman who mined in Brazil. Interesting – both miners who set my crystals free from their hiding places within Mother Earth were women. I half-wondered if I'd known them and Bev in Atlantis.

"This is an amazing crystal," Bev remarked as she handed me a stack of pages. I commented about how distracting it'd been during the channeling and bowl meditation. She laughed when I admitted that her performance had turned me into marshmallow. The crystal that had been relentless last night was now perfectly content and silent. Even Bev was surprised by the extent of the crystal's many different personalities, abilities, and purposes (which spoke volumes about this odd little crystal, given the thousands she'd come across). Even though my mind was clueless, my heart knew I needed this crystal. I decided against shipping the crystal. Now that it had found me, I didn't want to risk letting it out of my care.

While these gorgeous quartz crystals don't qualify as Master Teachers, they've proven to be very significant players in my life. I felt it important to share the synchronicity surrounding our coming together. Maybe they'll turn into Master Teachers when their student is finally ready to fully work with them!

Chapter 14

∞

Proof Positive

As a skeptic being jerked out of my comfort zone, in the beginning I required lots of proof of the effectiveness of what I was doing. The Universe understood my need for physical proof – proof I could see, hear, or touch. A parade of animals found their way to me, offering me positive validation that I was indeed having an effect not only with my communicating talents, but more importantly, with my more recently resurrected healing skills.

Animals appeared to prove that, without doubt, each new modality I was learning was highly effective and integral to my newfound path. The tales of my clients' animals will be recounted in my next book, for they have much to share. But while they are extremely significant and crucial to my growth as a communicator and healer, they aren't my Master Teachers. Except for Because Of Love, my Masters shared their lives with me, often enduring hardships in order to teach their human friend.

Deepak Chopra's synchrodestiny was hard at work on our farm, although it was years before he coined the term. Most days on the farm were just like they'd always been: Shadow and Licorice helping me with the barn work; the barn cats keeping the rodent and barn swallow populations under control; riding and training Squiggles and Junior when I could steal the time; and endless office work (mostly done after the sun went down). I begged the cats to leave the birds alone, but no one was listening to their communicator person.

Many friends called my life romantic, but those were the ones who didn't understand just how much work it involved. My life on Fair Chance Farm was idyllic, even though exhausting at times. To be surrounded by my animals – caring for them, foaling mares, and nursing sick horses back to health – was more than I'd ever hoped for. And then, my epiphany took everything to the next level. Interspersed within the mundane were occurrences that bordered on magic – and they always began in the most innocent of ways.

One summer morning in 1997, I walked to the pasture to bring in Junior – now 13 years old – for the farrier, who had just arrived to fit him with new shoes. A farrier trims horses' hooves and nails shoes on and does any corrective hoof work that's required. A blacksmith forges tools or other objects from hot iron or other metals. As Junior gingerly turned to face me, my heart sank. He showed all the signs of founder, a deadly disease of the foot. I looked at my farrier and declared, "But he was fine last night!" When one of mine is hurting, my objectivity disappears. I was trying not to panic, but I knew better than most the serious nature of founder. Depending on the severity, it can be extremely painful and oft-times end with euthanasia. I wanted neither for Junior, my beautiful-moving hunter and dear friend.

I located my husband and explained my crisis. He never questioned my diagnosis and came home immediately. Bob began all the usual medications to control Junior's pain and stop the progression of the disease. Founder and colic are the two conditions horseman fear most. Founder can result from any number of causes. Nothing had changed with Junior's feed or environment. There simply wasn't an explanation for his acute attack.

Laminitis is the medical term for this disease. It's believed to be caused by metabolic changes within the horse's system. Many different things can trigger an attack: getting into feed and over-eating, grazing for too long on rich spring grass, drinking unlimited amounts of cold water while hot from exercising, etc. And there are many other, more subtle, reasons. The bones of the foot are suspended within laminae (latticework of tissue) inside the hoof. When the laminae become inflamed they lose strength, and the bones sink or "rotate." The trick is to stop the rotation before the bones protrude through the sole of the hoof. I've only known one horse to survive once the coffin bone broke through the sole. She was a client's stakes-winning Thoroughbred race horse, who ended up shedding her entire hoof before growing a new healthy one. It took an inordinate amount of effort on the part of both the horse and her people to save her.

Radiographs revealed that Junior hadn't rotated yet, which was great news. The bad news was that despite high levels of analgesics he was still very sore. In an effort to support the soles of his hooves, we ordered a truckload of sand that cost over $1000. I didn't give it a second thought. Whatever Junior needed, I'd do. Over the years, I had cared for a number of horses in our hospital that struggled unsuccessfully to survive founder. I swore I wouldn't let Junior suffer. Bob and I agreed that as long as Junior was willing to try, so were we.

At least now we'd know exactly what Junior wanted. I communicated with him about whether he was trying to return to Spirit. I hated to ask, fearing what I might hear. I wasn't ready to say good-bye yet, but I knew that Junior wouldn't get better no matter what we did, if his wish was to go Home. *I'm not going anywhere.* I'm so relieved to hear that. I'm sorry you're in so much pain. *I am, but it's better with all that you and Bob have done. I'm sorry to cause you so much worry.* Don't apologize; it's not your fault. It's no one's fault. We'll do everything we can and as quickly as possible to get this under control. As long as I know you want to stay and try. *I do, and I trust you can fix my feet.* I'll do my very best!

Once again, my life was taken over by a critically ill horse, except this time it was my own horse, making it infinity harder. I cleared Junior of past-life negative energies that were contributing to his founder, using Spiritual Response Therapy. I also prepared a solution of flower essences and gem elixirs for him to promote healing. Thanks to my efforts, Bob's contribution with appropriate drugs to control Junior's pain and retard further progression of the founder, and the cushioning support of $1000 worth of sand under his tender feet, Junior was holding his own. He wasn't getting worse – still no rotation – but he wasn't improving either.

I had one last option I could try: a shamanic journey. After Michael Harner's course at Omega several months earlier, I'd practiced the journeying technique numerous times but never for anything as important as this. I was still skeptical about it and not at all experienced, but what did Junior and I have to lose? I did briefly ponder the timing of Junior's crisis and my having just taken "The Way of the Shaman" course.

I've never shared my journeys before, but the animals have asked me to share all I've learned from them. I believe I need to recount the entire journey in order for you to truly appreciate the astonishing power of the shaman to retrieve information and healing from "non-ordinary" reality. My method for journeying is to lie on my bed listening to a drumming tape. By focusing on the drumming, I'm able to enter "non-ordinary" reality. I describe what I'm hearing and feeling into a tape recorder. You can see from the details that my level of feeling is akin to seeing. In fact, I think it's even more accurate due to the presence of the emotions being experienced as well. After setting my intention for a healing for Junior, I turned on my drumming tape and began my journey.

I journey to the Lower-world for a healing for Junior's founder. I go down through the pond and water slide. I arrive in a prairie-like area, out in the West, very expansive. I ask if there is anyone here that can help me with my horse. A big, black horse (stallion) comes galloping up and stops next to me. Really pretty horse. He wants me to get on him. I have to figure out a way, he's so big (surreal big). Oh, I just sort of "flew" up on him. Such a muscular, powerful animal. We're almost like flying. We're going very fast. I don't know where we're going.

It's so smooth, like flying, but I feel his body galloping with no concussion. We're going down a canyon along a river. We're making turns as we follow the riverbed through the canyons. Oh, pretty. Looks like we've arrived at an Indian place; teepees and peaceful & beautiful. Indian families and Indian ponies – so beautiful. We're walking through the Indian village or whatever you would call it. We're stopping at a teepee. I'm getting down. There's an old Indian motioning me to come in. He's a man, a male Indian. It's like I've known him before. He wants me to sit down. He's serious, not threatening, pleasant but concerned. I ask him if I can get some help for my horse. Will he be able to help me?

He begins, *You have to stop doubting your abilities. There are many spirits available to help you. All you have to do is ask. There are many different ways to heal, but belief is the biggest part.* I really want to believe that we can heal him, but I get so discouraged, because I feel his pain. How can I help him? *You have to believe in your heart that he will get better, before he will believe in his heart that he will get better.*

He's going to mix up some kind of medicine for me to bring back. We're going out now to look for things. We're walking down by the riverbed. He's picking plants, very specific plants, that are along this riverbed. Some have flowers, but others don't. He's placing them in my hand to hold them. He's helping me along the riverbed, and he's very old! I don't know how he distinguishes one from the other. They all look like weeds to me. It's so peaceful and pleasant. The horses are just across the river, free and grazing. Beautiful! He's getting a little bit of the dirt from the river. Oh, yuck. That's kind of wet and mushy. He's putting it in my other hand. Looks like he's found everything he wants here. Just moving along. It's so pretty.

Where we are is very green, lush meadows; very beautiful, so peaceful. There is so much happiness. I'm glad they found this valley. We head toward the village. We stop in an area where there are some utensils. He's mashing up the plants and mixing with the mud to make like a salve. Now, he has a big, broadleaf thing that he's packaging up the concoction in so that I can carry it. I don't know how I should use this. He instructs, *You will carry it in your heart. When you're back in your reality, you will apply it with your heart and believe that he will be healed, and so it will be!*

I don't have anything to give him in return, which I'm telling him, other than my gratefulness. *Give me your belief in return and that will be more than enough.* He's such a wonderful old man! I have to go and take this healing back to Junior. Where's my stallion? He disappeared for a while, but now he's back. It's so pretty, yet so sad. It's so peaceful here. It's how it used to be. I have to go. I hate to leave, but I know I have to help Junior.

We're going back down the same riverbed. Flying along the river between the very high, steep walls. A very powerful, powerful animal. Now we're back out in the prairie where we first met. I have to get off this big, beautiful animal. I'm hugging and thanking him. He's nuzzling me and sending me back. He knows that I need to come back to help Junior. I'm coming back up the water slide. Back in the pond. I'm going out to apply this healing to Junior with my heart. . . whatever that means.

This journey was as real to me as my ordinary world experiences, as evidenced by my remark about the mud being yucky. While it wasn't my first shamanic journey, it was the most detailed and involved to date. Consciously, I was bewildered. How do I bring healing gifts back in my heart? How do I apply them? Obviously, another part of me knew exactly what to do: the part of my consciousness that had been a shaman before.

As I headed out to Junior, I grabbed the rocket quartz crystal. The shaman I once was knew quartz crystals are powerful amplifiers. Standing directly in front of Junior with the crystal over my heart chakra, I applied the healing I'd been given. The rocket crystal directed these healing gifts into Junior's ailing front feet. Then, I held up each foot and applied more healing through the rocket directly to the sole of each hoof. The entire process probably took ten minutes. Now I understood why I was drawn to this crystal a few months earlier. Ah, there is method to the madness if we listen to our hearts! As I finished Junior's healing that afternoon, my pharmacist-self thought: if anyone drives in and sees me, they'll have me committed for sure.

When Bob got home I played the entire journey tape for him and described how I applied the healing. Neither of us knew what to expect. My desire to help Junior fueled my hope. Did I really believe he would be healed? According to the medicine man, it was imperative that I believed that Junior would recover. The shaman part of me believed with my whole heart. The pharmacist part of me was guardedly optimistic based on the previous results I'd achieved with SRT and vibrational remedies.

The next morning, less than 24 hours later, Junior was devoid of *any* symptoms of laminitis. My husband and I looked at each other in utter disbelief. I hugged Junior and cried. Ironically, healing Junior's founder should have cost nothing more than an hour of my time. His recovery was virtually impossible based on everything known to our physical world. Junior was healed by energy from a world beyond our five senses. The impossible became possible before our very eyes.

Watching Junior trot soundly across his pasture solidified my belief – belief in myself, belief in my abilities that I was only just discovering, and belief in the unlimited possibilities that lay beyond the illusion that I'd been raised to believe in. It was a whole new world for this pharmacist-turned-communicator/healer.

Junior's willingness to endure significant pain in order to teach me about the healing power available from "non-ordinary" reality is worthy of a Master Teacher. There is incredible healing and information available to anyone with an open mind and heart. Start with a pure intent, ask for answers and/or healing, and then *believe*. Junior's efforts and lessons are honored every day in the healing work I do, and in my unwavering belief in limitless possibilities.

Chapter 15

∞

Strengthening the Connection

Given the success with Junior's founder, I decided to see if I could help him with some arthritis that had been giving him trouble. He wasn't constantly lame, but it seemed to be getting worse. So a week or so after my experience in the Lower-world, I set my intention and headed back to "non-ordinary" reality. I had no idea where I was going, but each of my previous journeys had encouraged me to come again.

I journey to the Upper-world for a healing for Junior's arthritis in his front feet, especially his right front foot. I have to go up three levels before I sense any help. When I get there I am in a beautiful area full of wildflowers, birds, trees, and a waterfall. It's very peaceful and calming.

Out from under the waterfall comes a man. He's approaching me. He's young, sort of 30–40 years old, ruggedly nice-looking. He motions for me to join him under a huge weeping willow tree by the side of the waterfall. It's so peaceful and beautiful. *I don't know why it took you so long to get here.* I ask his name. *Merlin.* He's much younger than the Merlin I imagine. Oh, well!

I ask if I can get a healing for the arthritis in Junior's front feet. *Why not?*, he asks. I am confused at how we can override the obvious bony (physical) structure. *You must realize that Spirit is behind everything. That nothing is impossible when Spirit is involved. Belief is paramount. Anything can be healed – follow me.*

We are moving through the woods. Walking, but gliding at

the same time. We've stopped by a tree. He is asking the tree if we might get some of its healing energy for my horse Junior. *Of course, you should take some of my bark.* It somehow strips itself of some bark and offers it to me. Thank you! *I am hawthorn.*

We continue on our way. It's so pretty and lush with songbirds serenading us. Now we've stopped by a mound of some kind of dirt. It's granular, really like tiny pebbles. We ask if we might have some of them to help my horse Junior. The mound starts to glow. Merlin scoops a small amount into my hand, and I put it into a pouch with the bark. Thank you!

We continue on, and we approach an opening in the forest with an old dead stump. All of a sudden, very silently, a giant golden eagle lands on the stump. He is as large as we are. I am almost pushed over by the power that emanates from him. He is *magnificent.* We ask if we might have some of his power to help heal my horse Junior. I have direct eye contact as I ask and begin to feel the same feeling of freedom I experienced when I flew as an eagle during a past-life recall. He lifts his wing and with his beak pulls out an under-feather and offers it to me. I'm not sure how to take it. I have no fear of him and Merlin motions me toward this huge bird. I hold out my hand and he very gently places it in my palm. It is so soft. Thank you!

Continuing along through the woods, we come to an up-surging of water, sort of like a spring, I guess. As we get closer, I notice that as the water reaches the top of its flow and starts to fall back, it changes into a rainbow of colors. Very different. I have never seen anything like this. (Like I've seen *any* of this before!) Merlin wants me to get a handful of this "water" to put in the pouch with the other gifts. It doesn't feel wet. I can't really explain what I feel; kind of energies, vibrations, like the color therapy. Thank You!

Now we're heading back to our place under the willow tree. Merlin says, *You now have healing offerings from all of the kingdoms that make up the physical world: plant, mineral, animal, water.* I look puzzled when he includes water. *You must remember that Spirit is behind everything. The color rays that you have brought* with you are simply the energy before it slows down to the frequency needed to become physical water. The essence is the same. The duality of nature. It is very important to accept this knowledge and have it become part of your knowing. I thought I had, but I guess not entirely. Take all these gifts back to your horse from all his brothers and sisters. You must realize that we are all here to help one another. We need each other in order to experience all that we have come to do. As we accept the help from another, the other being grows and evolves also. Everyone has something to contribute; none is greater than another. Each has its own part. All the parts come from the Whole and will return to it. When we truly realize this, we will have returned to the Whole.

How am I to apply this healing to Junior? *Carry it with love in your heart. When you get back, take your healing crystal...* The rocket? *Yes. Hold it over your heart chakra with both hands. Aim it at both front feet. Ask for the healing to be amplified and sent out through this crystal. Your love for this being will carry the healing gifts forth to him. This crystal will amplify and enhance the gifts from all the kingdoms. Believe it, and it will be!*

Merlin is leaving. He's heading back under the waterfall. I think I need to stay here in this energy for a little bit. It's so nourishing to my Spirit. The longer I'm here, the stronger and more confident I'm feeling. I think I'll just wade around in the water from the falls. It's so soothing; perfect temperature. What a surprise.

A doe deer has come to the water's edge to drink just downstream from me. She is so pretty and doesn't seem at all afraid of me. What a thrill! *Why should I fear you? There is nothing to fear here. That's what you feel – the absence of fear/negativity. You think this is such an unusual place. The feeling you have here can be anywhere. You can bring this back to your reality. It is your choice. This is how beings are supposed to experience being-ness. Just as the ripples move on this water, the ripples of energy move outward from your being. You are the center of these ripples of energies. You are the only one responsible for the energy you transmit; no one else. You can choose to have the feelings of our reality with you in yours. Just transmit ripples of love/positive energy. For as you send out only these vibrations, that is what will be attracted to you. Not only will you attract humans, but also the wild ones that you seek to spend time with. They will approach you the same as I do now. Use them as a reading as to what energy you are creating. They will be a mirror for you. If you are sending love, they will feel that and respond by approaching. If you are harboring any negativity, they will feel that also and move away. Remember, they are very sensitive and true. You can trust their actions for they use these instincts for their survival.*

The time now is very important in your reality to enhance and support the changes in vibrations upon your planet. There are many upon your planet now to help with this mission. You are responsible for your own energy. That is where it starts. Feel in your heart the essence of this place, remember it in your heart, and bring it back in your heart. It is the essence of the Divine Energy; it is unconditional love.

The whole time we are talking the doe approaches me and eventually kisses my hand that's holding the pouch. I begin stroking her. She is so soft. Her eyes are so beautiful. When we look in each other's eyes, I feel like she is holding my heart within her. She is truly *gentleness* in physicality. Not only is she physically gentle, but spiritually gentle. We could all learn so much from the way she lives her life. She leaves and walks out of the water and back into the woods. I look down; my pouch is glowing! It is a pale, pink glow – the color of love.

Well, I'm just going to draw in the essence of this place and bring it back as she has suggested. I hope I can learn to do what she has taught me. I'm so grateful. It all seems so incredible, yet so simple to do. It really does stem initially from your belief. It's the starting point for all our journeys in this life. Thank you to all who have shared with me!

I gained much more than healing for Junior from my journey. The wisdom shared by the doe was unexpected and so timely for both me and all of humanity. I applied the healing to Junior. He lost his occasional lameness despite the arthritic changes still appearing on his x-rays. I was quite perplexed by that. My left brain didn't understand how that was possible, but my shaman's brain understood perfectly well. The important thing was that Junior was more comfortable and happy.

Trying to find time in my day to pursue my young communication and healing business was almost impossible. I already covered the responsibilities of three people. Whenever we had a horse in the hospital everything else had to be put on hold. Discovering my life's purpose was a double-edged sword for me. On the one hand, I was thrilled to know what I'd come into this life to do, but on the other hand, I was already overcommitted. I simply didn't know how to balance it all, and that caused me great stress. Eventually, I decided to journey for *me*. What a novel concept! I would learn years later after I left my beautiful farm, how important the lesson of taking care of self first was.

So after one particularly stressful morning, I got out my drumming tape and tape recorder to seek answers to my predicament.

I journey to the Upper-world. I have to go up three levels. I keep asking if there is anyone who can help me. At the third level, I feel like I'm supposed to stay here. I don't see anyone. I am in a wilderness area with a huge lake surrounded by mountains in the distance. It's very quiet and peaceful. I still don't see or hear anyone.

As bizarre as this might sound, there is almost the image of a face in the lake. There *is* a face in the lake! It's a woman's face; a very pretty face. I'm going to go in the lake. Her face is kind of beckoning. Her face is kind of moving off from the shore like she wants me to follow. I'm going to wade in first, then dive.

The lake, when I go in underneath it, is not really water. I don't know what it is. It's like rainbows of colors under the surface. Many different colors, all together. I can breathe in it. It's just beautiful! Very soothing, all these colors. Swimming underwater just like I love to in the water back home. But I can stay underwater. I don't have to worry about going up for air. I feel supported and light. Everything is so easy, carefree. Oh, it's just wonderful!

The face is telling me, *That is the way you have to make your life. Make it so that it's carefree and wonderful. You have to make your mind still like the surface of the lake, so you can see within. When you still your mind like the lake, you can go within, just as you've done with this lake, and find all that you need to make life easy, to feel supported, and to heal.*

If you don't make your life easy, you will have all kinds of physical problems. Your back has started to bother you because your soul is crying out to go in a different direction. It feels the only way you are going to listen to it, is if it does something to keep you from going in the wrong direction, physically. If you keep ignoring what your Spirit really wants to do, you'll continue to have more physical problems. You have to be true to your own soul.

I'm telling her that I've been trying to have respect for everyone else's concerns during this time. *That is fine, but you have to have respect for yourself – that is the most important. For if you don't really respect yourself and be true to yourself, you can't truly respect someone else. You just say you're trying to respect them, but you're not doing that unconditionally. You're doing it with great resentment and anger. And all of that resentment and anger is settling in your body. If you don't release that and start to take action for yourself, you will just continue to create dis-ease and illness and pain in your body.* I tell her I know that, but it is very difficult to do when there are other people involved that you care about. *That's true and I understand. But, if you don't make yourself happy then no one around you will be happy.* I understand that, but . . .

I'm asking if there is anything that can be done outside me that can initiate getting everybody organized to make this change. *You have to be the one to truly believe that it is going to happen. You have to be the one to initiate it. It cannot be done from outside. It has to be done from inside.* I know all of these things. I just don't seem to be able to put them into action.

I'm just going to stay in this "Lake of Colors" for a while. I wonder if I'm being healed with color therapy. It's so wonderful. Everything is so easy; movement is so easy. It feels so good, like when I swim underwater. Only it's even better because I don't have to come up for air. I can just stay here. I'm just swimming through different areas of color now. Blues, oranges, oh, this is wonderful! I think I'm just going to come out here and sit on the shore a little bit.

This lake is so beautiful! The face is back on the surface. *You must love yourself. You must trust yourself. For only you know what is best for yourself. This is a very powerful lake. You may come back anytime that you want healing. You have a lot to do in the next few years, some of which will cause need for much healing. You only have to ask to be with the "Lady of the Lake." I will always be here for all who believe.*

As her face fades away, I thank her for her help and her healing. The lake is like glass. It is so still. I feel like I should drink some of this water. It feels like water going down; very pleasant. Just like you would imagine a clear, pristine mountain lake should taste. Very satisfying, although I can't say that I am thirsty; but maybe my soul is? I'm totally startled! A single dolphin leaps and dives. How unexpected! Dolphins aren't in mountain lakes, but then again, neither are faces and voices and colors.

For quite a while prior to my journey, I'd been trying to accept that our plan to sell the farm and relocate to the mountains of North Carolina wasn't going to happen anytime soon. My folks lived on the farm with us and initially agreed to move when we first shared our wish to relocate. Over the next several months, it became obvious that at their ages, they just weren't moving anywhere. I'd surrendered to their wishes, but I'd struggled for months to accept it. I was so disappointed. I was ready to make a change. The Lady's guidance was centered on these circumstances and the negative effects I was experiencing from my struggle.

Each time I return from a shamanic journey, I'm more astonished than the previous time. I never know where in "non-ordinary" reality my journey will take me or who I will meet. It hardly matters because each journey is unique unto itself. Who could ever imagine a lake such as this or the Lady of the Lake? The feelings, sensations, and conversations are as real as if they were happening in our ordinary reality. The fact that I'd never heard of such a place or such a Lady was more proof to me that this experience was not of my imagination.

I felt renewed and encouraged after my time in the lake. I understood the Lady's message, but implementing that back in this reality was easier said than done. I tried, but I must confess that our plan to move stayed buried until my folks died three years later. It's always about choice and free will. I just wasn't ready to put self first yet. It was an opportunity missed that would plague me down the road.

Chapter 16

∞

Those Little Voices

My days on the farm continued to be filled with mundane farm and vet-practice chores. I struggled to find even an hour in the day for my new endeavor of communication and healing. The Universe presented a continuous flow of animals that helped reinforce all that I was learning. Luckily for me, most of them were other people's pets. I honestly tried to incorporate the knowledge gained from the "Lady of the Lake" into my everyday life, but failed miserably. I was blind to my soul's need to make animal communication and healing the priority it was destined to be in my life.

The farm, hospital and vet practice, horses, and Bob took up most of my time. The inner struggle between my soul's wishes and my actual reality continued to create stress. I carried around a huge burden named responsibility. I was "the responsible one," and I hadn't a clue how to change it. So I chose not to – another decision that I'd regret later.

Over the years, I'd cleaned thousands of stalls. It's repetitive, mindless work that I did on autopilot. After I learned to meditate, I realized that mucking was a wonderful time to practice mindless meditation. I did some of my best "thinking" while cleaning the barn. Why was it the best? It was right-brain thinking – the intuitive rather than intellectual side.

While cleaning the barn and being entertained with my new kittens, Crystal and Merlin, I began getting thoughts about breeding Squiggles. Early in my development, I used to get confused about the little voices in my head. Were they my thoughts, information from the higher realms, or messages from the animals themselves? I decided their origin wasn't all that important.

From an early age Squiggles loved to watch all the mares and foals, and would gaze longingly at the babies. I could tell she really wanted one of her own, but we'd decided to stop breeding our own horses. When Squiggles was a four-year-old, a client's mare died from a ruptured stomach. It was sudden and sad. She had a lovely, three-month-old filly that I called Monday. Monday was drinking water and eating enough solid food that we felt she'd do fine without spending the client's money on a nurse mare, a surrogate mother for an orphan foal. He'd already suffered a huge financial loss when his broodmare died.

Monday was lonely, depressed, and not eating well. She just stood alone in the field without grazing, which broke my heart. Monday needed companionship, and she needed it fast. The only possible candidate was Squiggles. I told Bob about my idea to put them together. There was an advantage, since coincidentally Squiggles resembled Monday's mother. We know there are no coincidences by now, right? I just knew Squiggles loved babies and would be friendly and gentle.

This was years before I knew I could talk to animals, so I couldn't explain the situation to them. As soon as we turned them out together, Monday tried to suckle from Squiggles. Squigs didn't squeal, kick, or show any aggressive body language, but the filly got the message that Squiggles was just here as a friend. Monday's improvement was instantaneous. She started grazing and followed Squiggles everywhere. Her appetite improved dramatically and her depression lifted. Monday was a happy foal again.

Every time I'd look out and see Monday standing up against Squiggles, my heart smiled. It was as though Squiggles' love was flowing into the filly by osmosis. If you didn't know, you'd think they were mother and foal. I teased Squiggles that she'd gotten her baby without the effort of pregnancy and birth. Eventually Monday left our farm to be trained for racing, so Squiggles did feel the sting of loss.

Since we'd stopped breeding, I ignored the little voices for a while, but they just kept up. If I followed the thoughts, I'd ponder who to breed Squiggles to. Immediately I'd hear *Los Alamos*, a dressage training center a couple of miles from us. Engaging further, I commented No, he's a short, chestnut dressage stallion. Los Alamos' foundation stallion was a small, chestnut dressage horse – a very successful stallion, but not one I'd been interested in breeding Squigs to.

This went on for several weeks until we received a call from the owner of Los Alamos wanting an appointment for Bob to do a pre-purchase exam at her place. I should've seen this as significant since Bob rarely went to Los Alamos. I didn't see the synchronicity, because I didn't believe there was a stallion at Los Alamos for Squiggles. Oh, ye of little faith!

Bob woke up that morning with his back out and asked if I could go with him to carry the heavy x-ray equipment. I was happy to help – and still clueless. While Bob was examining the horse, our farrier (a person who trims horses' hooves and puts shoes on them), who also worked for Los Alamos, announced he was bringing out a stallion. Instead of seeing the chestnut horse I expected to walk by, Mark walked a tall, impressive-looking dark bay (brown almost black) stallion past us – my favorite equine color!

I was shocked and asked the farm owner who the horse was. She laughed and said he couldn't figure out if he was a dressage horse or a jumper. She then told me that he'd just returned from a successful stint on the Florida show circuit, where he'd been shown by someone I knew to be a very accomplished professional jumper rider. *"Really?"*

As soon as we finished x-raying, I packed up the equipment, loaded it into the car, and disappeared to find where Mark was shoeing the stallion. Mark had worked for us for years, so I knew he'd be candid with me about the stallion. "He's the real deal!" The stallion was quietly cross-tied in a barn with mares in stalls around him. Not only was he big and handsome, he radiated the most wonderful energy. In the horse world, we call it "presence." I was in *love!* Bob found me, and I shared the nagging thoughts I'd been having/receiving about breeding Squiggles. He quipped, "I figured as much. Well, you better not wait much longer." Squiggles was 13 years old now. A mare's fertility diminishes as she ages, especially if she's never had a foal before.

As the farm owner crossed her barnyard, I yelled that I might have a mare to breed to her stallion. She was surprised, but quite pleased. I told her I just needed to see a picture of the stallion jumping. "How about a video?" Even better. Apparently, all the videos were sent out. I told her a picture would do fine. She found one from his recent trip to Florida. As she handed it to me, I let out an uncensored gasp. He was young and inexperienced, but jumped in fantastic form! The next question dealt with stud fee, which was doable for me.

Bob drove home while I read the PR about the stallion that she handed me. I was amazed that the stud fee wasn't higher, as I learned about everything he'd already achieved. The more I read, the more I knew that this was the perfect match for Squiggles, who was also a very athletic jumper. I couldn't help but smile at the orchestration of the Universe to coerce me over to Los Alamos to meet the stallion of my dreams: LA Baltic Inspiration, Swedish Warmblood stallion, and future mate for Squiggles The Special.

Getting Squiggles to "catch" – a horseman's term for getting pregnant – turned out to be harder than anticipated. Being a sport horse, Spiro (his barn name) was bred artificially, which meant it wasn't crucial that Squiggles be receptive, but she needed to have a healthy reproductive system to conceive. Many mares stop cycling in the winter months. Squiggles' cycles were delayed that spring. Plus, she had a uterine infection that needed treatment before being inseminated.

Pretty much everything that could be a complication, was. But, I didn't give up. I knew how badly Squiggles wanted a foal and felt this breeding had been destined. She didn't conceive after the first insemination, which was a confusing disappointment for me. Squigs needed to be inseminated on the Fourth of July, which was the last attempt for the season. Luckily, she caught – making her foaling date early June (if she'd read the book on equine reproduction).

You can see that communication comes in many different forms. Belief and trust are paramount. I found it curious that the stallion's name was Inspiration, for that was what started the entire scenario. I was receiving inspiration from Squiggles about her deep desire to have a foal of her very own. These inspirations began a journey that none of us could have ever predicted – one of amazing highs and agonizing lows. Like I said at the beginning, it's been quite a ride!

Chapter 17

∞

Practice Makes Perfect

*W*hile I was being bombarded by thoughts of possibly breeding Squiggles, I noticed Rainbow trying to walk across the barnyard one afternoon. I say trying because he'd wobble for a few steps and fall over, wobble for a few steps and fall over. My barn cats were never any problem. I'd never seen anything like this in any animal before. My pharmacist's brain starting spewing out all sorts of thoughts about what could be affecting Rainbow. I put Rainbow in the car and headed to my vet-friend Gary's clinic.

Having all the confidence in the world in Gary, I knew he'd have the answer and he did: Geriatric Vestibular Syndrome. The name was bigger than the cat. The term "syndrome" meant to me that they really didn't know what it was. Apparently a seasonal condition, it affects the inner ear and balance of older animals; hence Rainbow's constant falling over. Supportive care and steroids were the appropriate treatment, along with time. Gary said some animals recover totally and others are left with impairments. Well, I didn't need a barn cat with impairments. Rainbow needed to be able to take care of himself.

Rainbow became a house cat temporarily, so I could monitor him closely. I needed to keep him from hurting himself or from being hurt by anyone else. I cleared Rainbow with Spiritual Response Therapy and tested him for vibrational remedies to help support and heal his body. Even though his prognosis was good, I wanted to do everything possible to speed up his recovery, since he was very unhappy about living inside. So out came my drumming tape and tape recorder. I would do a shamanic journey to acquire healing for Rainbow.

I head to the pond and down the water slide. I journey to the Lower-world. I arrive in a desert area. There's cactus and sand. It's very red, *very* warm. Really don't see too much happening yet. Just walking around to see if I can come across somebody or something. Off in the distance there must be a source of water. There are some cattle around it. I'm going to go over there and see if I can find anybody.

It's very hot, dry. There's an older woman with the cattle by the water. I'll ask her if she can help me with my cat. She shakes her head no and points in another direction. Off in the distance there's something travelling fast, creating a lot of dust. Oh, it's my friend, the big black stallion. He gets around, I guess. Okay, it's nice to see him again. He's so powerful. Let me get on him. He wants to take me somewhere.

Going back in the direction he came from. Down through the valley of the desert area. Galloping quickly but so smooth. Now, we're going up a little bit to what looks like an Indian village, but it's in the side of the red cliffs; sort of cave things. Going up into that area. We've stopped on a plateau ledge; very large though. It looks like a meeting area. There are a number of different Indians there. Everybody I ask if they can help me, points in a new direction. They just look at me blankly. I just keep following the different directions they're pointing in.

There seems to be one dwelling that's off a little, separate from the others. There's a man inside. He invites me in to sit down. Can you help me with a healing for my cat? He wants me to sit down! He's offering me something to drink. It's very tasty, whatever it is. I don't know what it is. It's some kind of juice, not water. I explain Rainbow's problem and ask if he can help.

He wants me to follow him outside. He's really not as old as he first appeared when we get out into the Sun; maybe 50s. We're climbing back down and heading out away from the rest of the abodes. He's getting some cactus; cut a small part off. He's going along and taking the flower from another type of cactus. Here's some other kind of plant that's very dry-looking.

We're climbing back up to his place. Going inside. Taking some other things out of pouches that he has. Not quite sure. He's mashing the flower of the one cactus and taking the fleshy inside of the other cactus to add to it, along with some type of powder. I'm asking what the powder is. *It is a special kind of ground earth from the nearby area. It has very special, strong healing powers.* It's almost brick red in color. He's using some of the liquid I drank to help combine them into a paste. Now, he's making it thinner, more liquid. It's getting quite syrupy-looking. He seems to be done with it.

He's smudging me (cleansing with the smoke of burning sage or sweet grass), offering prayers to the four directions, to the Father above, and the Mother below. He has a very kind, kind energy. When he touches me I feel very safe. I thank him for preparing this for my cat. I explain that when he gets up and tries to move he just falls over, and this causes me great sadness to see this because I love him. These are wonderful things that they know. I wish I had more wisdom.

Do not chide yourself. You have the wisdom to come and seek help. Many others don't even do that. There's help everywhere if you just ask for it. You don't have to have the knowing. You just have to know how to ask and know where to ask and who to ask. We all have our gifts to offer. I work with the natural gifts of this area in the desert where I live. I'm so grateful for his help. How should I use this? *Drink the mixture and bring the healing energies within you back to your cat-friend. And through the love in your heart the energies will pour from you into him. And he will be well. You are welcome to come back at any time.*

Well, I'm going to drink this mixture right now. I have no idea what it's going to taste like, but that's really unimportant. I need to do this for Rainbow. Really doesn't have much flavor; very chalky. Not bad at all. I thank him again for his help for my cat. I'm going out to find my good friend to take me back.

Please share the knowledge you have. We would like to help more people, but not many come anymore. And there's plenty of healing available if they only ask. You could tell others. If they're pure of heart, they will find their way. Not to worry, we are safe here. We want to help and only the pure of heart are allowed to enter. I'll share this when I get back so that others will know that you wait to help them. Thank you!

There's my horse. Looks like he's had a drink. Now we're going to head back to wherever it is I came from. Doesn't feel like a real super-happy place. They feel a little sad here. I think they'd like to be helping more. This is such a wonderful horse and so easy to sit on. Everything he does is so effortless. We're galloping back across the desert area. Boy, it's so barren. It looks like a very unforgiving place to live. Not a place I'd want to be at all.

Now we're back to where we started. I thank my horse-friend so much for bringing me. He always takes me to the most wonderful healers; so generous and kind. 'Til the next time, my friend. Thank you! Just coming up the water slide. Back at the pond. Heading downstairs to offer this healing to Rainbow.

Just as with my previous journeys, I am so touched by the generous nature of the people I meet. They are all so helpful and welcoming. I am always transformed by their giving spirit and their healing wisdom. I ask my inner shaman to apply the healing gifts from the Indian of the Red Cliffs (as I've decided to call him). I find it interesting that only when I specifically ask someone's name do they tell me their name. These are humble healers who need no personal aggrandizement. They merely want to help.

By the next day Rainbow is much improved, which had my pharmacist-mind spinning once more. While he was still wobbly, he was no longer falling over. His balance seemed to improve as the hours passed. In the afternoon, Rainbow was so much better that he jumped through the kitchen window's screen and escaped. I found him reclining in his barn. He tried to get away, but he wasn't that improved. I scolded him for ripping the screening while I carried him back to his prison. Neither of us was happy. (Well, I was somewhat because the healing received from the Indian of the Red Cliffs had certainly had a positive effect.)

Rainbow's escape got the better of him. I came downstairs the next morning to find one very sick kitty. He'd thrown up through the night, and now he wouldn't eat or drink. I knew he'd aggravated his vestibular syndrome that made his world spin, causing nausea. I felt bad for him, but he'd really done it to himself. I had no more healing to apply. Since he'd responded so successfully to my last journey, maybe too successfully, I decided to head off on another the following day.

I'm in the same desert area as the other day, but not the exact same spot. I don't really see what I saw the last time. It's different. It's very early in the morning. It's much cooler than the last time. Kind of dawn time. Just looking around to see. Oh, it's my cougar-friend! Well, isn't that a surprise. We're just greeting each other. She's leaned into me like a small cat would – but almost knocked me over. I haven't seen her in awhile. This is a nice treat.

She wants me to follow her. Well, this is interesting – I'm moving along just as fast as she is, just effortlessly. She's just bounding, loping; big bounding strides. I'm running but going as fast with no effort at all. Heading in the same area. Well, I must say she gets up the rocks a lot more adeptly than I do. It's the same area, but she's actually taking me to a different cave-like area. This one is quite hidden away. There's no way you could see it.

It's really dark. I'll just follow her inside. There's an older woman in here. I'm going to ask her if she can help me with a healing for my cat. She wants me to sit down, so I do. She offers me something to drink. It's different from the other day. This is kind of sour, but refreshing at the same time.

I'm telling her what's wrong with my cat. *The man that helped you the other day is my son.* I tell her that his healing was very good and it made the cat feel so much better that he jumped through our window screen and went outside. But now he doesn't feel well at all. He's not eating or drinking and can't hold down food. He's worse. *That's like a typical child that just thinks they know best.* She's right.

We're going outside to find some things that we need to make a brew. She has a *very* sweet energy; very gentle. Trying to climb down the embankment out of the hidden cave. Really rugged terrain for someone her age. Rugged terrain for me, and I'm not nearly her age. Going into a different area than before. More brushy, scrub-like area. Denser vegetation than where we got the other plants from. She's picking several different plants, different leaves.

Now we've come to an area with a little water. That's probably why they are gathered here with their homes. She's getting some kind of vine-like plant that grows more in the water than on the land. She's got three or four or maybe five different plants she wants me to hold. There's another flower; pretty purplish flower that she's getting – a desert wildflower. She's taking several of those flowers. *This is all we need.*

We're going back to her home. She's taking some water. She's putting several plants in the water over a fire. She's making a tea or some sort of extraction. She's put three of the five in the water over the fire for a little while. The other two plants and the purple flowers she's grinding all up. She's taking the water off the fire to sit for a little bit, I guess. She's still busy grinding up the other leaves and flowers.

Now she's getting some other things from further in her home. It's more of that same brick-red powder that her son had used. She's adding it to the smashed-up flowers and a couple of the other plants. She's making a dry mix out of that. Now she's putting the crushed-up plants and the red powder in a small clay dish. She wants me to bring it back that way, I guess. Now, she's working on the tea or whatever it is. She wants to cool it down some. She's taking the leaves and things out of the water. She's pouring some of the water into a glass. I don't know what you'd call it – like a pottery mug, I guess.

She's using some type of smudge. I don't know what it is. It's a different type of aroma than other things I've smelled. It's nice, but I don't know what it is. She's offering a prayer to the four directions, the Father above, and the Mother below.

Drink the tea! Wonder what this will taste like? Oh boy, is that bitter! Oh boy, ick! It made me burp. Oh, she wants me to have another cup. Oh, wow! (Sigh) Oh, that's enough of that. It's *really* bitter; awful. It gives me the shivers.

Bring the powder back just the way it is in the little earthen dish, so you can keep it. Don't use it all at once. Use some of it and save the rest. How do I do that? *Your heart knows how to apply it. Apply all of this healing though your heart. Your inner self knows how to use these. There's extra of this powder mixture. Only use some of it now and retain the rest. You may need to apply more of it tomorrow. See how your friend is. Apply the tea mixture and part of the powder mixture when you get back. Hold the other part of the powder mixture in reserve in case he needs that, so you won't have to come all the way back to get more.*

There are just some things my son has not learned yet, just as your cat has not learned to trust you and to let you help him until you know he's totally well. My son has done a very good job, but not a complete job. This was a little more involved than we realized. The cat has hopefully learned a very important lesson that he needs to let those that are trying to help him have a little more control. There's always a positive lesson to learn from the negative. It's too bad that he felt ill today, but he's probably learned a very important lesson from that, so it will be worth it. I'm so glad that you've come back for more healing. That you didn't get discouraged because he wasn't healed. Sometimes it takes more than one attempt. Many people get discouraged and they just don't believe and they don't come again.

I'm so grateful for their help. I have a lot of faith in this method. I've had wonderful results the few times I've done it. I'm so grateful that they're willing to share their knowledge with me and my friends. I will continue to come whenever I need help.

I'm going back with my cat-friend now. Gee, she's actually gotten a little larger in size and actually wants me to ride her. *You have to carry this healing and I don't want you to have to worry about how to get back to your spot.* Umm, we're just flying along. We're really not even running or loping. It's just very smooth and I'm holding my little bowl of goodies. I'm just thanking her for her help and telling her how glad I am to have seen her again.

I'm beginning to feel more at ease with these journeys and I hope to be doing many more in the future. I'm very grateful for her help. I give a kiss to her and she licks my hand. I go back into the water slide and come up to the pond. Now, I'll head downstairs and apply this healing to Rainbow and hope my inner self can regulate the amounts, but I do believe I know how to do this.

The old Indian woman was as wise as she was kind. The shaman part of me followed her instructions for applying Rainbow's healing. He seemed almost normal the next day – but made no attempt to escape. Of course, I kept the windows closed downstairs, but he could have easily scooted out the door. Cats are extremely fast and cagey. I hoped that his tolerance with being confined was a sign that he'd learned something from all of this. I certainly did, and I was grateful for Rainbow's teaching.

I decided to use the rest of the healing, mostly because I didn't want to waste the goodness of it. I waited another 24 hours before I returned Rainbow to the barn. He was so happy to have his freedom back. I was thrilled to watch him run across the barnyard with no residual impairment. Once again, I watched a miracle from non-ordinary reality. I couldn't help but wonder how we could have lost this most amazing ability to journey to "non-ordinary" reality for guidance and healing. What I heard was, *Fear!*

A knowing deep within me agreed. The shaman in me knew all too well the power of fear. If humanity can't see it, touch it, feel it, or hear it, then it simply isn't real. I hope to change that paradigm by sharing these powerful tales of my Master Teachers and the astonishing recoveries they each made – right before my pharmacist-eyes!

More synchronicity occurred several days later when I shared my journeys with my network chiropractor and dear friend. After I described my experiences, she remarked that it sounded like I'd visited the Anasazi – the Ancient Ones. I'd heard the name, but didn't know too much about them. She'd just seen a television program about them. They were cliff-dwellers. Well, my curiosity was piqued.

I searched the Internet and found out that these were an indigenous people of the American Southwest who lived from 1200 B.C. to A.D. 1300 and then mysteriously disappeared. The images of the ruins of their cliff dwellings were exactly what I had been to. I was astonished. The Anasazi hadn't disappeared. They had just relocated to "non-ordinary" reality and were waiting patiently to assist all who sought their wisdom and healing.

The revelation that I'd actually been invited into an Anasazi village and gifted with healings from two different "ancient ones" was almost more remarkable to me than the experiences themselves. I am honored that they chose to share their ancient wisdom with me and their healing with Rainbow. It's no wonder he recovered without incident. Thirteen years later as I write this, I am even more astounded. You just can't make this stuff up.

Chapter 18

∞

As Different as Night & Day

I am always amazed that full brothers and sisters (same father and mother) can be as different as night and day. That was the case with Junior and Squiggles. Junior was a gorgeous-moving hunter. Squiggles was an extremely athletic jumper who moved well. While they were both kind horses, Junior could be a bully at times. Although Squiggles was very self-confident, she had no need to prove who the boss was. There was no doubt that Squigs was the alpha mare. And as Junior himself admitted, Squiggles was the more tolerant and (I would add) the epitome of forgiveness – something Junior lacked.

Squiggles thrived during her first pregnancy. For a mare that had been through several life-threatening situations, she was the picture of health as she carried her first foal. She just blossomed, which I knew was the result of the joy of being in foal. A mare's gestation period is 11 months, so even though I was excited and anxious for the foal to arrive, I had settled in for the long wait.

While Squiggles radiated health, Junior began to have lameness issues with his hind legs. Junior was one of those horses that the smallest of injuries or illnesses turned into big deals. Some horses are just that way. Squiggles had had big issues for sure, but they began that way. We were managing Junior's discomfort with feed supplements and occasional analgesics when he became *really* lame. Feeling Junior's discomfort was upsetting to me. Since Junior had responded so well to the shamanic journey I'd done for his life-threatening founder and arthritic front feet a year-and-a-half earlier, I chose to journey for help with his advancing hind-leg discomfort.

I leave the pond through the waterslide to journey to the Lower-world for Junior's hind-leg discomfort. I've arrived in a very dense rainforest area. It's very humid, damp, hot. I'll walk around and see if I find anybody to help me. Birds and monkeys are everywhere. The vegetation is incredible! Huge-leafed plants, very different. Found kind of a path through the forest. I haven't really seen anybody yet, but I get the feeling I'm not alone. But it's not a worrisome feeling – just that I'm not alone.

There's some running water in the distance. I think I'll make my way toward that. Hopefully, somebody will be near the water. It's a beautiful, small waterfall that falls into a pool. Beautiful kind of water. Tremendous amount of energy in this area; almost electric. I can feel pulsations. Powerful, powerful area. It makes my whole body tingle. There's a lot of activity all around here. I hear birds and all kinds of activity, very vibrant and alive. Very powerful, radiating energy. Boy, it just feels like I'm being filled with Life Force. I've never really... I can just feel my whole body swelling with Life Force. (Sigh) Wow, what a sensation!

I'll just sit here for a little bit and see if I can get someone to approach to help me understand. This is sort of like what you'd consider the fountain of youth or something, I think. It's just amazing! The energy just wants to lift me. I'm so much lighter and alive. (Sigh) There's so much going on in the forest with the birds and the forest sounds. It's incredible. Everything is so amplified. It's just amazing! (Sigh) I feel like I'm totally filled with, with something like... my cells are just vibrating at an incredible rate of speed. It's amazing!

I keep asking if there's anyone here that can help me with my horse. I haven't found anyone yet, just feelings, energies. Just amazing. I think I hear someone. There's whistling coming from across the little pool. It's a boy; a teenager type of boy. Boy is he happy! I'm going to ask if he can help me. *I knew you were waiting. Something held me up. I'm glad you waited for me.* It gave me a chance to feel the energy of this place.

I'm telling him how powerful and exceptional this is. *It's because it's an area that's been untouched. It hasn't been interfered with by the negativity that you've created* (meaning all of humanity). *This is Nature in its truest sense. You could experience this everywhere if you hadn't created so much imbalance with the way that you've treated Nature. There really aren't very many places like this left in the physical. There are many such places left in the non-physical. They're available for your benefit whenever you need it. All you need do is ask for help. What you're feeling is the pure Life Force unaffected by anything. It's in pure balance. It can perform incredible healing tasks.*

The real key is for you to stay in balance all the time and you would have this force within you. Because of the way you choose to live your lives, you've muted this power so greatly. In its muted state, it's within all of you and all of Nature. Its pure form, which you sense here, is what you all should have but you don't. You're welcome to bring this back and instill it in your horse to help heal the areas that have become imbalanced within him. It's pure positive energy. You are welcome to come at any time.

I wonder to myself if this is Pan (mythical God of Nature). I ask if he has a name that I might call him. *Just call me Pan!* (Wow) *I appear in whatever form is most comfortable for the visitor.* For whatever reason he chose a teenage boy for me, which I don't understand, but... *You just need to bring this energy back within you.* I'm telling him about my crystal. *It would be good to use the crystal. The crystal will amplify the energy even more. Whatever might be lost in your journey back, the crystal will negate any lessening as you come back into the energy of the physical, which immediately reduces the vibration and the power of the Life Force. The crystal will amplify it back up to more positive healing vibrations. But what you're feeling is what you should be feeling all the time. It's at the level that you should be vibrating. You're welcome to come back any time and just be in the energy if you feel you need benefit of this for your own self. Just ask to come back to the Pool of Light.*

As he said that, he kind of took his arm and swung it all past... and the waterfall turned into rainbows of colors. It wasn't water anymore. I think he somehow kind of sped up the energies even more and it turned into rainbows of light; the energy precursors to the water. *That's right. You're definitely learning.* I'm thanking him for his help. *Glad to help anytime. Just call on me. I have some other business to attend to, so I'll travel on. But, you're welcome to stay as long as you want to and come back whenever you want to.*

This is available for all to use as long as one comes with pure intent and a clear heart and belief that everything is possible. Only the pure of heart can find their way here, so you need not worry if you share this with someone not of pure heart, they can't enter. They won't have access. They won't be able to harm it. He could sense that I was concerned about that. *This is protected. Not all have access. It is very important to remember to always come with pure intent.*

I'm just going to sit here for a little while longer. The rainbow light has changed back into water. It's so sweepingly beautiful, very nourishing. A place I could just stay at. I don't really want to come back, but I know I have a purpose with this mission and I need to come back and fulfill that for Junior. If I don't, then my intent isn't pure; it's selfish.

This whole forest is filled with life. It's so vibrant. It just makes you really realize how lacking in vibrancy our physical world is. We don't even know what it should be like. It should be miraculous! Just drawing in all the energy from the "Pool of Light." Bringing it into me and into my heart chakra to carry back and offer to my horse, Junior, to allow him to heal the difficulties he's having in his hind legs, so he won't be in pain all the time. I'm so grateful to Pan, to the energies here, the "Pool of Light," and all the beings around it for I know there are many – the seen and the unseen – that are helping. We both appreciate them.

I'm going to head back down the path to find my way back home. It's funny; when I was by the pool I didn't feel all the heat and humidity of the forest. It was just perfect. As I'm heading down the path, I can feel the humidity. It's like a sauna. (Sigh) Coming up out of the pond now. I'll go apply this to Junior with the crystal.

I headed out to the barn with my crystal and the healing in my heart for Junior from the "Pool of Light." The shaman-part of my consciousness applied the gifts from Pan, which hopefully would be as effective as the first two healings that I'd secured for Junior from "non-ordinary" reality. I always returned from my journeys remembering the most important ingredient for a successful result – belief! Within a day's time, Junior appeared 90 percent improved after the healing. Each time, I was blown away by the magic taking place before my very eyes.

I was astonished that Pan, who I considered the Spirit of Nature, appeared on this journey to offer me his wisdom and the healing gifts of the "Pool of Light." It just seemed that he'd have more important things to tend to, but then I'm thinking from the perspective of ordinary reality. I'd read much about the meetings between Pan and Michael Roads in Michael's books that I'd brought back from the Omega Institute five years earlier. To have had the privilege of sharing time with Pan was humbling for me.

Remembering the vibrant energy of the rainforest was exhilarating, but also disheartening. To compare what our world should feel like to what our reality actually felt like was troublesome. The loss of Life Force in ordinary reality was disturbing on so many levels. Knowing that I was always welcome to enter the rainforest and the "Pool of Light" made me proud of the shaman/healer I was becoming. Now if I could only find more time . . .

Chapter 19

∞

Staying Positive

Not long after I journeyed for Junior, my little feline comedian, Merlin, became seriously ill and died. I wasn't given the opportunity to seek help from "non-ordinary" reality for my entertaining companion. Merlin fell ill and transitioned within 24 hours, creating a feeling of helplessness within me. I missed Merlin's antics that amused me each morning as I cleaned the barn. Although small in stature, my little black cat cast a large shadow.

Merlin chose to depart about halfway through Squiggles' pregnancy. I was in my infancy of embracing the Universal Law that our thoughts create our reality. If in fact it was true, I didn't want to create anything negative surrounding Squiggles' upcoming big event. Merlin's transition didn't help me stay positive.

Even though we hadn't bred any of our own horses in the past 14 years, we still foaled numerous clients' mares each year. In fact, it is what I miss most since leaving Fair Chance Farm. The thrill of helping a newborn into the world never gets old. It is simply a miracle each and every time. The anticipation of assisting Squiggles' foal helped soften the sadness of losing Merlin at such a young age.

Never having enough time in the day to accomplish all my obligations helped keep me away from thoughts about Squiggles' unhealthy past. Squiggles was the last foal of our own, having arrived in 1985. Although she was a big, impressive Thoroughbred who looked the picture of heath, she'd almost died a few times on us. In all my years of having horses, I'd never had another horse with even one serious illness, no less multiple ones.

It had been six years since Squiggles' stopped eating and drinking for 18 days. She'd been relatively healthy ever since (except for a few minor cuts and injuries that horses always seem to get). Being healthy for that long made my decision to breed Squiggles that much easier. The synchronicity of the events leading up to Squiggles' pregnancy fueled my optimism.

As the months wore on, my eagerness to get on with Squiggles' foaling got the better of me. Over the years, we'd had many critically ill foals born at our farm. I used to obsess over why. I assumed responsibility for everything that went "wrong." I did everything humanly possible to avoid problems, but they still haunted us. Many foals survived thanks to Bob's medical expertise, my nursing care, and the foals' willingness to be helped. Some died and each took a small part of me with them when they left.

Once I opened to my spiritual path, my understanding broadened. I came to realize that we cared for so many sick foals at our hospital because we had the skills necessary to save the foals that chose to stay. Many years later, I finally understood that there is always a reason for everything – including foals that are stillborn, born but die a few days later, fetuses that are aborted, and foals that are born healthy but die weeks or months later.

For whatever reason, I felt it easier to accept the abortions, especially if they were very early in the pregnancy; not that it was ever easy. I remember the agony that Squiggles' mother, May Ban, and I experienced when May aborted twins after six months gestation. I'd trailered May and her first foal, Mr. Watch It, ten-plus hours to upper New York state to be bred to a relative new-comer, Abdullah, who showed great promise. This was 1981 before the advent of using ultrasound to check for twins. May had aborted twins at ten months for the clients we'd bought her from. I'd warned the farm owner about her potential for twins.

It's rare that twins survive due to the lack of size of the mare's uterus; most are aborted. If they are born, one is usually smaller and may be sick. Mares weren't created to support two babies like many other species, so it falls to their people to feed and care for one of them. Normally, I did bed-check on the horses to be sure everyone was happy and healthy before I ended my day. Bob checked one night and returned saying, "I have some very sad news." We'd bought a very old, incredibly well-bred

Thoroughbred broodmare, Larkswing, a year earlier. I figured he was going to tell me that she had died.

I'll never forget his words. "May Ban slipped twins!" I felt nauseous as I ran to her. My dream of an Abdullah baby was shattered, but I was more concerned for May. She'd had many foals and was a fabulous mother. I knew she understood what she'd lost. I knew she was more devastated than I. Bob had removed the fetuses from her stall immediately to lessen her anguish. Well, I cried with her for the next week.

Although May kept eating, she was visibly emotionally depressed for months. About three months after her abortion, she just looked "off" one afternoon. Her blood count was almost inconsistent with life. This was when I learned about the stoicism in May Ban's bloodline. Thanks to Bob's medical care and May's big heart, she survived. This was ages before I had any idea of the skills I could have contributed. May Ban got right back in foal the next year with no problem.

Not only had I learned about May's stoicism – which was important to know about her offspring and their offspring – but May's response to her abortion half-way through her pregnancy solidified my belief that animals possess a wide range of emotions. May Ban and I grieved together over her devastating loss. I avoided foaling calls with Bob for a long time. My pain was too raw. Eventually, the foals born on our farm healed my heartbreak. I had salt rubbed in my wound several years later when Abdullah won an individual Silver Medal and a team Gold Medal at the Los Angeles Olympics.

Being years away from realizing that everything happens for a reason and for our highest good, I couldn't understand why this had happened to *me*. I was supposed to have a young Abdullah out in the barn to train. I tried to quell my grief with the knowledge that I'd made a great decision about who to breed to, even though it wasn't meant to be. Over the years I learned that it's *not* always about me/us. In fact, it's usually not about me/us. With time and experience comes wisdom. It always seemed more tragic to lose a completely formed, perfect-looking foal. At least the Universe prevented that from happening. Thanks to Bob's compassion, I never saw the fetuses, so my memory is free of that dreadful picture.

Of course, it wasn't about which was easiest to accept, it was about the lessons that souls gain from each scenario. When you're the one trying to keep them alive, it's exhausting and devastating when you *fail*. And fail is what I thought I'd done for much of my life on Fair Chance Farm. Learning from my client's animals that it's not always about healing the physical, but more importantly the spiritual, i.e., the soul, has helped me accept the failures – but it doesn't lessen the sadness surrounding the losses.

As Squiggles' foaling date approached, my anxiety heightened. Not because I thought anything bad would happen, rather the opposite. I was convinced that this was destiny and everything would just flow in perfection. This was a blessed event that I just couldn't wait for. I was imagining what the foal would look like. Would it be a colt or filly? I didn't care as long as he/she was healthy. That's all I wanted: a healthy mare and foal and a smooth, natural foaling.

I put Squiggles under our closed-circuit TV camera about a month early, so she could get accustomed to the low-level light that would remain on in her stall to allow the camera to operate. Most mares foal at night and prefer being alone. They are masters at holding off the first stages of labor until the barn is quiet and free of distractions, i.e., people.

The average time from breaking their water to having the foal out is about 20 minutes. It's a very fast birthing process with powerful contractions. If the foal isn't presented properly, the mare can be in big trouble fast! Correcting a mal-presented foal is easiest done before the foal moves too far into the birth canal. So it's extremely important to be in the barn ready to assist the mare if she needs it. But quietly aside so as not to disturb her. A camera is the only way to accomplish this.

Many years and many mares taught me the signs of a mare that was soon to give birth. I remember the first mare of ours that I watched. I didn't know what I was looking for. I'd drag Bob to the barn, because I was sure she had "wax" on her udder. Horsemen use the term "wax" for milk that's accumulated on the outside of a mare's teat. Wax is what every foaling person is waiting to see. It heralds the much-anticipated birth. Most mares get it, but not all.

Bob would patiently tell me, "No, that's dander." I'd be so disappointed. This went on for weeks. By the time the mare foaled a month later, I hardly cared. I was exhausted from a month with very little sleep. After years of foaling mares, I'd become adept at watching mares and still being able to sleep during the night.

For me, predicting a mare's readiness to foal is based mostly on her udder. Udder development in mares begins about six weeks prior to foaling. It will enlarge at night when she's stalled and go down during the day while she's out in the pasture. I'd check this twice daily, so that I'd be aware of when it didn't go down while she was outside. Once the udder was large enough that I thought there was actually fluid in it, I'd start stripping a little out to check its consistency. The liquid begins almost urine color, changing to clear, to hazy, to cloudy, and then to frank milk. The progression was different with each mare. Some would go through all the stages over a few weeks, some a few days, some in a day, and some while they were foaling.

One thing I had grasped from my many years of foaling on Fair Chance Farm was that you can't trust a broodmare. Just when you think you've got them figured out, the next one will do just the opposite. One thing I found to be a constant was the rate of change between the stages of milk. If the mare took two days to go from yellow to clear, she'd probably take the same time for the rest of the stages. Notice the word probably – nothing is written in stone with broodmares.

Most mares don't foal until they have milk, but enough mares will that you have to be ready regardless. Hence, the importance of a camera. I've been with mares that had nothing in their udder as they started to foal and were streaming milk by the time the foal was out – Nature provides what her children need. Once a mare had milk in her udder, I was fairly certain she'd foal that night. . . though we had one mare that dripped milk for two weeks before she foaled. We were concerned that she was losing vital colostrum, but the foal did just fine once it arrived. Mares that didn't have milk prior to foaling were the hardest to judge. Attitude changes helped alert us to their impending event.

Squiggles had no worries about foaling alone. I'd become fairly skilled at knowing when a mare was ready, and I was "the responsible one." There was no way I'd miss this! Squiggles was full of dapples (different shades of a horse's color formed in circular patterns) advertising her excellent health as she approached her due date. The gestation period for horses is 335–345 days. So as not to miss anything, we calculated due dates from the lesser number. This allowed us to back off one month from their breeding date, making Squiggles due on June fourth.

Squiggles didn't foal on the fourth, but she did have milk in her udder, so I was sure she would. Well, she made me wait and watch for another exhausting and worrisome four days. After dinner on June 8th, I sat in our bedroom watching TV with one eye, and the other on Squiggles in her stall. There was just something about her behavior that made me head across the barnyard to check on her. When I went into her stall she told me, *I'm not feeling very well.* I stroked her and told her that I thought her foal had decided it was time to come out. Bob and I would be right here to assist her if she needed it. *I really want to see my baby, but I'm afraid.* You're gonna do just fine. We're here. There's no reason to fret. I called Bob and alerted him to what was going on. He said he'd be right over.

Most maiden (first time pregnant) mares don't have a clue what's happening to them. They show all the signs of colic as their labor proceeds. Being able to communicate with Squiggles was a godsend to help her realize why she was hurting; it was good pain. Given her history of serious colic and colic surgery, I wanted to be sure she wasn't having any flashbacks. Some maiden mares are actually afraid of their foals initially, which is kind of comical. One of my favorite things is seeing the look in a maiden mare's eye when she sees her foal for the first time. There's simply nothing else to compare it to. It's so heartwarming and touching.

Squiggles foaled fairly quickly, once breaking her water. Her mother had averaged about seven minutes each time she foaled, which didn't give you much time to run to the barn to assist. I wanted to be quietly waiting for Squiggles. I needed to be, in order to keep my emotions in check. After all, my "grandchild" was about to enter the world.

At 9:47 p.m., Squiggles gave birth to a large bay colt with a small white spot on his forehead. I didn't know who was happiest, Squiggles or me. *She* was, I'm sure, but I was over-the-moon happy that her foaling went without complications. The tears fell as I heard Squiggles nicker to her foal with the tender voice that mares reserve for their foals *only*. I'd been treated to this sweet, loving voice for years, but hearing Squiggles' mother-voice opened the floodgates of my emotions All those memories of almost losing her, saving her, and almost losing her again, filled my mind.

Most people think the hard part is over once the foal is out, but that's when the real work begins. Squiggles was feeling pain from her intense contractions, so Bob gave her an injection of pain-killer. I dried the foal somewhat, leaving enough for Squiggles to clean to assure their bonding. I knew I had no worries there – Squiggles was born to be a mother. Most large foals are slower to stand just due to the long legs they need to coordinate. Squiggles' colt was busy trying to stand, so I stayed around for a bit to lend a hand and revel in the wonder of this miraculous event.

I had chosen the name *Truly Inspired* for registration with the Swedish-breed organization. I felt it was perfect, given the influence of the Universe and the sire's name – LA Baltic Inspiration. I don't pick barn names for my animals until I get to know them. Usually an appropriate name appears seemingly out of nowhere. Having discovered my skills in communication, I now understood that names weren't coming from nowhere. They either came from the animal itself or from the spiritual beings that surrounded me and my animals.

It was near midnight when I decided to watch the pair from my bedroom. I wanted them to have some time to themselves to get to know one another. I finished cleaning up the barn from the mess created from cleaning Squigs' stall, so they'd have clean, fresh straw to rest in. I watered and threw some extra hay to the other horses who were all quite interested in what was going on in Squigs' stall. I told Junior, "You're an uncle now!" He just grabbed the hay from me and started chewing. Not at all impressed with what his sister had just done.

As I was rolling up the hose, my mind started to wander. I wonder what I'll name him. Instantaneously, I heard *Dash*. I knew immediately what that meant: Merlin was back! It had to be. The day he left, I'd received the poem on the Internet entitled "The Dash." Sounded like a great name to me. I took one final look at Squiggles and Dash. My heart was full. I felt blessed. I turned out the lights and headed to the house to rest a little before the real work began.

Chapter 20

∞

Murphy's Law

I knew from my years of foaling that I'd better catch some rest before we reached some of the milestones of newborn foals. Foals should stand within the first hour and nurse within the next two hours. *We* never let a foal go that long without eating, but I had a vet in the house, which made it relatively easy to feed mare's milk through a stomach tube if the foal was slow to nurse.

The larger the foal was, the harder for them to nurse. They had to learn how to bend their head and neck to fit under the mare's body and then tip their mouth up to the udder. Trying to help a foal find the mare's teat is *the* most exasperating task. Some foals find it and latch on after one or two attempts, while others look like they'll never figure it out. The worrisome foals were the ones that didn't have a clue – trying to suckle from the mare's knee, her side, the stall wall, or the water bucket. Those foals usually turned out to be sick.

Getting a maiden mare to stand still to allow the foal to nurse was crucial. A mare's udder is bursting with milk and very sensitive. The maiden mare doesn't understand what's going on and can be aggressive towards the foal. Engorged teats are very difficult for a newborn to get its tiny, inexperienced mouth around, causing great discomfort to the mare. Once the foal suckles, the pressure is released and the mare's pain diminishes. She begins to relax as her anxiety softens. Her eyes glaze over, showing her enjoyment.

I knew Squiggles wanted desperately to be a mother, but I wasn't sure how she'd accept Dash banging into her tight udder. I watched them from the house until Dash was steady enough on his feet to begin searching for food. I couldn't tell anything from the house. I needed to be in the stall with them. My rest period was over.

Squiggles looked so content when I entered her stall. She trusted me completely, so she wasn't overly protective like some mares can be. I held her still so Dash could find her teats without her walking in circles – an evasive mechanism of mares. For as large as he was, Dash was really pretty close to accomplishing his goal by the time I arrived. I sighed with relief as he began suckling. He moved from one teat to the other fairly handily for his young age – not quite two hours old. I was so proud of Squiggles and Dash for achieving this crucial milestone so easily – but then this had been destined!

The day after foaling, Squiggles looked slightly off to me. Newborn foals nurse about every half-hour in the beginning and the rest of the time they sleep. As they age, the time they stay on their feet increases. A sleeping foal is a sure sign that he/she is getting an adequate amount of milk. I'd been noticing that Dash seemed to be nursing constantly, which usually means there is a problem. Squiggles' udder seemed small in size and never looked full, which also concerned me. I checked her temperature – 104°. No wonder she looked off!

We drew blood from both of them and started them on antibiotics, based on their abnormal blood results. They were fighting a virus. We hydrated Squiggles with fluids by stomach tube in the hope to help her questionable milk production. To enhance her milk production, I added as much protein to her feed as I dared, given her past history of colic. My heart plummeted as Squigs' first foaling experience became anything but normal and healthy.

I was incredibly discouraged and totally bewildered. While I always had some concern in the back of my mind about complications surrounding foalings, I had felt none of those with Squiggles and expected an easy time. My confusion sent me to the best place I knew for understanding – the spiritual realm. Just as I had for many clients, I flowed "insights & guidance" regarding the truth behind Squiggles' and Dash's situation. I knew there's always a reason, and I needed to understand what it was for the future. So I channeled information using automatic writing from my Guides and Teachers.

I was astonished with the insights I gained from my communication with my spiritual partners. It seemed that over many, many lifetimes Squiggles had *never* had any offspring survive. Tears fell and my heart broke for Squigs when I read the message. (The information doesn't come from my consciousness, so I don't know what I've written until I read it.) I couldn't believe she had the courage and desire to be a mother after what she'd experienced in her many incarnations – a perfect example of why we forget our previous lives when we incarnate. So many things fell into place with this knowledge.

Years earlier, I'd decided to sell Squiggles' mother since we were getting out of the breeding business due to too many tragedies for us. May Ban was carrying Squiggles at the time. After Squiggles was born, a client bought May to breed to her own stallion. Had someone bought May Ban while she was in foal with Squiggles, then Squigs might never have gotten the opportunity to achieve the soul purpose that was shared with me – having offspring survive. It truly was destiny that Bob and I chose to breed her. Keeping Squigs and Dash healthy had huge ramifications beyond just keeping dear friends in our lives. Our job had just become infinitely more significant. To be able to assist with someone achieving their soul's purpose was gratifying, but a little scary too – no pressure!

Squiggles' soul's history provided a perfect explanation for her insufficient supply of milk. I was so grateful for the information that I'd been given by my spiritual friends, and for the ability I possessed to access it. It offered so many answers to my questions of why we'd had so many serious occurrences with Squiggles The Special.

The emphasis on Dash, who was less ill than Squiggles, soared to a whole new level given the information I'd just received. I wasn't going to let anything happen to this baby that had taken Squiggles' soul many lifetimes to achieve – a live offspring. Foals cannot make antibodies until they're about four months old. The only protection they have comes from antibodies in the mare's colostrum, which can only be absorbed within the first 24 hours. We ran a routine antibody test on Dash to be sure he'd gotten antibodies from Squiggles' colostrum. The results were too low, which fit with his infection. Dash received an intravenous liter of commercially prepared serum to boost his immune system.

Both Squiggles and Dash were responding favorably to the medical treatments, healing energy sessions, and vibrational remedies, albeit slowly. I was worried and discouraged. Once again, I was challenged with a sick mare and foal, only this time they were my own. I knew just how stoic Squiggles' family-line was – which motivated me to journey for a healing for Squiggles and more answers for me.

I journey to the Lower-world down from the pond through the waterslide. I arrive coming up out of a lake. Along the lakeside, it's kind of green and grassy. My black horse-friend is there waiting. It's good to see him again. He seems sort of anxious though. He doesn't want to take any time for a greeting. So, I'll climb upon him.

He starts galloping really fast like he's in a big rush. It's very smooth. Getting over towards a mountainous area. We're climbing up some pretty rugged trails, pretty fast. Coming back down the other side of a ridgeline. It's a big meadow inside. It reminds me of that area that we went to before with all the animals, but I don't really see anything right now. But we're coming down into the meadows. We're going along fast.

Oh, we've found a mare foaling (oh my gosh, it's Squiggles – really?). *That's* why he was in such a hurry. The foal looks like Dash. This must be some – I don't know what, but anyway. He's taking me somewhere. It's another part of the meadow where Dash is older and everybody looks really well, fat, and happy. Dash looks to be about a month old and is as fresh as can be. Squiggles looks happy; carrying a lot of weight. He's nursing away. There doesn't look like there are any restrictions in his milk. Great!

Now we're moving to another area. Dash is even older, three to four months. He's really pretty. He's shedding out his coat, and he's dark. He really is pretty. They're doing really well. They look great.

Going down to another area. Dash looks even older now. It looks like they're weaned. They look really, really good, and Squiggles is happy. Dash looks wonderful. He's getting really handsome. He looks to be about eight to nine months old. Really pretty horse!

Moving on again. Squigs is foaling again. Maybe we're back at the first scene. She's foaling and everything seems to be fine. Oh, this is another foal. This foal has a white stripe on its face. They both seem to be fine. The foal's standing and nursing really quickly. It looks like the foal's a few days older, maybe a week, and everybody's doing fine. Squiggles isn't sick. There are no problems here. There's plenty of milk. This baby's very busy. Looks like a little girl. Looks like a little Squiggles. She's really pretty. It's just wonderful. It's really pretty here. Now we're leaving.

Going back up the mountain and down the other side. Now we're going very fast. Coming to the same old Indian's village. Stopping by his teepee. There he is. So good to see him again. He's a small man. He's happy to see me again. I think I need your help for my horse Squiggles and her baby. She's had such trouble with this birthing. I know it's her purpose to work through this, and we're trying to help her. Can you send me back with a healing?

You've been gifted with the sight of her future, and it's the knowingness that she can produce and sustain her baby that will change her future. It's within this knowingness that the healing resides. You need to go back to her and show her the future that you saw for her and help her to believe as you believe that this will be her future. It will end the lifetimes of tragedies she has experienced, for she doesn't believe this yet. If you take this information back and show her through your heart the scenes that you've seen, she will believe you because of the love that you share. The difficulty she's having now is basically because she's unsure of herself. Once you show her the scenes and explain what you've seen, that will complete the healing. For it's in her thoughts and in her belief that she creates the discord. She needs to be shown the future. She is unable to do that herself. It is a gift that you have that you may give to her for you have seen her future. And it is wonderful, and it is perfect, and it is Love. It is through the love you have for each other that she will believe and recreate her future. I'm just thanking the Indian for his help and understanding with what I saw. I'm getting back on Destiny (I asked his name in an earlier journey) and we're heading back to the lake. He's so powerful. Thanking Destiny for his help. I'm back in the lake and heading home. Now I'll go out and help Squiggles see her future.

For it's in her thoughts and in her belief that she creates the discord. Here it was again, more evidence of the Law of Attraction. The old Indian Shaman said that in order to prevent any complications for Squiggles in the future *she* had to change her thoughts and her beliefs. Nothing that I did, or did not do, created Squiggles' difficulties. Her thoughts and beliefs were the culprit! Even though I'd been on my path for six years, I still struggled with this particular universal law. Professor Squiggles was providing me the opportunity to embrace it once and for all.

It's within this knowingness that the healing resides. It is through the love you have for each other that she will believe and recreate her future. It's the domino effect – change Squiggles' belief ⟶ change her thoughts ⟶ change her future. I could be of assistance, but ultimately, no one can heal Squiggles' soul of its heartbreaking lifetimes of loss except for Squiggles herself. The assistance available in "non-ordinary" reality was nothing short of phenomenal.

After I showed Squiggles my vision through my heart, I also communicated with her about what I'd experienced to be sure she got the message loud and clear – she would be a successful mother as long as she believed it to be so. *Believe it, and it will be!* I'd heard it and read it so many times. Now, I desperately needed Squiggles to embrace it. As my old Indian friend advised, *If you take this information back and show her through your heart the scenes that you've seen, she will believe you because of the love that you share.* Time would tell.

Receiving this knowledge about Squiggles' many past lifetimes of tragedy cried out for Spiritual Response Therapy. I had the perfect healing modality to couple with the "healing of knowingness" from my shamanic journey. I asked my spiritual partners to work with Squiggles' soul to clear everything that was contributing to her belief that it was not possible for her to have any offspring survive and thrive. Squiggles was affording me another opportunity to learn the true power of the SRT process.

Murphy's Law – *anything that can go wrong will go wrong* – was hard at work, but with the combination of Bob's medical expertise, my communication and healing skills, and the determined wills of Squiggles and Dash, we handled the immediate crisis. Even after Squiggles recovered, she didn't make a tremendous amount of milk despite all the supplements I'd added to her diet. The information gathered on my journey helped me understand and accept why. The best thing for her was grass, so she was out as long as possible each day.

I muzzled Dash one afternoon just to be sure Squigs was making milk. He was very angry despite my explaining to him why he was wearing the muzzle. *This is in my way. Get it off me. Why are you doing this? Mom has milk. Let me drink!* Dash only wore it for about an hour until I was satisfied that Squiggles' udder showed that milk was accumulating. She could make milk, but it just didn't seem like enough to satisfy this hungry little guy.

Dash had begun trying to steal Squiggles' feed when he was just a few days old, which is quite unusual. Most foals won't try to eat grain until they are three to four months old. A milk pellet is manufactured for orphan foals, so I bought some for Dash. He fiddled around with it in his foal feeder for several days until he figured out it was good to eat. I thought it might help lessen the burden placed on Squiggles' udder.

Due to Squiggles' late foaling date of June (and her illness), we didn't breed her again as I'd wanted too. My plan had been to breed Squiggles a second time for a "keeper," as we horsemen call a horse that isn't for the market. I felt selling one would help defray the cost of breeding two. I wanted to be sure she recovered completely from this foaling before we began another pregnancy. Squiggles' health was the most important. I didn't want to do anything to put her in jeopardy.

Squiggles and Dash thrived over the summer and fall, just as they had in my vision in "non-ordinary" reality. Dash was growing into a gorgeous, well-built Warmblood. When friends came to visit them, I could tell Squiggles was so proud of her baby. No one but Squiggles' soul, Bob, and I knew the deeper truth that fueled her tremendous pride and sense of accomplishment. Often she'd say to me, *Isn't he handsome? I just love him so much. Thank you for letting me have a baby. I want another one!* I tried to explain to her why she had to wait. *I'm fine. I don't need to wait.* Just be patient! Breeding season will be here soon enough.

Even though Squiggles was Thoroughbred, Dash could be registered as a Swedish Warmblood like his father – as long as he passed inspection by the breed organization. They only came to our area every other year, which meant I had to trailer Squiggles and Dash to the breeding farm near us to have him inspected when he was only three-and-a-half months old. I don't know who this was more stressful for. It was definitely harder on me. Now I was the one who needed remedies!

One of the greatest benefits of communicating is being able to assist foals with their first time on a horse trailer. It totally changed our experiences with shipping foals. In the past, we'd have to practically lift them onto the trailers with their mothers in tow. The foals were afraid, which then worried the mares. It was *always* very stressful. It was my job to keep my animals safe – a job I took extremely seriously.

The first time I communicated with a client's filly foal about trailering, I was stunned with the results. I explained to the filly about the "big box that moves and carries them to other places." I led her out towards the trailer, getting ready to have to push her onto the trailer. I was astonished when she just looked at the trailer, tested the ramp with one foot, and then walked right up into it! No fear, no anxiety; just cooperation, trust, and understanding. Tears filled my eyes. I could now do what I'd always dreamed of doing – helping an animal confront a frightening situation without cause for concern. I couldn't ask for more.

Dash loaded onto my horse trailer as easily as that first foal I counseled years earlier. His willing acceptance of the trailer calmed both his mother and me. We made the two-mile journey to inspection with no problems. Dash passed with flying colors – everyone praising what a lovely mare and foal I had. Then Dash was branded with a hot iron, which definitely bothered *me* more than him. I was so proud of my "daughter" and my "grandson," who showed what a difference love, patience, trust, and communication can make.

When Dash reached four months of age, we began his vaccinations since he was now immuno-competent. At five months, we weaned Dash from Squigs, which was another very stressful time for everyone. Being able to communicate with them helped, but they were still upset. More vibrational remedies reduced their emotional stress. After a couple of weeks without seeing one another, the separation was accepted. I was happy to be able to turn them out in fields next to one another. I could feel Squiggles' anxiety dissipate as she watched Dash romp and play with his pasture mate – her first experience of producing a live baby.

I couldn't have asked for a nicer colt, so I planned to breed Squiggles to the same stallion in the spring. I was hoping for an improvement on the post-foaling scenario, but all in all we'd been lucky. I figured we'd had our tussle with Murphy's Law and Squigs' past life misfortunes during this first attempt at motherhood. We were a great team who'd worked together to help Squiggles achieve her soul's purpose, which was more gratifying than words can ever express. It also helped me understand why she kept on badgering me for another one. *Isn't he handsome...?* Yes, he is! I was ecstatic for all of us, especially for Squiggles – mother extraordinaire. I only hoped that she started to believe in herself as a successful mother. Change her beliefs ⟶ change her thoughts ⟶ change her creations.

Chapter 21

∞

The New Millennium

After Dash's inspection, I turned my attention towards my father's worrisome weight loss. While he needed to lose weight, he wasn't trying to – which concerned me. Over the summer, he'd lost his desire to be outside working on his end of the farm, which was unheard of for him. He'd always been able to work Bob and I into the ground.

The end of our 20th century was consumed with doctor appointments and diagnostic procedures. As the 21st century began, Dad headed to Columbia Presbyterian Hospital in Manhattan for surgery to remove an abdominal tumor, which hadn't yet been classified as malignant. I'd known before we started the parade of appointments that it was exactly that – cancer. Biopsies during surgery confirmed what I'd already known – Dad had stomach/gall bladder cancer. Sometimes I just hated the accuracy of my intuition.

My mother had been losing her health long before my dad. While she'd been seeing her doctor for the past couple of years about weakness and fatigue, nothing concrete was ever diagnosed. After dad's surgery, I finally convinced Mom that she needed to get a CT scan. I told her that as soon as Dad recovered from surgery, he'd want to be going on a road trip. We needed to know what was causing her lethargy and fatigue.

Thank goodness I had my animals around to comfort and support me through this difficult time. I'd watch Dash playing in the pasture and my day would brighten. Late afternoons, I'd play frisbee in the big paddock with Shadow and Licorice. Without those brief moments of joy each day, I'm not sure I could've done all that I did.

Mom's work-up revealed liver cancer. I brought her scans to Dad's surgeon when we went back for a follow-up with him. The surgeon felt her tumor was inoperable. Now I had two parents diagnosed with cancer. I'd always felt they would transition close together, since they'd been inseparable most of their lives. What I hadn't anticipated was the strain of caring for two dying parents. At the same time, my mother's younger sister was dealing with pancreatic and lung cancer, and her husband was suffering from a deteriorating heart condition.

Having my four closest relatives relying on me for medical assistance was too time-consuming for my already packed days. I had to give up something. Ironically, I gave up what I knew to be my purpose for this lifetime. I chose to stop my burgeoning communication and healing business. It was the easiest thing to drop from my day – but years later I'd learn that easy isn't always wise.

As we entered this new millennium, I had issues in my animal family as well. While Dash was growing and thriving, his uncle Junior was doing the opposite. Junior was beginning to look much older than his 16 years. We ran blood work to try to diagnose a reason for his premature aging. We suspected Cushing's disease, which is a metabolic disorder caused by an over-production of hormone by the pituitary gland. We'd been seeing it in more and more horses.

Junior's blood results showed some evidence of Cushing's, so we began medication to slow the condition. There is no known cure for it. All we hoped to do was slow its progress. Laminitis is a complication of Cushing's disease, which worried me given Junior's previous experience with founder. However, my knowing that he had developed founder to teach me the true power of healing obtained from "non-ordinary" reality, eased my concerns. Junior had endured pain already in order for me to learn; I did not want him to endure any more on my behalf.

So far, the millennium was nothing to celebrate.

My parents weren't interested in doing any type of treatment to prolong the inevitable, which I understood. I encouraged them to go to Fox Chase Cancer Hospital in Philadelphia to hear the latest available treatments for their cancers. I knew that every day new things were being discovered for the treatment of cancer, and I wanted to be sure we didn't overlook anything.

My aunt joined us as we all trooped to Fox Chase to hear what they had to offer. At least this way they'd be making an informed decision. Our time with the doctors at Fox Chase didn't offer my folks anything that changed their minds about treatment. Being younger, my aunt decided to begin chemotherapy at a satellite of Fox Chase in our area. When she tried to explain her choice, I told her that no one, including her doctors, should tell her what to do. All she needed to do was follow her heart.

Fully recovered from his surgery, my dad and mom headed off on what we all knew would be their last road trip. . . just as we all knew that the previous Christmas was our last as a family. I got through each day by following the animals' lesson of living in the moment. If I let my mind wander, I'd become bathed in sadness at what lay ahead for our family.

As my folks left for parts unknown, it was time to focus on Squiggles' next pregnancy – the perfect distraction. I had put off breeding her until April, trying to take full advantage of Mother Nature. I didn't want to wait any longer in case she didn't "catch" the first time. I'd begun an herbal hormone product four months earlier to improve Squiggles' efficiency in getting pregnant. Based on what we learned from her first pregnancy and foaling, I wanted to do everything possible to make this an easy and successful attempt.

Squiggles got in foal on our first attempt with no trouble. She was inseminated in late April, making her due in late March. This was a huge improvement upon her first breeding experience. I could tell almost immediately by her behavior that she had caught. Long before her first pregnancy check at 18 days she told me, *I'm so happy I'm having another baby. I'm glad I don't have to wait any longer. Thank you for giving me this.* I wondered if she was creating that look-a-like filly that I'd seen on my shamanic journey; time would tell.

Not long after Squiggles became pregnant, my dear cat Rainbow disappeared from the farm. Of all our cats, he was the one who never left the property. I called and called, telepathically tried to communicate. There was no response, but still I kept waiting for him to appear. After several days, I knew he wasn't returning. Rainbow was the first animal that had ever left in this way.

I used to comment that it would be nice not to have to euthanize a dear friend. Rainbow taught me the falsity of this wish. As hard as it is to put an animal down, I've learned it's far more agonizing *not* to know what happened to a dear friend, not to know where they are, whether they suffered. I missed Rainbow so much. It was almost like he was giving me a gift: practice how to truly let go of a loved one – something I'd be challenged to do in the not-to-distant future with my dad, mom, aunt, and uncle.

Chapter 22

∞

Dreaming at Omega

The Universe provided me with a wonderful respite from the woes of cancer, Cushing's disease, and my missing cat-friend. I couldn't believe what I was reading when the flyer came promoting Omega's workshop, *Entering the Dreaming*, taught by an Aboriginal couple. Could I really experience this culture within my own backyard, a mere three-and-a-half hours away? One of my dreams has always been to visit Australia; but finding someone to share their beliefs with you once you've made the journey is another thing. Now it looked as though I could achieve part of my dream in the very special atmosphere of the Omega Institute.

Of course, my first thoughts were of my folks. Since they were doing well, and Squiggles was safely in foal, and Junior was coping with his Cushing's, I felt comfortable booking the five-day workshop. I really wasn't sure what to expect, but I anticipated a unique experience. Dreamtime! I had read several books on the subject over the years and had always been intrigued, but never satisfied. These were the true "first people" sharing what they knew to be the *Truth* of their culture. The Universe and my soul knew how important it would be for me. What an opportunity!

We had the perfect group, as always. There were 17 attendees with different backgrounds from all over the States. All were united with open hearts to learn from these wisest of teachers. I can assure you that all would attest to the value of the time we spent with Leah, Lee, and their liaison, Diana. These three were so far from their home, very personable, somewhat shy, but always approachable. They shared incredible amounts of information through discussions, slides, videos, and ceremony. They showed great flexibility during the week, allowing the needs of the group to be reflected in their scheduling. I came to realize this was a necessary trait of living in their world, one that we in the States really need to work on.

I learned tons about our differences and our similarities. I learned things about myself that I never expected to. We were asked to introduce ourselves in the Aboriginal way. Where did we come from? Who were our family? Nothing that had to do with what we do, which is a stark contrast to what we focus on in this country. I lived within a two-hour radius from where most of my family has lived for five generations. Diana said to me, "That's *your* Tjukurpa – *your* Dreaming." Now that was something to contemplate.

I learned about *Kinship*. Kinship, with a capital K. Aboriginal life revolves around family, community, and the land. I realized after listening to many of the group introductions that most Americans don't live anywhere for very long. Our families are fragmented, living all over the world. We also don't know much about our ancestors beyond what country they may have come from originally. I had a small family that wasn't very close, so the distinction between aboriginal family and my own was quite obvious.

During a guided meditation that Lee led us on, we were asked to visualize gifts from different family members. After we finished the meditation anyone who wanted to share their experiences could. I'd become quite friendly with Diana and had shared with her about my folks' failing health. She saw the tears flowing as I followed Lee's meditation. She asked if I'd like to share my meditation, knowing that expressing my deep emotions was healthier than keeping them hidden.

The most difficult part for me was when Lee asked us to take a gift from our father. I was handed an ornate mirror with many jewels all around its frame. I was very confused, because this was more like something my mother would give me. The gift became clear when I looked into the mirror, saw my reflection, and heard, *Your father gave you the gift of You and is very proud of the Who You've Become.* As I spoke the words to the group, I broke down in tears and couldn't finish. My new, dear friend Diana, explained my emotions to everyone. It was the first time I'd confronted my dad's mortality, and the first time I'd shed any tears; but it wasn't the last. I felt better and was humbled by all the hugs and good wishes the group offered me afterwards.

Lessons and communication come in many ways and forms. Following our heart's lead allows us to get exactly what we need, when we need it, and how we need it. If I hadn't taken the time to come to Omega, to enter the dreaming, I'd have never been given this most precious gift.

Knowing what my family was getting ready to go through back home placed even more emphasis on the significance of family to me.

I learned about the *Land*. Like the Aborigines, I'm very connected to the land. I talk to the animals, the trees, and the land that comprised our farm. I thought I loved the land and felt responsible towards it. I did, but to a minute degree of how the Aborigine are connected to their land. The Land is everything to them; it *is* them. They are true custodians of the Land. I understood better now, which ignited a greater sense of custodianship, producing stronger and deeper feelings for my farm.

I learned about *Ceremony*. One glorious morning on the shore of the lake at Omega, we did Ceremony! We had learned the songs and dances of the Wati Ngintaka, the song line of the country where Lee and Leah lived. We were painted with ochre brought from Australia to reflect the skin of the Perentie Lizard Man. We were dancing to guarantee a successful crop of mistletoe berries. Our ceremony was also to keep the Wati Ngintaka song line alive, as well as the Land and the People.

While this was a serious ceremony, it was done with great humor and joy among us all, especially our Aboriginal teachers. When the men appeared with Lee painted and in full headdress, I was transported away from Omega to somewhere long ago and far away. The power of ceremony was fully experienced by all of us. For me, it was fantastic. Once again, Omega provided me with an incredible spiritual experience in the perfect timing.

I learned about the *Dreaming*. Did I enter the Dreaming? To be sure, I entered it during my meditation and on the shores of a lake in New York State. The Dreaming is *everywhere*. It's not some special place that you reach after a specific exercise that transports you there. I think some of us came looking for the *way* to this other-world. Lee and Leah taught us that *the Dreaming is always everywhere!* It's happening whether we're a part of it or not.

We can experience the Dreaming by acknowledging it and keeping it alive around us. It is always present, regardless of our awareness. We all have our own Dreaming that we can choose to nourish, or not. Dreamtime isn't restricted to the Australian Aborigine. They've remembered and remained faithful to the Creation Law of their Land. They've kept it alive, and I am forever grateful for their willingness to cross the world to share their wisdom with me.

I learned about *History* – what it feels like to make History. I don't think any of us realized before we came that we would be a part of history. Thanks to the vision of Leah's Mother, Nganyinytja, we became the first group in North America to be taught the wisdom of the Pitjantjatjara people. After our ceremony at the lake, Lee smiled and said, "That's the first time the Wati Ngintaka has been danced outside of the Land."

One of our group picked some local flowers, grasses, and herbs to share with Lee, Leah, and Diana, to show them our gratitude – a simple gesture of friendship and love that turned out to have a much deeper significance. Whenever someone in Lee's family died, Lee received flowers in some way. The next day, we learned that Lee's grandfather had passed away. As Lee explained this to us, he said, "That's the first time Spirit has used a non-aborigine to send me a message." *History!*

Nganyinytja's spirit was with us throughout the workshop, and I know she was pleased with what she saw. Her dream was being realized. Spirit works through all of us: black, white, yellow, red. It knows no color. What better evidence of this than Lee's messenger, a gentle white woman from New York City with a message from Down Under that a loved one had passed away.

I couldn't help but think of my folks, aunt, and uncle, who would soon be making that same journey back Home. It was quite a week. I still hope to one day make a trip to Australia. I was so grateful to Nganyinytja for not listening to the other Elders when she shared her vision with them. The other Elders were against sharing their aboriginal culture with the outside world, but Nganyinytja believed that the only way people will be better able to live together on this Earth is through understanding each other. Who better to try to understand than the People who were Earth's first inhabitants? I was heading back to the farm to make the most of the rest of the days my family had left, with a new perspective on living – a gift from Down Under, the Universe, and my soul.

Chapter 23

∞

The Parade Begins

Not long after I returned from my foray into Dreamtime, my dad celebrated his 83rd birthday. Nothing was said by anyone, but we all knew it would be his last. I had a collection of relatives gathered around my dining table, who were getting ready to make their transitions. I made my dad's favorite birthday cake – ice box cake. You know, the chocolate cookie wafers drowned in whipped cream? Each year, I'd use a different food coloring to make it more festive.

While making it the night before, I was besieged with thoughts about life without Dad. I tried so hard throughout this long period of waiting to stay present. I struggled to keep my mind away from thoughts of the dismal future that lay ahead. What was second nature to my animals was so difficult for me. I guess I just wasn't being a very good student.

I knew my animal family could sense the increasing negativity and sadness within me, especially Shadow and Licorice. We were so close. They felt my every mood. They simply wouldn't leave me alone each afternoon until we ventured into the big paddock, after the horses were in the barn eating. They wanted me to play and focus on nothing but that moment. To be happy!

Dash was growing into a handsome yearling, albeit a little challenging. I had wondered when Merlin's soul popped into Dash, how that would be. Merlin had been such a trickster, which wasn't an issue in a ten-pound cat. However, that mischievous soul residing in an 800-pound yearling colt was a whole different creature. I was so glad everyone had stayed long enough to experience Dash. I have a fabulous picture that Bob took of my folks, my aunt and uncle, and me watching Dash's father in a big jumper class. I didn't realize at the time that in less than a year I'd be the only one left living. The photograph sits near my dining table today, so I feel like I'm never eating alone. Memories – our most precious treasure.

At night in the barn, I'd renew my spirit for the next day. Listening in the dark stillness to the horse sounds always brought me great peace. I needed peace and centering now more than ever. The sounds of the horse's chewing, breathing, moving about their stalls, snorting hay dust out of their noses, was something very spiritual for me. It always touched my soul deeply. I'd draw in all the strength I could from my horses, dearest Junior, Dash, and Squiggles.

As I visited each one saying good-night, I felt so fortunate for my life and especially for my folks, who encouraged my path by providing riding lessons for an eager eight-year-old, and granting the wish of a 13-year-old for her own horse. My folks had encouraged and supported me my entire life, even when I chose to leave my family's pharmacy to return to a life of horses on Fair Chance Farm. Their support continued a year later, when my folks sold their home on the water and bought half the property, so we could keep the farm and hospital. Thankfully, it took another 20 years to realize one of the perks of sharing the farm – being there when they *needed* us.

For most of my life, they had always been there for me. Now, it was payback time. I think it brought them great peace to know they would die on their farm. Our combined medical expertise allowed us to care for them at home. It was the least I could do for the people who'd given me everything.

I'd spend time at night with Squiggles, trying to focus on the life just beginning inside her and not on those getting ready to end. She and I had always been very close. There was something unique about Squiggles. She was indeed *Special*. And it wasn't just me. People who'd been to our farm *always* asked about Squiggles. The loving energy she flowed into me didn't need any words. Just *being* with her replenished my weary spirit. Nothing more was needed. I truly don't think I'd have gotten through the next ten months without the support and unconditional love of my animals. Bob was a tremendous help as well, but my animals were my lifeline.

Having my folks live just down the lane on our farm made caring for them infinitely easier, physically. Emotionally, their loss would create a huge void in my every day. One afternoon, it felt right so I opened up a discussion about what kind of tree they would like to "be." Whenever we buried one of our animals, we planted a tree or bush to honor them. We'd already determined that my folks would be cremated, so I needed their input on the tree they wanted their cremains spread around. It sounds morose, but it was so helpful later to know their wishes. I told them to think about it and nothing more was said.

While watching TV with them a few days later, my dad (with eyes riveted on the TV) announced, "I'd like to be an oak tree!" I fought desperately to control my tears. He'd chosen the exact tree I would have for him – the mighty oak that symbolizes strength and courage. Our family was one that didn't openly express their emotions, so I fought hard to control mine so as not to make him uncomfortable. Mom just said, "I'm not sure yet."

My dad lived a month and a day beyond his 83rd birthday. That precious month gave us several emotional exchanges that I treasure. Having only *heard* once that he loved me, after my wedding, these declarations of the love we shared were priceless. My entire life my dad showed me through his actions, generosity, and support just how much I was loved. I never doubted it for a moment. Expressing it was just too difficult for him.

Unlike with my animals, I didn't feel compelled to be with my dad when he transitioned. I think his soul was telling mine that it would be too hard for us both. I knew his time was very close when Bob and I prepared to head back to our house for the night. I knew I wouldn't see him again. I took control of my emotions and told him, "Look for the bright light. Go into the Light and you'll find friends and family waiting for you."

To be telling an atheist not to be afraid and to go into the Light was incongruous, but I knew once his soul left his body he'd *remember*. I just wanted his journey to be effortless. Of course, I'd already cleared him with SRT to assure an easy return to Spirit. I felt huge relief as Bob and I headed to our house. I *knew* Dad would leave before morning. I couldn't believe I wasn't staying with him, but I let my heart direct me.

My cell phone rang at 5:20 am. The health care worker called to say my dad had passed. I ran to the house to be with my mother. I sat on her bed and began to cry. She said, "There's nothing to cry about. At least, he's not suffering anymore." I was astonished that my mom, who spent most of her almost 85 years with my dad, could sit there, seemingly devoid of emotion.

Several days later, I heard an unusual bird call outside near the big pasture. I looked out and found a small bird of prey that I couldn't identify sitting on the gate to the pasture. It was just screeching at the house. I showed it to Bob, but he didn't recognize it either. Having gotten many messages from hawks, I decided to ask if it had a message for me. *It's Dad. I just wanted to tell you that everything you said came true. You were right about it all!*

I was overcome with emotion when I heard my dad's words. It was the first time I'd cried since *that* morning. I never ever thought I'd have any contact with his spirit. It wasn't something I'd ever experienced before. As the bird flew off, I thanked him for letting me know. Sadness erupted like a volcano from somewhere deep inside. It was as though the knowledge that I'd never see my dad again hit home. I cried for quite a while, feeling infinitely better when I'd finished. Dad was the first close person I'd ever lost. While I'd had lots of practice letting go of animal family members, Dad began the parade of people leaving me behind.

Two days later, the squawky little bird was back on the gate yelling for me. I was so happy as I asked what it wanted. *I felt your sadness the other day when you thought you'd never see me again. You won't see me, but I will always be around you. I wanted you to know that. I don't want you to be sad. I love you!* There weren't any tears this time, just comfort knowing that my dad will always be with me, just in a different way. When the bird flew off this time, I understood I'd never see it again or "hear" from my dad, but I was okay with it now. I have never seen that type of bird again anywhere.

As fall approached, I needed to get an answer from my mom about her tree choice. I explained fall was the best time to plant; so what did she think? She still seemed undecided, which wasn't a surprise since she was the same way when she shopped. She'd come back from a road trip having seen something she liked, but didn't get. Not long after, Dad would be telling me they were headed on the road again to get the thing "your mother couldn't make up her mind about."

So I took a lesson from Dad and told her because of her love for flowers, I thought a weeping cherry tree would be perfect. She smiled and agreed. For the first time, I hired landscapers to plant Dad's white oak tree and Mom's weeping cherry in two special spots near their house. I didn't want to take any chances that the trees wouldn't survive. At least my mom got to see where the trees were planted.

Mom struggled with her transition. The day before she passed, she appeared to be leaving in the afternoon. The healthcare worker and I were with her; I told her the same thing I'd told my dad about the Light. Her eyes were closed, but I sensed her fear and her fighting it. Eventually, she relaxed, having won her battle to stay a little longer. Later that day, the healthcare worker told me that Mom yelled out a couple of times, "It's too bright! It's too bright!" I found this astounding.

Right to the end, my mom exerted her control. My niece had arrived the day before, which is why I figured my mom was fighting to stay. I'd told Mom her granddaughter was on her way. I was in the kitchen when my niece said she thought Nannie was dead. I rushed in to check. Mom was gone. She had waited until no one was with her, which was so typical of Ruth. I had to believe the reason was because it was easier for Mom's soul. Mom died a week before her 85th birthday, not quite three months after my dad's transition.

Dad's ashes had been patiently waiting, because I wanted to spread them together. Taking both their ashes, Bob and I had our own little ceremony along with Shadow and Licorice, who loved my folks, most especially my dad. I spread my dad's ashes around the base of his oak tree while Bob spread Mom's around her weeping cherry. We saved a small portion of each to spread with the other's ashes. Neither of my folks wanted funerals, so this gave me some private closure.

Five weeks later, my uncle died in Florida. I flew down the week after, figuring my aunt would need some company after all the funeral people left. Little did I know how accurate my intuition would be again. The stress over my uncle's passing combined with her pancreatic and lung cancers were too much for her. Luckily, I was there to notice her shallow, labored breathing one evening. I spoke with her oncologist and ran for a prescription.

The next day, we saw her doctor so he could examine her and adjust any meds. I felt so much better having met him. He was an excellent doctor and very caring. I teased him that I thought only horse vets handled calls at night. My aunt recovered without complication and I scheduled another trip in a month so we could have some fun. We enjoyed a wonderful visit the following month, creating many great memories that I cherish today.

Chapter 24

∞

Emotional Roller Coaster

I kept in touch with my aunt's healthcare people by phone. Squiggles' foaling date was late March. I was hoping to be able to visit my aunt in Florida one more time, but I wasn't going anywhere until Squiggles foaled. We'd added a Canadian herbal supplement, Broodmare, to Squiggles' feed to help facilitate foaling and milk production. Squiggles was glowing. Being pregnant definitely agreed with her. I dreamed that this time she'd have the perfect, normal foaling that I'd seen on my shamanic journey. I couldn't wait to see if she was going to give birth to the little version of her I'd met in "non-ordinary" reality.

Dash was now a two-year-old, and I was anticipating beginning his training later in the year. I couldn't wait to get on him and see how he felt. He'd grown into an impressive young horse, albeit with a devilish attitude. Junior was concerning me. Despite having him on meds to slow the progress of his Cushing's, he looked five years older than he actually was. Arthritic changes in his hind-leg joints had been causing him grief. He was also receiving herbal supplements to lessen his Cushing's symptoms and relieve joint pain.

March came and went with no new member of my animal family. Squiggles was truly teaching me the lesson of patience. I knew mares had some control over the first stages of labor, but I didn't think they could stop it completely. Squiggles radiated such an amazing energy when she was pregnant that I feared she'd never let her baby emerge. Finally, three weeks after her due date, she started to foal. At 11:20 pm on April 21st, Squiggles gave birth to a huge black (like her) foal.

As the foal's head appeared, I saw a small white spot on its forehead – no large white stripe as in my journey. As soon as the foal was fully out, I discovered it was another colt. Oh well, maybe the filly was in her future. As large as this colt was, I figured he would be very slow to rise and nurse. Like I said earlier, just when you think you've figured horses out, they teach you you're not as smart as you think. The colt got up and began nursing in an hour, which was astonishing. I thought this was a great omen for this foaling.

Knowing Squiggles' soul's history and seeing her with another baby was very emotional for me. Assisting souls to come into their life experience (as well as leaving it) is perhaps the most profound work I do. Birth is magical and transition is a time of mixed emotions. When a soul departs I'm sad for those left behind, but thrilled for the being that is returning Home. Birth is pure joy each and every time for all awaiting the individual's arrival. It never gets old. To be helping with my "grandchild's" entry into this world was as good as it gets. Squiggles' soul's purpose added a tremendous amount of pressure to the event. There was a huge goal to be gained with each of Squiggles' offspring that survived – immense spiritual growth.

I'd already decided that the colt's registered name would be *Fashionably Late*, because he was. I asked the colt what he wished to be called. *Randy!* I questioned it. *Yes, Randy – short for Randolph*. I chuckled when I heard his assured explanation, because Randolph was the name of the road the farm was on. I doubted that it was a coincidence since there are none.

As soon as the name issue was settled, I asked if he'd been with me before. *I just left. I was Rainbow*, which meant he had also been Gentle Ben, my first Yellow Lab. I had an inkling because as soon as the colt got up and I began interacting with him, I felt a strong love that signaled an old friend had returned. I couldn't have been happier that it was Ben/Rainbow. I'd wondered when Rainbow disappeared if he might possibly be considering returning in Squiggles' foal. The time between Ben and Rainbow had been years, so I hadn't been too hopeful.

Squiggles milk production was still deficient, so I began a thyroid supplement to stimulate milk production. Otherwise Squiggles was doing better than after her first foaling. She didn't seem sick at all. Randy wasn't right though. I could just tell. We ran blood tests, which showed a viral infection. Just as with Dash, Randy's antibody test was too low, so he received the same plasma transfusion. I'd started them on vibrational remedies and cleared both with SRT hoping to eliminate any doubt in Squiggles' mind arising from her past life failures.

Randy wasn't nursing enough, so I purchased a commercially available milk replacement, Foalac, to be fed by stomach tube. A small diameter soft tube was threaded up through Randy's nostril, along his naval cavity, past his epiglottis, down his esophagus, and into his stomach. It was a ticklish and uncomfortable procedure. Bob had tubed thousands of horses and foals, so Randy had an expert guiding the tube into the proper place. I explained to Randy what we were doing and why. I felt bad that a baby was being subjected to this, but he needed the added nourishment to keep him healthy and alive.

Randy was fed three times daily. He also was on two different antibiotic injections multiple times a day. Being able to communicate with him allowed me to explain why we were "mistreating" him so. He was very forgiving and grateful for our help. It took a week of antibiotics and tube feedings before Randy was strong enough to nurse adequately from his mom.

As his white blood count improved, the frequency of his tube feedings was reduced until at ten days old he was nursing from Squiggles and starting to enjoy the same foal pellets I'd fed to Dash. I felt a great deal of relief when Randy turned into a hungry colt suckling readily from his mom.

I'd been in touch with my aunt's caregivers in Florida throughout this time. She wasn't doing very well, but Randy hadn't been either. With Randy's improvement, I began to consider making a quick trip to see my aunt one last time. One hot afternoon while trying to cool off Dash with a cold shower, he pulled me off balance. It really didn't seem like a big thing. He wasn't being bad, just a youngster. Apparently, the odd movement pulled my hip out of place. Within a few minutes, I felt extreme pain in my left hip.

I called my gifted network chiropractor and began seeing him several times a day. I'd never experienced a hip issue before. I learned that when your hip isn't where it's meant to be, you aren't comfortable sitting, standing, lying, or sleeping. I was miserable. It required many visits to my chiropractor before the area relaxed enough to allow my hip to slide back to where it belonged. Eventually, my chiropractor lifted my leg in an odd fashion and I heard and felt a slight movement. Violà! It was aligned. I couldn't believe such a slight degree of mal-alignment could create so much pain.

Sadly, this was when my aunt chose to transition. I was so upset that I couldn't go to Florida, but I couldn't have handled the flight. My enjoyable last-visit memories would have to be enough. It was as though the Universe said, "Enough! This woman doesn't need to watch her fourth human family member return to Spirit." I had Dash to thank for his hand in keeping me home, which became even more significant the next day.

As we left for a chiropractor appointment, I was watching Junior in the pasture. He'd been having more and more problems with his hind-leg arthritis since winter. Junior was enjoying a roll in the grass, which horses often do. I cringed as he tried to stand, watching him almost fall over due to the pain in his hind legs. I *felt* his pain.

In that moment, I knew it was time. An hour before, I wouldn't have told you he was ready to leave, but in that moment it became obvious. I looked at Bob and told him what we needed to do. He never questioned me. We postponed the chiropractor so we could give Junior the last great gift that we could – an easy transition. When I reached him in the pasture, I explained what we were planning. *I thought I could stay longer for you. I know you've been dealing with the new baby. I know you've been unwell yourself. These legs just don't work anymore.*

Crying, I told him how much I loved him and didn't want him to be in pain. He'd been a wonderful horse, and I'd appreciated the pain he endured when he taught me about journeying. I'd never forget everything he'd taught me. *It's been an honor. You've been a great teacher and student. Thank you for helping me now.* It's an honor.

Assisting Junior on his journey Home caused flashbacks to my folks' transitions. Since they were humans, I couldn't offer them an easy transition. I watched my dad starve to death over an eight-day period, because the opening between his stomach and small intestine had been closed by tumor tissue. To me, it was inhumane and barbaric. I wanted nothing more than to slip a needle into his arm and set him free. With my mom, it was a little easier. She only suffered for two days. Neither should have suffered for a moment, but they were human. If we treated animals like that, we'd be brought up on charges of abuse. Obviously, you can see I haven't let go of the anger surrounding these events.

I felt as though I was on a roller coaster. Thrilled that Squiggles had foaled, frustrated that Randy was sick, happy that Squiggles wasn't, disappointed that her milk wasn't better, relieved that Randy recovered, aggravated about my hip, distraught I couldn't reach my aunt, saddened by her loss, devastated over losing Junior, but so happy that my aunt and Junior had returned to Spirit. My roller coaster of emotions took another severe turn when Bob decided we shouldn't breed Squiggles again.

Squiggles' two foalings had been anything but ideal, but her second one was definitely an improvement upon her first, in that only Randy had been sick. Squiggles' only issue was her measly milk supply, but we had viable solutions for that. Bob's concerns were for Squiggles. He felt the foalings were hard on her. I really didn't agree, but I needed him to be on board with the plan. I really wanted a filly out of Squiggles, in order to have the option of continuing the bloodline that I'd begun in the early 80s.

Once I acquiesced to Bob, I was overcome with grief. I felt as though a good friend had just died. I was utterly depressed, despite having Randy to play with. Compounding my sadness, Randy developed a diarrhea when he was three weeks old. His white count bottomed out again, alerting us to another virus. We began appropriate meds and ran another antibody test, which was once again too low. So Randy received a second liter of plasma to replace the protection he'd apparently used up battling his first viral infection. We had never had to infuse a foal more than once with plasma, so I felt Murphy's Law was once again hard at work on Fair Chance Farm.

Despite Randy recovering very quickly from the second virus, I was still depressed about not breeding Squiggles. Several of my friends asked me what Squiggles thought about the decision. Honestly, I hadn't even communicated with her. I think I was too close to even realize it. So, I decided to seek assistance from my Guides and Teachers before speaking with Squiggles. I channeled the following message from them.

Dear One – You have been in a time of great turmoil and change around you; not only of others but yourself as well. You have responded to all in a magnificent manner and should feel so proud. Even though at times you've felt disconnected, in truth, one never is. Simply, one's awareness can be dulled due to the extremes of the physical world. We sense a strengthening in your love of self, which is the key to all. That must be strong in order for you to embark on your chosen path.

We feel your sadness. Have you not learned the truthfulness that your heart speaks? Has your heart ever led you astray? When you have been led astray by the mind and solid reasoning hasn't it always been your heart that's directed you back? Trust! Trust!

This painful decision you've made with your mind that has broken your heart contains concerns for your 'special' one, and she is truly that, which are based in great love for her. But you have not even asked her what she thinks. And we know you are expert at this!

Do you think what she has experienced at each of her births is any worse than the earlier health challenges she faced? We think not. Do you see worsening or improvement? Did you really expect to cleanse her of lifetimes of tragedies in one experience? Disappointment comes from your Ego – get rid of it! Be grateful for all you have gained for her, and it is much. Be proud that you accept the job of supporter.

If your friend was in the wild and Nature was in control, she would have had countless pregnancies because of the way of the animals. Not many would have survived, no doubt, and her legacy of lifetimes would have continued. Look what an effect you have had. Such gifts you have given one another. Talk with your friend, and then let your hearts lead the way. Let love make your decision. Just keep following your heart. Trust! Trust!

I was humbled and encouraged by the message flowed from the spiritual realms. I had hoped to create perfect foaling experiences for Squiggles, which had been naïve. While I focused on the improvement, Bob focused on Randy's complications. If we just took Squiggles into consideration, there'd been a vast improvement between the two foalings. I communicated with Squiggles next.

I felt a strong, positive, upbeat energy when I connected with her. Hi, Squigs, I love you so much! *Isn't he beautiful?* Truly. How do you feel? *Much better today, and so does my baby. I was so worried.* I know. *What did you give him?* More plasma. *I don't know why my milk is too little.* You have to eat everything and not worry. *I will.* I want to ask you something important. Do you ever want to have another baby?

I felt her confusion and worry. My heart chakra tightened, which occurs when one goes into fear. *Why not? Why wouldn't I? Do you know what it feels like to love someone this much?* Maybe not. You and Junior and the other animals are my children, but I didn't give birth to you. *Well, I feel sorry for you, because it is the most glorious feeling. It makes living worthwhile. So, why wouldn't I want to do it again?* I worry that it is so hard on you. *It's worth it. Do you not want me to have another baby?* No, I just don't want to do anything that will hurt you as you're getting older. I love you so much!

As long as you can help me with the times that I need help, I couldn't think of anything I'd rather do. If you decide you don't want to help anymore . . . well, I'll understand. Isn't he beautiful? True Joy! I felt my burdened heart lighten. Now, all I needed to do was convince Bob. I showed him both the channeling and my conversation with Squiggles, which I'd written down like many of the communications I'd done for my clients. With some hesitancy, Bob agreed to one more pregnancy for Squiggles.

This would be Squiggles' last foal, because Bob wanted to retire in three years. We'd already begun to search for property in the mountains of North Carolina. Somewhere deep within, I just knew Squiggles needed this third foaling opportunity in order to solidify her belief that she was indeed a successful mother and producer of offspring that survived. Bob's change of heart also kept alive my dream of a filly with a large white stripe!

Chapter 25

∞

Stop the World

Despite my joy over breeding Squiggles again, I was besieged by feelings of loss after her brother passed. Junior had been on our farm for 17 years. He'd taught me so much in that time. He was absolutely the easiest horse I'd ever ridden, once he embraced his job of jumping. I knew he could have been a wonderfully successful show hunter, but my schedule hardly gave me time to ride on the farm, no less show.

I remembered the afternoons we'd go to the showground that was close to the farm so that we could school – a horseman's term for practice. We'd jump after the classes were finished, before the jumps were removed. I used to tease that it was "poor man's (or woman's, as it were) horse showing." For me, those times were more fun than showing. It was a way to judge my training program without the investment of time and money that showing demanded. We'd made great memories together, and I missed Junior's presence in my life tremendously.

Two weeks after Junior returned Home, we inseminated Squiggles with more semen from Inspiration. I had two gorgeous colts; why change now? When I arrived to pick up the semen, they were still processing it after collecting it from the stallion. Part of the processing requires that it be strained through gauze to remove particulate matter. I teased the gal that I hoped she was straining out those little boy sperms – only filly sperms, please!

Randy was doing just fine. His pasture antics cheered me each day. My biggest problem was finding enough time to watch and enjoy him, but my heart knew how healing it was for me. Watching young foals begin to play and experiment with all that their little bodies can do is pure joy. They run, buck, rear, fall down, get up, run, twist, buck, run, rear, run. Foals are unadulterated joy, just like youngsters of all species. Life is all about one thing – play! It is impossible to stay sad around them. I felt blessed to have Dash and Randy, and hopefully another on the way. Life was challenging but good.

Once Randy turned the corner, I switched my focus to Dash. I decided it was time to start his training. We purchased a round pen to make the training process easier. Since I was older now and was hopeful to have three to start, it made sense to make the considerable investment. While I loved my little comedian cat, Merlin, having his soul in Dash was tough. Using the pen would allow me to do the necessary groundwork with Dash, so we could develop a clear line of understanding without the frustration of having too much area for him to fool around in. Dash was extremely intelligent, which made working with him a pleasure.

A week after he began his lessons, I decided it was time for our summer turnout schedule, which meant out in the pasture at night while it was cool and in the stalls during the heat of the day. My plan not to castrate (geld) Dash necessitated that he be turned out alone. That first night I left him in the same pasture he'd been in for weeks, thinking nothing of it. Life struck harshly the next morning, crushing my dreams.

Dash was standing by the fence when I went to bring him in. He always came to the gate, because he knew his next meal was coming. He didn't make a move toward me. I called him – nothing. I sensed an odd energy from him, so I communicated. What's wrong? As I walked towards him I heard, *I can't move. I've hurt myself.* When his side opposite from me came into view, I saw broken skin and a tremendous swelling over his hip that was very hot and sore. My heart sank as I tried to get him to walk. *I can't. It's too painful!* I felt the intensity of his pain, which frightened me. I ran to the house to get Bob. I just couldn't believe what I was seeing. It really looked like I was about to lose Dash. I simply wouldn't survive another good-bye. I *wouldn't!*

Bob administered the highest dose of pain-killer possible. He was afraid of a broken hip as well, but we couldn't do much unless we could get Dash into the barn. Our portable x-ray equipment wasn't powerful enough to image a horse's hip. We gave the drug time to work and then I coaxed Dash inside. He came carefully and very slowly, but he eventually made it into his stall, which was a huge relief to me.

Once inside, I began what would turn out to be several months' worth of intensive nursing care. We gave him everything imaginable for pain relief. I cold-packed his injured hip to reduce the heat from the inflammation. While I was cold-packing him, I asked what happened. *I hit the barn wall.* He wouldn't say any more than that, but I could feel his embarrassment through his pain.

We went out to his pasture to look for evidence of what happened. On the edge of the barn wall that jutted out into his field, we saw hair and dried blood. He'd hit the cement block wall just like I'd heard. By the next day, Dash seemed much more comfortable, but then he was on tons of medications and oral pain supplements – whatever it took. I added remedies to promote healing and SRT just in case there were any past life influences.

Dash behaved just like any male horse that wasn't gelded. I'd learned much about stallion behavior from Squiggles' and Junior's father, Brave Emperor, who I nicknamed Studly. We stood him for a syndicate of stallion owners for five years. He was *the* smartest horse I'd ever handled. Studly always needed to know where all the horses on the farm were. If he couldn't see them, he'd run to wherever he could see them. I'd watched Dash do the same thing, so it was always important that he be able to see somebody. I believe Dash was running to the other end of his pasture to find the other horses when he had his accident with the barn wall. It was hard to imagine since horses have fantastic night vision.

The day after Dash's catastrophe, Squiggles had a favorable pregnancy check. My joy was muffled due to the tragedy I was being confronted with by her first-born. The following day, we had Squiggles ultrasounded by a local vet-friend to confirm her pregnancy. Bob hadn't wanted to make the investment in ultrasound equipment (which is very pricy), knowing his plans to retire. We showed our friend Dash's injury and asked his opinion about trying to ultrasound it since we couldn't x-ray the area. He'd never ultrasounded a hip, so we decided to wait and see what transpired over time. Time was usually our greatest ally.

Four days after Dash's "accident," his pain flared and he wouldn't move. When I checked his temperature, it was 105.3° indicating an infection in his wound. We ran a blood count and started two antibiotics and a medication to help with his pain and lower his temperature from its dangerously high level. Several hours later his temperature was 103°, which was still high but much less alarming. I was now living a Broadway play that we'd seen years earlier, *Stop the World, I Want to Get Off.* I was back on my emotional roller coaster ride, and I wanted off right now!

After several days on antibiotics, Dash's wound opened in a second spot, draining bloody ooze. Once this happened, he began to improve. His pain lessened, his temperature returned to normal, and he was willing to move freely. His infected wound necessitated that I flush it twice daily. The daily flushing and antibiotics were just the ticket. I could see Dash's wound shrinking in size. Within a week, it was 50 percent smaller. Ten days later, it was a tiny hole with slight drainage, so we stopped his antibiotic therapy. Miraculously, he was sound (not lame).

I continued to flush the area since he had some drainage. We didn't want another infection to get started. The better Dash felt, the harder he was to treat. It didn't matter how much I communicated to him about the need for the flushes. We began a real test of wills throughout the next month. I was flooded with guilt over his injury, which was unfounded. He was in a perfectly safe environment that he knew well. He'd lived out at night each of his previous two summers, so this was nothing new.

I was also angry about the injury, his lost potential, and my lost dream. My belief that everything happens for a reason and in our best interest was dealt a hard blow with Dash's injury. I couldn't find any good reason for it, and certainly couldn't begin to see how this was in *anyone's* best interest – not Dash's or mine. Being so angry wasn't beneficial while trying to treat Dash. We ended up battling for most of the summer. We were so much alike. It was the first time I didn't find much help from communicating. Dash didn't care to engage telepathically, but he had no trouble letting me know just what he thought of my treatment regime with his disagreeable behavior.

Bob and I took a week in July to visit the region in the North Carolina mountains where we wanted to retire. I'd made a list of properties to look at – just land, since our dream was to build a round house to spend the rest of our lives in. As luck would have it, we bought the second piece we stepped upon. I knew almost immediately that my soul had found its home – on my dad's birthday, no less, which I felt was serendipitous.

While I loved my farm, the heavy work had taken a toll on my aging body. I knew I couldn't keep up the pace for too many more years. Bob was older than me by 13 ½ years, so he was anticipating retiring. I felt bad about that since he was a talented horse vet and the horses would be the losers when he stopped practicing. But I'd learned the hard way that in order to be happy you have to follow your heart. I was in love with the mountain property and excited about our future in North Carolina.

By mid-August, two months after Dash's impact with the barn wall, he was still draining. Given all that had been done for him, it meant that he had broken bone fragments preventing healing and closure of the wound. He was also verging on dangerous to treat, so we made arrangements for our vet-friend to try to ultrasound the area. As I'm writing this, I'm looking at the ultrasound scans showing three large bone chips in Dash's hip. It explained what we'd experienced over the past two months with him.

Dash couldn't live with an open wound, and I couldn't risk getting injured trying to help him. So Bob called the surgeon who'd saved Squiggles years earlier for us. I told Bob that the surgeon might as well geld Dash while he had him on the table. His injury was probably going to prevent him from being sold as a jumper prospect, so keeping him a stallion was a moot point.

Two weeks later, I had a long telepathic conversation with Dash about his possible surgery just like I'd done for many clients' animals that were facing worrisome medical procedures. Being able to counsel animals about procedures reduced their anxieties and helped them understand what to expect. I explain absolutely everything that will happen so nothing will be a surprise.

I explained to Dash about the surgery prep, the anesthesia, and most importantly, coming out of anesthesia – which can be deadly for a horse due to their size and weight. Dogs and cats don't suffer the same risk of injury in recovery. One of the most famous deaths due to an anesthesia disaster was the talented Thoroughbred mare, Ruffian, at Belmont racetrack.

Bob had spoken with one of Ruffian's surgeons a few months after the tragedy. He learned that the strong, determined heart that had made her a fabulous racehorse cost her dearly. When she felt the weight of the steel cast on her damaged leg through the haze of anesthesia, she fought it. Her battle with the cast shattered her leg further and she was euthanized as soon as the radiographs showed the irreparable damage she'd done to herself.

A horse's entire sense of safety and survival resides in their ability to run. After surgery, many horses attempt to stand and struggle to walk before they're awake enough. This is when the injuries happen. It's as dangerous for the people trying to help them as for the horse itself. I was always extremely nervous until we got a surgery horse safely back into their stall. Knowing Dash's strong will and sense of fight, it was imperative that he waited until he was ready to stand. I spent a long time on this during our conversation. I could only hope that he listened to my advice. We'd know the next day. I also explained about the horse trailer again, because he hadn't been anywhere since his inspection adventure as a weanling.

We trailered Dash to the referral clinic for more diagnostics and possible surgery. I put Dash in a stall, and we waited in the lounge area for the surgeon to arrive. The surgeon must have come in the back and did a quick exam of Dash, because as he ran to his office he said, "I can see why you want to do brain surgery on him!" He was referring to the castration, which many horsemen call brain surgery due to the vast improvement in behavior after the procedure. "You mean you've already looked at him? I told your staff I'd handle him for you, because he can be a handful!"

The referral clinic's larger x-ray equipment could radiograph the area, which showed bone fragments. Their ultrasound showed more than the three chips we'd seen at home. The surgeon was reluctant to geld Dash because of the potential for his wound infection to contaminate his castration. I wasn't happy, but I understood the concerns about cross-contamination.

Bob assisted with the surgery and I was in the OR as well. Orthopedic surgery can be pretty rough. Dash's was no exception. We all were astonished as the surgeon filled a large plastic cup with bone chips. There was one piece that he and Bob worked on, but couldn't get free from the bone. They were afraid of causing more damage and chose to leave it, hoping the body would remodel it over time – our ally.

The surgeon couldn't believe that Dash was sound with all the damage to his hip bone. Knowing his DNA, I wasn't at all surprised. His mother and grandmother were the queens of stoicism. Luckily, the damage was to the outer edge of the lip of the bigger bone – the tuber coxae, or point of the hip. The joint itself was undamaged, or Dash wouldn't have been sound. There would've been no other answer but to euthanize him. So, while the injury was unfortunate, Dash and I were lucky in some respects. Once again, I was thanking this wonderful surgeon for giving me back a dear friend, albeit still a stallion.

Dash came home on two different injectable antibiotics to counter any residual infection and a drain (sterile gauze packing) along his incision to help facilitate drainage. The drain would remain for at least a week. Reduction in drainage would determine when it could be removed. Keeping this devil-catcher from pulling the drain out with his teeth was my next ordeal.

The best way to assure that Dash didn't disturb the drain was to use a "cradle." A cradle looks torturous on, but it really isn't. It's akin to a necklace of long wooden poles that run the length of the neck, preventing the horse from reaching around to his side to pull a drain out or down to his legs to remove bandages. It doesn't interfere with grazing, eating, or drinking, but I can guarantee you – it's annoying. Dash's attitude wasn't conducive to cradle use, but I didn't have a choice.

Dash had to be restricted for the first week or so. His turn-out was limited to a small pen in front of our barn. He recovered very quickly from the anesthesia and surgery and thought being confined was cruel and unusual punishment. I explained the reasoning, but he wasn't happy. He definitely had *not* inherited Squiggles' cherished traits of tolerance and forgiveness.

On the third day of confinement, our battle of wills turned into war. I entered the pen to bring Dash in for the night, but he wouldn't let me catch him. His body language showed anger and defiance. Even though he was supposed to stay quiet, I asked him to move away, driving him forward in circles – a training technique to regain control.

At one point, Dash stopped and faced me, but instead of yielding to me, he was defying me. In my 38 years of training horses, I'd never seen the look that was in his eye – the look of a younger stallion confronting the leader of his herd. It was chilling. To show any fear would have been a huge mistake on my part. Instead, I chased Dash away from me. We went round and round until he finally stopped and let me quietly walk up and catch him. I explained to Bob what Dash had done and that he needed to be gelded before someone (me) got hurt. To this day, I can still see the look in his eye. Luckily, I've never seen it again.

The next morning, Dash was a gelding. Exercise is very important after a horse is castrated, which was in direct conflict with his restricted exercise due to surgery. We compromised by sedating Dash so he could move around, albeit quietly, in his pasture. My anger at him had subsided and I felt sorry for all he'd been through, so I decided to give him a break with the cradle while he was outside sedated. I watched for a while after I removed it. He seemed so much happier and was just grazing away. I went about my chores, figuring I'd check on him periodically. Big mistake – the drain was gone when I returned. He was so smart, waiting for me to be distracted before ridding himself of the annoying drain. Fortunately, his incision healed without any complications.

Months before Dash's battle with the barn wall, we'd made plans to visit Colorado for ten days. Several years earlier, our friends who introduced me to SRT and crystals had moved to a town near Boulder. We exchanged a timeshare week for a resort in Rocky Mountain Park. Dash's incision was improving each day. His attitude would take more time, but I had a surplus of time. Despite Dash's rapid improvement, I had a *bad* feeling about going on our trip. I'd made arrangements with a very reliable gal to care for the farm and its critters, so it wasn't that. I couldn't explain why. It was a foreboding feeling – a *very* strong one.

I couldn't shake the sense of doubt and dread about the trip and shared it with Bob. After living with me for a quarter of a century, he knew better than to ignore my feelings. Too many times we'd been sorry we hadn't paid better attention to my intuition. So I canceled the flights and resort, listening to the uncomfortable feelings – which stopped the moment I acted on their message. Our friends were as disappointed as we were, but very understanding.

I'd received a flyer a few weeks earlier about a one-night concert on Broadway by one of my favorite singers, Mandy Patinkin. It was the night before our flight to Colorado, so I had thrown it out. Trying to assuage my disappointment, I called the theater on the outside chance there might still be seats. I doubted it since it was only a few days away. Imagine my surprise when I purchased the last two orchestra seats. My entire being smiled, knowing that these had been saved just for us – a reward from the Universe for listening to my intuition.

Knowing we were going to the city to see Mandy's concert helped lift my deflated spirit. Dash was doing just fine, so I really didn't understand what I'd been feeling. As we drove into Manhattan for the concert, we experienced a thunderstorm. We dodged the rain as we parked and made our way to the theater. Mandy was absolutely spectacular. He closed the show with a very emotional song, which conveyed conflict between faiths: Jewish, which Mandy is, and Arab. It was a beautiful, powerful, and thought-provoking closing number.

The rain had stopped, and as we emerged from the Lincoln Tunnel and rounded the curve towards New Jersey, the skyline of New York City stretched out before us. The clearness of the air after the storms made the night lights even more spectacular. I remember telling Bob that despite Manhattan's dysfunction, it was exceptionally gorgeous at night. I drove home happy with the memories created with Mandy on Broadway. It was a magical salve for my wound of not leaving for Colorado in the morning.

The next morning, my housekeeper came to the barn for some cleaning supplies and said that she'd heard on the car radio that a plane crashed into one of the Twin Towers. I didn't know what she was talking about. Concerned, I walked down to the house to find Bob riveted to the TV watching a smoking Tower. I was astonished that a pilot could hit something so big on a perfectly clear morning. The reality of what had happened changed the moment we saw a second jet hit the other Tower. Instantly, we understood that it was a terrorist attack.

Bob's sister and her husband worked in the New York and American Stock Exchanges which are located right there! Bob began trying to reach his sister, with no luck. I needed to get the barn cleaned, so I returned to my chores. I got the barn cleaned out and returned to find out if Bob had reached anyone. He told me the Twin Towers had fallen. "What are you talking about?" Just wait. The TV showed the Towers crashing to the ground – first one and then the other. My fear for my sister-in-law and brother-in-law intensified as my tears fell. This was inconceivable!

As much as I wanted to stay, I couldn't bear to watch the replays of the disaster – it was too heartbreaking. I returned to finish the barn and sought solace with my dogs and horses. I answered the phone to hear my other sister-in-law from California telling me that she was all right. In my confusion, I asked what she meant. Unbeknownst to us, she was currently in Manhattan on business. She had watched the first plane hit from her room in the Millennium Hotel, which was damaged as well. She hadn't been able to reach her sister either.

Five hours after the first plane hit, we got a call from Bob's local sister. She and her husband had escaped by walking over the Brooklyn Bridge and taking the Staten Island ferry to her dad's house – where they arrived covered in white ash and shaken to the core. Several days later, my California sister-in-law found a car service that brought her to our farm. I watched a tearful reunion of the two sisters on our peaceful and serene farm located 50 miles from the Trade Center, which was now a massive pile of rubble and lost souls. Terror was the absolute perfect word for what had occurred. The terror in both women was palpable. I was so grateful that they were both alive. So many families lost so much that day. Our family had been truly blessed.

It wasn't until about four days later that I realized the fateful message my soul had delivered the previous week. My foreboding feelings had nothing to do with my horse's health. Our flight to Colorado departed at 8:15 am from Newark Airport on September 11th! We would've been just in the air when the first plane struck its target and then downed in who-knows-where until our airspace reopened. Wow!

Your intuition is incredibly important to pay attention to; I just can't stress that enough. I received a warning days earlier about something that was unimaginable. I'd learned a crucial lesson about *always* taking serious the feelings that come from my heart. I had to thank Dash as well for keeping me safe on our farm. It was my love and concern for his well-being that made me listen to my feelings and my intuition. Dash became a Master Teacher with just this lesson alone, yet there were many more in our future.

Mandy Patinkin's closing song, performed less than 12 hours before the world as we knew it was changed forever, was haunting. I kept hearing Mandy's version over and over in my head. Bob and I hadn't been to a New York theater in many years. Who would've ever thought that we were enjoying that landmark skyline for the last time? By morning, New York City would never look the same or be the same – none of us would. *Stop the world, I want to get off!*

Chapter 26

∞

Starting Dash

As our country tried to comprehend the terrorist assault on the World Trade Center, I found solace with my animals and my daily routine on Fair Chance Farm. Animals are masters of the moment and during the turmoil on our shores, the present moment was the *only* place to reside. Playing with Shadow and Licorice each afternoon with a frisbee or ball in the big pasture brought a smile to my face. Stealing time to watch Randy cavorting in his pasture with Squiggles (and knowing she was once more in foal) filled me with joy.

The best thing to keep me present and away from the turbulence of our *new* world was starting Dash. Working with horses demands that you are fully present in the moment or you risk injury. Horses are extremely quick to react and some can be volatile. Allowing your mind to wander while working with a horse can lead to disastrous results. Staying present was second nature to me, since I'd been involved with horses for most of my life.

I was 50 years old and hadn't started a young horse since dearest Squiggles – 14 years earlier. I gave Dash six weeks to fully recover from surgery before starting his training again. I hadn't accomplished much before that fateful night, so it was like starting from scratch. Given the conflicts I'd encountered over the summer, I wanted him back in training before winter arrived. I didn't want Dash to get any older and possibly more stubborn. Admittedly, his attitude had vastly improved after his "brain surgery."

This would be the first horse I'd started since I'd uncovered my skill in telepathic communication. I really wasn't sure what part it might play in his training. I go slowly when I start a youngster, spending whatever time is necessary to put them at ease before I introduce saddle, bridle, and rider. As I mentioned earlier, Dash definitely inherited both his parents' intelligence. There is nothing more frustrating than working with a dumb student, no matter what species. Ignorance wasn't going to be an issue with Dash, although his strong will could be another story.

Patience and flexibility are prerequisites of a good horse trainer. I followed my intuition to determine when Dash was ready to move to the next level, as I'd always done. Dash possessed a keen willingness to please, which was a relief. Using the round pen made training much easier and safer. Much of the time I was alone on the farm, so the pen was essential. Once I decided Dash was ready for me to sit on him, I coordinated with Bob's schedule so he'd be available to help.

All the horses that I'd started before were Thoroughbreds. Before you get on a Thoroughbred, they need to be fluent in *Whoa!* Much of the groundwork I did focused on voice commands (whoa, walk, trot, canter, whoa) and controlling the direction the horse is moving. But to start, my main concern is trusting that the horse will stop when he's asked. I could tell Dash was getting bored with the groundwork, so I alerted Bob that it was time to get on him.

I communicated with Dash about what I was going to do before we headed to the pen. He wasn't a talker, which I'd learned over the summer, but he thought it sounded okay. I was so anxious – good anxious – to get on Dash. This was my first young horse project in 14 years. I worked very hard to stay calm so as not to alarm him. Horses sense a rider's emotions and react accordingly. It's one of the added benefits of working with horses. They force you to leave all your own emotional baggage behind. If you don't, you'll pay for it.

I wasn't sure what to expect since Dash was half Thoroughbred and half Swedish Warmblood. Thoroughbreds are hot-blooded – quick to react, often nervous, especially if they've had race training. Warmbloods are calmer, but known to be stubborn and less intelligent, hence the nickname "dumbbloods" they've been given by some horsemen. Dash was possibly too intelligent. The more intelligent horses are more challenging to train.

They become bored quickly and anticipate everything.

I'd been given a crash course in training exceedingly smart horses by Dash's mother and uncles. Watch It, Junior, and Squiggles were the most intelligent horses I'd ever started. They inherited their brains from their sire, Brave Emperor, the smartest horse ever. I'd had some very nice horses prior to this group of siblings, but none were so exacting. It's pretty bad when the rider feels like her horse quite possibly could be the smarter of the two.

My training routine had never been so focused mentally as when I worked with Watch It, Junior, and Squiggles. I had to remember what I'd done the previous day with each of them and *not* repeat it the next day. I constantly had to change things up, or their anticipation of what they thought came next would take control. While training this first generation had the mental pressure to stay ahead of them, it was an incredible joy to work with horses that remembered what they'd learned each and every day.

The less intelligent horses don't remember from day to day what they've learned. Training becomes somewhat like the movie, "Ground Hog Day" – unending repetition. Eventually, the learning-challenged horse gets it, but until then it takes immense patience and discipline on the part of the rider.

Dash's stubbornness had been quite apparent during our summer of wound flushing and nursing care. I'd also heard some stories about his sire's attitude from clients who boarded at the dressage center where Inspiration lived. It sounded as if he could be quite confrontational when asked to do something he didn't want to. The picture they painted was one of a stallion who wasn't afraid to express his feelings. I'd certainly seen some of that in Dash during our summer-from-hell. I filed away our clients' warnings for the future. I'd had enough confrontation with Dash just after his surgery. I never wanted to see that look in his eye again, *ever!*

I eased myself into the saddle that first time, getting ready for whatever reaction Dash might have. He rushed forward until the confines of the pen stopped him. I spoke calmly and quietly to him to ease his anxiety, all the while stroking his neck with my one hand. That was it! I really couldn't believe that was all he was going to do. I asked him to walk, but he'd only take a few steps and stop, a few steps and stop. I could feel how intimidated he was with my weight on his back, which was normal. I got off, praising him for being such a good boy. I didn't want to overdo it with Dash. The last thing I needed was a confrontation at this early stage of his training.

Consistency and patience are the keys to success with horses. Like most animals, horses are creatures of habit – good and bad. It was my job to create only good habits in my young horses, which required a continual program. Animals in general and horses in particular thrive on routine, so I got on Dash every day when Bob was around.

The first couple of times you get on a green (inexperienced) horse, they're usually intimidated. It's several days later, as the horse gets accustomed to the rider's weight, that the fireworks might start. None of that happened with Dash. In fact, after three days of trying to get him to walk without stopping every few steps, I called the dressage trainer who had Dash's sire.

I explained what I'd been experiencing with Dash, which was so different from all the other babies I'd started. She laughed and said, "That's a Warmblood. Just don't push him too hard. You don't want him to explode suddenly or rear!" Sounded like good advice to me. I didn't need any of that to happen. Battling with Dash on the ground had been tough enough; I didn't want to start a war while sitting on him.

Dash continued to be intimidated, which, given his self-assured nature, was odd. He hadn't shown any interest in bucking, rearing, or running off, which was a great thing. I had a feeling that it was the small enclosure that was intimidating him rather than the weight on his back. I'd always been a very balanced and centered rider despite having not ridden in quite some time, so I knew it wasn't me. My intuition told me I could trust Dash outside the pen.

I explained my plan to Bob – I'd get on in the pen, and then see if I could get Dash to walk out of the pen into the pasture. Hopefully, the larger space would encourage him to walk forward without stopping. I knew Bob was anxious about my plan, but I felt very safe on Dash. I can't explain it, but I was convinced Dash was ready. He hadn't done a thing to show me otherwise.

While Murphy's Law affected some areas on our farm, it hadn't found its way into my training programs; at least not yet. Allowing Dash the freedom of the more expansive front pasture made all the difference. He began to walk willingly without feeling cramped by the small area of the round pen. I wasn't sure how much to attribute to Warmblood mentality and how much to the round pen itself, since this was my first experience with both.

After several days of walking, stopping, and turning exercises, I encouraged Dash to move into a trot. This was where all the time on the ground using voice commands paid off. Reluctantly, Dash trotted for a brief time. I'd been waiting for this moment for what seemed like an eternity – to feel the character of his movement. When I had found him unable to move four months earlier, I thought I might never know. But now, even though it was only for a short distance, I felt the impulsion behind his trot, which was crucial for a successful hunter/jumper.

Each day, Dash felt more comfortable in the pasture and trotted freely and willingly. I thought about Squiggles' colic surgery and other serious medical conditions, Dash's and Squiggles' complications at foaling, and then almost losing Dash to his severe hip injury. Feeling the power and smoothness of his trot was reward enough for all I'd been through. I didn't need anything else. The Universe had given me a heavenly gift.

There was no unsoundness in Dash's surgery leg, which astonished me. I was so grateful to Bob and the surgeon for giving me back my "grandson," who might yet have jumping in his future. Practicing the art of living in the moment kept me out of that future, which was the best place to stay. Numerous times I'd get teary as I rode him, knowing all that Dash and I had been through. It appeared that he had inherited a little of Squiggles' forgiveness. I never felt any resentment in him as we worked together each day.

Working with Dash, fooling around with Shadow and Licorice, watching Squiggles with her *second* foal Randy, and managing the farm and vet office kept me focused on my serene setting in central New Jersey. The world outside the gates of Fair Chance Farm was still reeling in the aftermath of September 11th. In November, Dash's training ended when we joined client-friends on their gorgeous sailboat in the Virgin Islands.

We'd canceled the trip twice due to my parents' cancers and didn't want to seem ungrateful for their generous offer, so we threw caution to the wind and booked flights to St. Thomas. We'd been to St. Thomas twice before, but not in a very long while. I felt it was just what I needed to recoup from my summer of strife.

While I wasn't thrilled about flying, given the recent terrorist attack on the Twin Towers, I figured it was probably the safest time in our history to fly. As our departure date drew nearer, I felt no forebodings like those I felt before our Colorado trip. In fact, I was really looking forward to this sailing adventure. I found an experienced gal to look after the farm and our animals, so I could leave without any second thoughts.

Being able to communicate with all my animals about our trip really eased everyone's minds. My routine is to "speak" with each of them before I leave, then again when I arrive at my destination, and lastly when I'm beginning the trip back. Sometimes on a two-week vacation, I'll check-in with them after a week; sometimes I don't. I rely on my trustworthy intuition to let me know if I need to communicate with anyone. I'm excellent at communicating when I've solicited the conversation, but not so great receiving unsolicited communications. The animals have taught me that if thoughts about a specific individual keep popping into my mind, I need to get in touch with them. Each time this has occurred, the animal had been trying to communicate with me.

There have been times when I've had to shield myself against the distress feelings I was receiving from racehorses during the stifling heat and humidity of the New Jersey summers. Our farm was located between a Thoroughbred track and a Standardbred track. My teacher in Manhattan taught me how to insulate myself from the "cries" of the stressed racehorses. Being an empath makes one much more susceptible to others' discomfort.

Reality struck when Bob and I entered the terminal at Newark Airport, which was filled with National Guard soldiers with rifles. As we moved through security, I felt like I was in another country, not in the USA. I thanked the soldiers we passed for being there for us. It was such an eerie feeling. I'd been isolated on my peaceful farm since the attack. The scene at the airport was like something out of a movie and brought our new world reality to the forefront.

We enjoyed *the* most relaxed two weeks sailing throughout the US and British Virgins with our lovely client-friends. My biggest decision during the two weeks was whether I wanted to swim before or after breakfast or lunch. Our friends shared all of their favorite spots with us. I never felt more like "the rich and famous" than when we were the only boat anchored in a quiet cove. Staring up at the spectacular night sky filled with zillions of stars was truly magical.

All the trials and tribulations of my parents', my aunt's, and my uncle's transitions; Squiggles', Dash's, and Randy's foaling challenges; and Dash's broken hip just drifted away on the Caribbean trade winds. The timing of this trip was absolutely perfect. I enjoyed two weeks of living strictly in the present moment, enjoying all that this gorgeous part of the world had to offer. The time in the BVIs on this lovely sailboat replenished my weary spirit. I felt the stresses and anxieties of the past few years melt away in the sun, the gentle tropical breezes, the shimmering turquoise water, and the twinkling, starlit skies.

Living on a boat (albeit a magnificent 49-foot sailboat) is a real test of friendship. Our friends were generous and gracious hosts. Two weeks flew by! I can honestly say that they became more than client-friends, they were *friends* by the time they dropped us at St. Thomas Airport for our flight back to reality. I can never thank them enough for the opportunity they gave me to feel like "the rich and famous," and to create fabulous memories. Not just great ones – *fabulous* ones!

Chapter 27

∞

Living the Dream

I returned from the Caribbean with a renewed spirit, and feeling blessed with the lifestyle I'd chosen so many years earlier. Gratefully, I got more training time with Dash before the harsh weather stopped us. He was being so pleasant and cooperative that it made the remainder of my year very fulfilling.

Randy was born a very large foal and kept right on growing into a strapping weanling. Knowing that Ben/Rainbow had returned in his huge body made the time I spent with him more special. To think a soul would want to continue to share its lives with me was very humbling.

Once again, Squiggles absolutely flourished being in foal. She never looked better or seemed happier than during her pregnancies. I created only good thoughts about her upcoming foaling, truly believing the old adage, "the third time's the charm" – none of those "three strikes and you're out" thoughts. Sharing time with my growing equine family fueled my feelings of satisfaction with life on Fair Chance Farm and helped the winter months pass.

Spring arrived with another breeding and foaling season in New Jersey. For me, I knew this would be the last foal for us in New Jersey. If I was blessed to meet that carbon-copy of Squiggles that I'd seen in "non-ordinary" reality, I might have another go at it with my "granddaughter" in the distant future. Time would tell. Our plans would keep us on the farm for another couple of years, so I'd no doubt foal some clients' mares, but this would be *my* last foal.

I was anxious to get Dash into training, but the responsibilities of the farm and vet practice didn't allow me much time. I lost a little of spring to other obligations before I felt I could be consistent with Dash. Now that Dash was three, he was ready for more work, but still only four days a week. Like I said, I'm very conservative with my youngsters. I couldn't wait to get him fit enough to add cantering to our regime.

I started to work Dash in our largest pasture hoping the added space would encourage him to move forward when I did ask for the canter. Still foremost in my mind was his reluctance to move forward initially. Whatever I could do to make it easier on my young horses I did. I loved watching Randy watch me and Dash work. Dash had never seen someone sitting on a horse since I had no one to ride when he was a yearling – Junior was too arthritic and Squigs was in foal. I felt it was an advantage for Randy to see that people sit on horses.

Randy was maturing into a spectacular-moving horse despite his young age. When he trotted across our big pasture, I *had* to stop everything to watch. Randy possessed a huge (just like him) stride, but instead of hitting hard like you might expect with a horse of his size, he barely touched the ground, as though simply floating across it. Randy's trot was so magnificent that I'd turn to see him – and sigh. I dreamed of what he'd feel like one day, and I only had another year to wait!

While I waited for Squiggles' due date, I continued Dash's education. I didn't encounter any problem getting Dash to move up into the canter. He had a wonderful canter, which boded well for his jumping future, which I felt he still had. Begin an empath, I was acutely sensitive to others' discomfort. I didn't sense anything from Dash's hip injury that impeded his training, so I remained hopeful that it was behind us. I felt so fortunate that Dash had dodged that bullet.

Dash taught me that my communication abilities had been operational all along when I rode. I didn't do anything differently when I rode since becoming aware of my skill. I did initiate conversations about new concepts before I got on, but while I was riding I functioned the same way as always, showing me that I'd been doing this for years unconsciously. What I felt and sensed with my horses while riding hadn't altered just because my awareness had changed.

What did change was that I better understood my capabilities. For years, Bob would ask me to get on clients' horses with obscure lameness. I'd be able to feel where they had problems even though it wasn't noticeable to the eye. Many times, I'd ask Bob to look at one of our horses, telling him he or she was dead lame. He'd watch me trot and have a hard time seeing the lameness, diagnosing them as slightly off. I'd be amazed because they felt awful to me.

Back in the early days, I'd criticize people because they seemed so oblivious to their animal's problem, lameness, bad behavior, etc. I judged them harshly for not being more aware and caring towards their animal. Shame on me. It took years and much study to broaden my perspective and become a more enlightened individual. I just thought everyone could feel and sense exactly what I could; I thought they didn't care like I did.

It was only after Love opened the door to my new reality that I understood. While I'm no better than another, I am more gifted with animals than most. It's my purpose to feel and sense and understand their pain and needs and feelings. Once I accepted this, I then understood that those I'd been judging were caring people; they just didn't receive everything I did as an empathetic healer and animal communicator.

Just as with her previous two foals, Squigs needed more time to gestate. At least this year, she was only two weeks and two days past her due date. I was having a tough time on Mother's Day since my mom had passed fairly recently – the sad memories were still fresh. The weather was beginning to get stormy, so I walked up to our bedroom after dinner to check Squigs' on the camera. There are many tales of mares foaling during thunderstorms, although in 25 years I hadn't had that experience.

Squiggles' brought me out of my doldrums. She appeared to be sweating and was pacing in circles, so I flew to the barn as the "Thunder Beings" played a symphony. On Mother's Day, May 12th, at 7:43 pm, I welcomed my last grandchild to Fair Chance Farm. As I helped Squiggles foal, once again I saw only a white star on the wet, shiny head. I remained hopeful that it could still be a filly. As soon as the foal was totally out, I checked and found that I wasn't meeting the filly I'd dreamt of. While momentarily disappointed, I was extremely grateful for an easy foaling and proud of Squiggles' achievement of creating a strikingly handsome *colt*.

While the Universe didn't grant my wish, I thought it so appropriate that this mother extraordinaire would foal on Mother's Day. It was perfect!

The colt was bigger than Dash at birth, but not as tall as Randy. I only hoped he was as proficient at standing and nursing as Randy was. He was. He stood within 50 minutes and nursed 20 minutes later. *Follow Your Heart* was going to be his registered name, because if I hadn't done that, he wouldn't have been born. Given the weather conditions that heralded the arrival of Squiggles' third colt, I chose the barn name Stormy.

The next day, I asked Stormy if he like his name. *I love it!* I asked my Guides and Teachers if Stormy was someone I'd known before, but he wasn't. This was our first time together in this life. I was secretly hoping that my old jumper, Jolly Man, might have chosen to return. Squiggles was doing better than with her previous foalings, although her milk supply was still marginal. For the first time, we got a low *normal* antibody test for Stormy, which would have been acceptable for any other broodmare's foal. Stormy's blood count showed a depressed white count, so we started him on antibiotics and gave him a liter of serum for safety's sake. His antibody test after the transfusion was sky-high, so one liter would be enough.

Stormy was born with a slight umbilical hernia, which some foals suffer. Our hope was with time it would close on its own. If not, we'd deal with it. It wasn't anything to fret about. We'd dealt with numerous ones over the years. There wasn't anything to jeopardize the third of Squiggles' successful foalings – hopefully proving to her that she had broken the chain of lifetimes without any live offspring. Being a part of such a momentous achievement was very humbling for me.

Just as with Squiggles and her three siblings, I was amazed at how her three colts could look so different. Dash was good-size and stockier looking, much like his Warmblood sire. Randy was taller and lighter boned, much like his Thoroughbred dam (mother). And Stormy was the ideal combination of Warmblood and Thoroughbred. He was the most striking of Squiggles' three colts. Despite not being a filly, Stormy was perfect in every other way. Squiggles and I couldn't have been happier. *Isn't he handsome?* Yes, he's gorgeous!

As we got further along from Squiggles' foaling with no other complications, I felt vindicated for my decision to breed Squiggles once more. Her third foaling, while it wasn't *normal*, it was the most normal of all. I felt her soul had finally embraced the persona of a producer of healthy offspring, achieving her soul's purpose. I couldn't have been more proud of Squiggles, Dash, Randy, Stormy, Bob, and I. This couldn't have been accomplished without our whole team. I was so grateful and honored that Squiggles chose me to assist with such a noble task. No one deserved it more than Squiggles The Special!

Since all was well by July, Bob and I went to the Carolina mountains for a week to find a stable for the horses. The area we were moving to didn't have many acceptable horse farms. I found a perfect place, but we were told they were closing their boarding business in the fall. We searched for a week and came up empty. I returned home disappointed, but figured once we moved I'd have more time to search for an appropriate home for my horses. Although we'd bought 54 acres of land, it was the top and shoulder of a mountain – not amenable to keeping horses. I didn't want another farm. My body needed a break, and my animal communication and healing business would take priority in North Carolina.

I'd started my college education at the University of North Carolina in Greensboro before transferring to Chapel Hill for Pharmacy School. I ended up leaving Chapel Hill and eventually graduated from Rutgers College of Pharmacy near my home in New Jersey. I'd kept my horses at a wonderful barn in Greensboro, so I contacted them about boarding there when we moved, until I could locate a closer barn. The daughter of the woman who owned the barn was running it. We'd been friends for years and she was thrilled to board my horses whenever I wanted. It wasn't perfect, but it was a solution.

Chapter 28

Summer Struggles

Once again, the barn at Fair Chance Farm contained important family members. It'd been a long time between generations, and I'd forgotten how satisfying working with your own stock can be. I was filled with joy, mucking stalls each day with Shadow and Licorice assisting. (If I could only figure out how to teach them to dump the wheelbarrows for me.) My barn-cat crew of Bandit, Butchie, Lucky, and Crystal kept the mouse population under control and were committed to eliminating all the barn swallows as well. I tried to get them to understand how valuable the swallows were for insect control, but they were determined to rid our farm of the stealth bombers of the bird world.

I'd watch one of the cats lying in the barnyard as the swallows dive-bombed them from above. Whichever cat it was would reach up, trying to catch the bird in flight, but never making contact. The barn swallows were amazing athletes. As I mowed the pastures, hoards of swallows zoomed around me, feeding on the insects that the mower stirred up. They were quite entertaining and helped pass the hours on the tractor.

As Randy and Stormy grazed and grew over the summer, Dash and I trained. I was so pleased with Dash's attitude. He was a smart and willing partner, which made working with him a joy, especially after the rocky start we'd had. For me, riding and jumping horses had been my passion since I was a small child. To start Dash now, as I was turning 50, was very satisfying for me, especially given his collision with the cement block wall. Continuing with his education was reward for all we'd both been through.

Early in August at almost two months old, Stormy's hernia hadn't closed, so we needed to intervene. Normally we'd have done surgery at our hospital, but our anesthesia machine was broken. With Bob retiring in two years, we weren't interested in purchasing an expensive replacement. Instead we placed a hernia clamp on Stormy as we had done very successfully for many clients' foals over the years. Bob administered a short-acting barbiturate, which allowed him to roll Stormy on his back. Once Stormy was on his back, Bob made sure all of his tissues were inside the abdominal wall before placing the clamp on.

I'd always hated hernia clamps due to the archaic way they work. The clamp cuts off the blood supply to the tissues that have been pulled through the clamp, causing them to die. As the tissues die, the clamp eventually falls off. The destruction to the tissues causes inflammation, signaling the body to repair the damaged area with new, healthy tissue, thereby closing the hernia in the abdominal wall. But once the clamp falls off, you have an open wound to treat until the skin heals completely.

Stormy's clamp was lost in the pasture after only six days, which was sooner than expected. He helped me find it as we walked the pasture together searching. The clamp didn't work as intended, so once his hernia wound was healed he'd be headed to Squigs' and Dash's surgeon for a proper repair job. Leave it to Murphy's Law – all our clients' hernias had been repaired by the clamp method. I had hoped Stormy's would as well, but down deep I didn't believe it would. So did I create this failure with my thoughts? I had started Stormy on remedies prior to his clamping to promote healing, but alas, a *simple* repair wasn't meant to be. I apologized to Stormy telling him we'd be going on a little trip soon.

Things were going exceedingly well with Dash's training until the third week of August. All of a sudden he became very cranky and resistant to everything I asked of him, which was nothing more than we'd been doing all summer. I tried to get him to communicate with me, but he never was very talkative. I wasn't picking up any pain from him, so I figured it was some of his father's attitude rearing its ugly head. A three-year-old horse is akin to a teenager, so I thought he was just testing boundaries.

I discussed the situation with Bob. We decided to run blood tests to eliminate any medical conditions. I gave him some Butazolidin (analgesic) to see if there was a component of pain that I was missing. After two days of Bute, Dash was more willing, so there was discomfort involved. I didn't feel anything strange in his way of going and he didn't appear lame, so it was hard to know since all he'd do was grumble when I tried to ask him. He was just an unhappy camper, which made me one, too.

When I was grooming and bathing him, I noticed that the scar on Dash's hip looked odd. The scar didn't seem sensitive, but something was different about it. My heart sank with the fear that Murphy's Law was still about on Fair Chance Farm. Twelve days after Dash's grouchiness began, his scar opened and started to drain. I was so discouraged, knowing this meant that Dash probably had more bone chips. I figured maybe the fragment that couldn't be loosened and removed during last year's surgery had finally broken free.

While Bob called the surgeon, I was once again having the same discussion with Dash about surgery – why he needed it and all the things to expect. I began appropriate remedies to boost Dash's ability to heal and lessen his resistance to the confinement afterwards. On September 3, 2002, Dash underwent more surgery on his hip. The area was debrided (removal of devitalized or contaminated tissue), three small bone chips were removed, and a bacterial culture and antibiotic sensitivity was taken of the wound tract to identify any infection present and determine the proper antibiotic therapy. The larger piece was still in place, so that was *not* the culprit. The remaining hip bone felt good to the surgeon. Dash recovered from anesthesia and surgery without any complications. We alerted the surgeon that he'd be doing a hernia repair on Squiggles' last colt in the near future.

Dash returned with the same drains in his incision as last year, only this time I knew not to trust him to leave it alone – no relief from the cradle until the drains were removed. He handled the post-surgical wound treatment better than after the first surgery. I felt last year's castration contributed greatly to his enhanced level of acceptance and cooperative spirit. Still, my optimism took a nose drive. I no longer believed that Dash would have the future I'd dreamed of – a talented and successful jumper.

Three weeks later, on Bob's 65th birthday, we were back at the referral clinic with Stormy for his hernia repair. Several days before our appointment, I spoke with Stormy about the horse trailer, explaining all about it. We practiced getting on and off with his mother, which he did very willingly. I didn't want his first time on it to be a trip for surgery. The day before surgery, I explained all the specifics of his surgery and the reason he had to have it. I started remedies for Stormy to promote healing and to alleviate any anxiety about his surgery and his confinement after surgery.

Animals live in the moment, not remembering much of the past, so I always counsel animals on an event as close to its occurrence as possible. I also don't want them worrying any longer than necessary. I explained to Squiggles about Stormy's surgery. Since Stormy was too young to be weaned, Squigs would come with him. Being the protective mother than she was, I worried that she would be overly stressed despite my explanation. She would be left in a stall sedated during Stormy's surgery.

Both Squigs and Stormy shipped wonderfully. The surgeon did a excellent closure of the umbilical hernia, and Storm recovered from anesthesia without incident. Since his incision was along his mid-line, I wasn't concerned about Stormy causing it any harm. Prior to his mother's colic surgery, I'd never had a horse that had needed major surgery. Now, I'd had three major surgeries within 13 months.

Unlike the year before, I wasn't able to get Dash back into work before the winter weather took hold. The attention required by him and Stormy after their surgeries didn't allow for much else besides my barn and office duties. Both recovered without any complications, for which I was extremely grateful. I knew Stormy's surgery solved his hernia issue – it was history. Dash's hip was another story. I didn't know what to expect with it. Having thought we'd solved his problem the year before (and hadn't) really hammered my confidence for his future. All I could do was allow time, the great healer, to do its thing.

About a month after Stormy's surgery, it was weaning time. I didn't have any other foals to wean him with, so I approached Bob with the idea of weaning him with his brother, Randy. Normally, you wouldn't put a weanling and yearling together since one is so much bigger and might be too dominant towards the baby. Randy had a wonderful spirit and hadn't shown anything that concerned me about putting them together. He was a sweet soul, and one I'd known for a long time.

My idea was to reunite Randy with his mother and Stormy. Even though Randy was Squiggles' son, she would protect Stormy if need be. Once Squiggles stopped getting between the two and they formed a bond, we'd remove Squiggles. Bob decided it was worth trying, especially since I'd be communicating with all of them and dosing them with remedies to lessen the emotional stresses between them. My intuition told me this was the best scenario for Randy and Stormy.

We sedated Squiggles and Randy before we put Randy in the pasture with his mother and brother. Stormy wasn't going to do anything to Randy, and I felt he needed to be fully aware if he needed to retreat quickly. After a few days, the three were a tight-knit little herd. As I looked out at Squiggles totally content with her two sons by her side, my heart filled with gratitude and joy for all she had taught me. I left them together until Stormy and Randy were good pals – about two weeks.

I was sad that Squiggles had to be taken from that serene picture. After two weeks without being able to see Stormy, I turned them out within sight of one another. Squigs was a little anxious, but settled quickly, happily gazing over at her two handsome sons. She and I were both unhappy that there'd be no more foals in our futures, but everything is always about timing!

Chapter 29

∞

Enough Already

While I'd been dealing with Dash's and Stormy's surgeries, I'd also been observing some odd movements in Randy's hind end. It was mostly at night while I was checking on them before bed. He'd move around the stall and make some suspicious movements with his hind legs – like a horse with stifle problems. The horse's stifle is the knee joint of the hind leg. It contains something called the "stay-apparatus," which allows the joint to lock in place, relaxing all of the horse's muscles so it can rest while standing.

Squiggles had had a stifle issue when she was young, which made me worry more about Randy. We'd tried all the conservative measures to correct Squiggles' issue without success. When she was three years old, Bob cut her stifle cords – a minor surgery he'd done routinely on clients' horses whose cords were too tight, causing them trouble. The horse is sedated and the cords are cut while the horse remains standing. Exercise after surgery is crucial to prevent the cords from healing too quickly.

The goal is for the cords to lengthen as they heal, alleviating the horse's discomfort. Squiggles recovered from her surgery without any complications and never had any trouble again. I was hoping to avoid this with Randy, but he was beginning to show increasing evidence of a stifle problem as he approached his second birthday.

We sedated Randy and radiographed his stifles before we contemplated cutting anything. We needed to rule out any bony issues, which seemed unlikely in a two-year-old. It was imperative that Randy stay very still while we x-rayed him. The muscles around the stifle joint are at the limit of what our portable machine could image through, so his cooperation was crucial. The views of Randy's stifles showed no evidence of any bony changes in either stifle joint, so cutting his cords looked to be a viable option.

I still hadn't found time to get Dash back into work despite the fact that we were well into April. I was anticipating getting on him any day, but I decided to wait until after his brother's surgery. When I turned Dash out in his pasture the day after Randy's x-rays, he trotted off slightly lame. I walked out to look at him, but didn't see anything obvious. I told Bob what I'd seen and that I wanted him to look at Dash when he came back from his farm calls.

When Bob got back and I went for Dash, I found his scar opened in a small spot and draining. By the time I reached Bob in the barn, the tears were falling. I felt so defeated and confused. I simply couldn't put Dash or us through a third surgery – I *couldn't!* Bob agreed, so on April 24th, six weeks before his fourth birthday, we sent Dash Home. With my heart broken, I communicated with him through floods of tears about the situation.

It's okay. Don't cry. You did everything you could, but it didn't work. I don't want another surgery, so you're doing me a favor. I'm sorry to have caused you such trouble. At least you have my brothers to heal your heart. Really, I'm happy to return to Spirit! I was so grateful that he engaged in a conversation – this non-talkative horse of mine. I'd learned from the many horses we'd euthanized for clients that they are all happy to go Home. I wished I could share his joy, but I was devastated over losing him at such a young age. I felt guilty for not taking better care of him, which was ludicrous because we'd done more than most people would have.

I held tight to Dash's lead to ease his head to the ground when the euthanasia solution took effect. I tried to stay telepathically connected to his spirit, but my raw emotions and torrents of tears prevented me. I *needed* to feel his joy, exhilaration, and freedom, which I'd felt in many clients' horses when the soul released from the body. I knew Dash was experiencing glorious feelings (which our language is incapable of describing) even if I couldn't feel them, which brought me a modicum of peace. I'd never lost such a youngster except for Merlin, my comic cat, who died at nine months of age and whose soul had returned in Dash. I was heartbroken with a crushed spirit. I simply couldn't understand any reason for Dash's transition and how it could possibly be in anyone's best interest, least of all mine.

My dear Shadow and Licorice tried to console me, as did Bob, but I was devastated over Dash's short life. I regretted not riding him after his second surgery, but my responsibilities and the weather prevented it. To think I'd never ride him again or experience jumping him fueled my tears. I just couldn't accept this dire end to a breeding that I felt was destined from the start – more like doomed. Both his parents were phenomenally athletic jumpers, so I felt he would be as well.

As they say, life goes on. I didn't have the luxury of wallowing in my grief; I had others who depended on me. Licorice had developed an on-and-off lameness, which was probably due to arthritis in our almost 12-year-old Lab. Our vet-friend, Gary, had started to study acupuncture around the same time I was learning about my animal-communication skills. Acupuncture was helping Licorice somewhat, but not totally, which fit with the idea of arthritic pain. We'd been feeding him and his brother, Shadow, Glycoflex – a joint supplement we'd used successfully in dogs and horses.

My immediate and main concern was Randy's stifles. Given the increased frequency of his stifle symptoms combined with his clean radiographs, Bob felt the next step was to cut his stifle cords like we'd done for his mother years earlier. I had a long discussion with Randy the day before his procedure explaining what we were going to do and why. Randy sensed my dismal mood, which I'd been in since sending Dash Home two days earlier. *You're so sad. Don't worry about me. Do whatever you think will help. I don't want you to be sad anymore.* Randy's compassion started my tears again. It was going to take a long time for me to get over this loss. I really needed things to turn around for my animal family – and *fast!*

So, four days after Dash left, Bob sedated Randy and cut his stifle cords. The procedure that he'd done numerous times went as well as it could. I was relieved when it was over. Even though considered minor surgery, I was always nervous with any surgery. I felt bad for Squiggles' sons because we had to separate Randy and Stormy due to the postoperative care that Randy would require. We sedated them several days before and weaned them from each other. Life is oft times cruel.

I was very optimistic about Randy's cord surgery, because it had always relieved the discomfort in the stifle, allowing the horse to move unencumbered. Despite all our prior successes, two days later Randy was in *extreme* pain. We increased his pain-killers to try to lessen his discomfort. Nothing seemed to help. I was consumed with guilt for subjecting Randy to this much pain. I was barraged with flashbacks of the pain Jolly Man suffered after his tooth extraction, only this was much worse. We'd never seen a reaction like this. Damn you, Murphy!

Randy was so uncomfortable that I'd come home from errands to find him lying down, which was not the norm for him. The exercise necessary to keep his cords from healing too fast was agonizing for me to do. Instead of asking him to trot, I'd just walk him for extra time. I simply couldn't ask him to do any more than that. I was drowning in guilt over both him and Dash, accepting full responsibility for these two disasters. I blamed myself and no one else. It was my job to keep my animals healthy and out of harm's way. I had failed Dash and Randy miserably. I was a beaten horsewoman.

I apologized to Randy daily. Nothing we did seemed to control his discomfort. Bob was totally confused and didn't understand what had happened. He felt the procedure had gone very well. I was exhausted from sensing Randy's pain. I couldn't imagine how he coped with it. *It's very sore, but I am feeling a little better. I don't want you to blame yourself, or Bob either. I've heard all your discussions about previous surgeries going fine. I don't know why this happened. I don't blame you. I love you! I'll be fine, but I need you to believe that. I need you to stop being sad and be happy. That's the best medicine for both of us. Dash wouldn't want you to feel so sad.* Obviously, Randy had inherited a huge dose of Squiggles' quality of forgiveness. I wished I'd learned it from her.

Randy's pain lessened over time, but it was taking forever as far as I was concerned. I decided I needed to seek help from "non-ordinary" reality. I hadn't done a shamanic journey since my parents were diagnosed with cancer four years earlier. I was a little anxious about journeying, but it had been two weeks and Randy's improvement had been minimal. I wasn't sure how effective I'd be, because I was consumed with grief and sorrow over Dash; and regret, guilt, and blame over Randy. But I couldn't wait any longer to be in a better frame of mind before I attempted to enter "non-ordinary" reality. I only hoped my negative energy didn't keep me from obtaining healing for both Randy and Licorice. As long as I was going, I'd seek healing for both my dear boys.

I set my intention for a healing for Licorice and Randy and was told to journey to the Upper-world to find assistance. I left from the top of our mountain property in North Carolina, where we'd be living the following year.

I have to go up four levels and then I see a little girl – *me*, when I was little. *Do you want to come and play?* I tell her that I've come for my dog, Licorice, and my horse, Randy, to help them with their problems. She giggles and says, *I know that but you need help first. How can you help them if you can't help yourself? You have to start to put yourself first, or you won't be of any use to anyone.* She just seems so happy.

She's taking me by the hand, and she's dragging me somewhere. Typical! I guess what I was like as a child, just on the move. We're just going along, going along, I don't know where we're going to end up?? It's just her and me. Now we've come to sort of a playground area by a little lake, pond area. We're going to get on the little horses that you can swing back and forth on. What else?

I can feel all the sense of responsibility floating away, and I am coming back to that sense of the wonderment of a child. Just the playfulness. Just going from thing to thing. That spinning top thing that you run along on. I don't have any restrictions. I can play on everything, my knee works, my shoulder works. I just feel so much lighter.

Of course, I guess at this time of my life, I didn't really have anything I needed to be responsible for. All I needed was to play, be happy, and joyful. It's been a *long* time. I have so many things that weigh me down, things I have to do. (Sigh!) It has my heart so heavy. I can just feel it. It's *so* heavy when I think about it. It's not like what I feel with this little girl. I just have so much sadness inside of it.

I miss my folks and I miss Dash... I miss Dash so much (tears begin). I don't understand why that happened. I *loved* him! Oh, now the little girl has come over to comfort me. *Don't cry, you have to be happy. You have to learn to live in joy, and not to be sad. All the Beings that you miss are happy. They're very happy where they are and are grateful that they got to know you* (more tears) *and got to spend some of their time with you. You need to be happy and spend some time with you.* I'm feeling a little better now. I'm feeling lighter again and not so sad. Oh now she's just run into the pond. I'm gonna follow her over. Oh, the water's so nice and warm. I feel so good.

You just need to swim around here and wash all the sadness and anger out, because it's creating so many blocks within your physical body. You're storing it in all your joints and it's doing nothing but causing you great pain in the physical. You need to release that anger and sadness and not to question, because it's really not always only about you. These other Beings had purposes, and they've served their purposes in life and they've returned back to Spirit. That's the only reason to come into the physical is to work on a given purpose, and once it's achieved, there's really no point in staying since it's so much harder to be in the physical.

I just can't imagine what purpose Dash had achieved. But then that's for another time... *You must realize that that Being is in a place of great joy and love for you.* We're coming back out of the pond. I'm feeling so much better. I'm asking her if she thinks she can help me with the healing for Licorice and Randy. She says, *No! My purpose is to try and help you remember who you are and that the child within you needs to feel happy and joyful again. You need to do things that create joy in your life.*

I explain about our move. I'm really looking forward to that change. *It is long overdue, and I know that every time you focus on that house I can feel the joy in you. It's going to be a tremendous change for you, and it's something you need to do in order to fulfill your life purpose. The time has come and things will be put in line* and you will be in great joy. You need to start to focus on that now. I thank her for having come. I thank her for reminding me of how I used to feel and letting me know that Dash is all right. I feel like I really want to move on and find who can help me.

Oh God, here comes *Dash!* (torrents of tears, gasping breaths). Oh, Dash, I've missed you so much. *Don't cry! I needed to go. I'm sorry that I caused you so much sadness, but you shouldn't be sad, because it was what I wanted. Get on!* Oh, God, I've missed this (sighs and floods of tears). *I'm taking take you to where you can find some healing for Randy and for Licorice, and where we can be in joy together.*

You shouldn't think of what could have been for me. I learned a great deal in the short time that we spent together and that was what I came to do. I'm sorry I put you through so much. But I think we both learned a lot, and it was time for me to go.

Oh God, he feels *so great* to be on. I'm so happy that he's happy. *You have two wonderful horses, and they want to be with you for a long time.* We're just cantering across the fields, and we're jumping jumps *(extreme emotion!!).* He jumps just like a deer. *I wanted to give you this gift, so you could feel what you believed should have been.* Do you know how much fun it is? Now I have been able to do what I felt so sad that I couldn't do with Dash. This is *wonderful,* and I will always have that with me.

It's my gift to you for what you've done for me. I don't think I've done much. *You did much; you went through so much for me. You shouldn't feel angry.* He had given me so much. He had taught *me! You taught me so much about love both as a cat and a horse. You went through so much to try to help me both times. That was the greatest gift you could have given me, which is why I wanted to do this for you!* Now we're saying good-bye! (*Hysterical,* flooded with tears.) I know I'm never going to see him again!!! But, I'm so grateful for this time. And now, he's just galloping off. Oh God, that was so wonderful! Oh, *wow!*

I have to start thinking about Randy and Licorice. I wonder where I am now. Oh, gosh, I'm in a valley. Whew. I'm just going to walk around here and see if I can find someone who can help me. Oh, it's so pretty and peaceful here. Oh, I'm really tired after that. I keep looking around and asking. Hello – just trying to find someone or something!

Well, there's a little path here that goes into the forest a little ways. I think I'll follow the pathway and see. Oh, it's very refreshing in here. Actually, I'm getting a little more focus here on what's going on as I'm walking through the woods. It's very beautiful. I can hear some water off in the distance. I think I'll head towards that.

Oh, boy, I'm feeling better and better as I'm going along. Oh my, there's a bridge over a pretty brook. Oh, there's an absolutely stunning Indian girl sitting on the opposite bank with an absolutely beautiful, beaded buckskin dress. She's just gorgeous. I'm going to walk over and talk with her.

I ask her if she can help me with my dog and my horse. *Yes! I've been waiting for you. I was so afraid you weren't going to come.* I told her I've been… I've been meaning to. I've just had so many other things, but I'm here. She's hugging me. *Don't feel bad everything always happens in its perfect timing. Follow me.* We're going down the path on the other side. It's opening into an absolutely beautiful meadow where there are Indian tepees and people and horses all over and flowers. It's just a beautiful place. It's just very, very lovely.

The weather's beautiful and everybody's pleasant. *Hello! Hello! We're glad you've come. We've been waiting for you.* This isn't the same Indian Village where the old male Indian-friend is. This is another. The girl wants me to follow her. We're going up and there's a tepee up a slight rise that's sort of away from the bulk of where everyone is gathered. *Go inside, someone is waiting for you.* I thank her and ask if I will see her again. *Yes, I will take you back to the bridge.*

I go inside. Hello. A very old Indian lady with very long, gray hair motions me to sit down. I tell her why I've come: to seek healing for my dog and my horse. Can she help me with either of them? She takes my hands into her hands. She has wonderful energy. *First, we must heal your heart, for until your heart is healed, you can't help anyone. It is from your heart that all healing comes forth.* I can just feel her pulling, pulling all my sadness out. I can feel my heart is getting stronger. I can feel the hole is closing that I've had in my heart. It's just becoming stronger and younger and *free*.

It's phenomenal, but I'm concerned that she's taking all this negativity into herself. *I'm not. Spirit is behind me and it will just be transmuted through me and changed into positive, Love energy, which will circulate throughout and forever.* My God, I feel so much different. She has the most beautiful eyes. I'm just staring into her eyes and feeling the energy flow out of my hands and into her body. All of my cells are just feeling more alive. Everything is getting more vibrant. I'm just so aware of *everything*.

The drums are getting louder in the background. The air is so wonderful. She's taking my hands and putting them on her heart. The energy is phenomenal. I feel energy pouring into my body. It's just super-charging my body. She's just pure energy, coming into my body. I can feel everything; every cell is alive and vibrating at an incredibly high vibration – an incredible vibration. I feel so much younger. It's wonderful. I've never experienced anything so powerful. This lady looks old… and has power beyond anything. I'm thanking her so much.

You must go back outside and you'll be taken to someone else who will help you with the dog and the horse. I have been here for you. Morningstar is my name. You need to be watchful of the amount of negativity that you take in. It's causing great harm to your physical body. You really can't take much anymore. I've transmuted all of it and filled it back up with positive Love energy. You need to be mindful and take good care of your body and fill it with only positive energy. I will try very hard to do that. I thank her. Going back outside now.

I'm greeted by Dancing Hawk, my Guide. Oh, he's giving me a big hug. I could just melt right into his body. It feels so wonderful. I feel like he can take care of everything. *I've missed you so much! You really haven't come to visit in a while.* I know. I don't know why… I just don't know why. I have no excuses. *I've been worried about you. I see great sadness and anger. I try to help.* I know. I know. I know you're there! All the time, I can feel you. I'm sorry I haven't come to visit. It's foolish. *Yes, Morningstar has done wonders with you.* She's truly remarkable.

Come on; let's go find some healing for your friends. For now you're ready to handle that. You have to focus on that. You have so much power and ability of your own, but you keep giving it away. You keep covering it over with negative emotions: sadness and anger and resentment. Your power is buried. Yes, I do feel it's back. *Come on let's go.* Okay, I'm ready. Where are we going? *We'll take a couple of ponies and just ride.* Of course, I get the Paint, my favorite color (sarcasm – my least favorite). Dancing Hawk's on a gorgeous Appaloosa – a bay with a blanket, really pretty. I have a very pretty bay-and-white horse.

Okay, we're cantering along the meadows, so beautiful with all the flowers. Now we've come to a river we're going to ford. Pretty chilly. Now, we're going up a steep trail up to the top of a ridgeline. Oh my gosh, we're looking out over an immense expanse of land. It's incredible. It's beyond anything, its beauty. Oh my God, now we're going down (you know me and down – hate it) a twisty little trail to a glacial lake.

Almost as gorgeous as Lake Louise. Just phenomenal. Looks like this is where we're going to stop. Dancing Hawk wants me to come to the shore of the lake. Just beautiful!! Now he has a vessel, like a pottery thing, that he's putting water from the lake in – just stunning, turquoise glacial water. *Let's walk in the water.* I tell him it'll be freezing. *Don't be surprised . . .* Well, it's cool but certainly bearable. Not cold at all.

Now he's bending down and gathers four stones from the bottom of the shoreline. They're actually very interesting looking. Two are turquoise in color, one jet black, and one variegated green color. He's handing them to me. He's giving me the vessel of water. Oh, the water! I'm feeling better and better and better. I'm feeling wonderful!

We have a couple more things to gather here. Wait, wait, let me thank the lake for its gifts for my friends. We're walking away from the lake towards some bushes. One is a shrub-looking thing growing along here, and he's picking the leaves. He's putting them in the vessel with the water – oh, flower essences – ah ha! Next, he's going to a tree. Taking a small branch (twig) off the tree. He's putting some of the branch in the vessel, not the leaves.

We've gone further into a wooded area. He's gathered some fern from the floor, also in the vessel. Heading back out again. I'm asking Dancing Hawk how he knows what things to use. *I don't. You're telling me.* You're kidding? I don't know what they are. *The Greater You knows what they are. You have all these secrets locked away. It's time that your knowledge is set free for there's so many that can benefit from it.* I have no idea of what any of this is. *You're directing me.*

Well, that's interesting! We're headed back to the ponies. We're going back to the village the same way. I just need to look at the lake one more time. It's just phenomenal. We're going back down to the village. Dancing Hawk, how am I going to use these? *I don't know, you know. You need to go deep within and find that knowledge and information. It is coming from you, not from outside of you. You just need to believe – believe that you have the knowledge within you and that you can heal not only yourself but others. You can allow others the opportunity to heal if they choose to. For that's what it's truly about, no one can heal them but themselves. You've done this before.* I know I've done this before. *Bring these back with you and you'll know what to do with them.* He gives me another hug. *Visit more often!* I promise I will.

The pretty, young girl is taking me back to the bridge. Oh, I hate to leave but I have to come back to try to help Randy and Licorice. I have the vessel with me with all the healing in it, and I have the four stones from the lake. Now, I just have to try to figure out what to do with them. I know for sure that I bring them back in my *heart*. I thank the young girl.

I walk over the bridge and out into the valley. I'm feeling so much better than when I first started. I thank everything and everyone for their help. I ask to bring all these back with me and to help me remember how to use them and apply them. Now I'm back on top of the mountain, *my* mountain in North Carolina. Where my future waits. Where my power will truly come into its own. Where much work will be done!

Little did I know when I entered "non-ordinary" reality that I'd be the recipient of such a powerful healing. I felt infinitely better upon my return. The encounter with Dash was totally unexpected and allowed me to bring some closure to his loss. Feeling his prowess over the jumps we shared together was immensely gratifying. Knowing that he'd accomplished what he'd come into this life to do, made me happy. I didn't know exactly what that was, but as long as he achieved his purpose, what more could I ask? I still didn't like that he was no longer in my life, but I understood and accepted it. I never, ever expected to meet him on my journey; but what shaman ever expects the things that happen on their journeys?

I applied the healing gifts that my dear Guide, Dancing Hawk, gathered for me to Randy and Licorice. Licorice became sound and stayed that way for quite a long while. Randy, on the other hand, improved from the acute pain of his cord surgery, but still showed evidence of a stifle issue, which completely confounded both Bob and me.

With Dash's death and Randy's stifle issue, I was once again left with no horse to train. Stormy was just a yearling, albeit a gorgeous one. Stormy was the nicest horse at the Swedish inspection later that fall. I received so many compliments about him at inspection. I was very proud to be his "grandmother." Given the tragedies that had befallen his two brothers so far, I secretly worried about what lay ahead for Stormy and me. I only hoped Murphy would find another farm to harass. Time would tell.

Chapter 30

∞

And Then There Were Two

*I*n an effort to support Randy's stifles, we started several feed supplements for joint health, along with a series of injectable medication to strengthen all of his joints. At least the acute pain from his stifle surgery was gone, allowing him to graze comfortably. Randy was really tall, and I wondered if that played a part in his problem. Whatever we felt Randy needed, he got.

Stormy was doing just great. He was the most handsome of all of Squiggles' sons. Although our souls had never met before, I felt very bonded to him. He was so much fun to have in the barn. I was beginning to worry about his mother, though. Squigs had started to display some of the symptoms of Cushing's Disease that her brother, Junior, had developed. One of the symptoms is a heavier winter coat of hair, which doesn't shed easily in the spring. We started Squiggles on the same medications and herbal supplements that Junior had received. Luckily, she wasn't looking older than her 18 years, so I was thankful for that.

I'd spent most of my spare time over the past two years researching everything about house-building. I wanted to be prepared for our move the following year. Most of my summer was spent in negotiations with our Town about them possibly purchasing our farm. The previous owners of our farm had given almost 100 acres of the farm to the County for agriculture and conservation usage. Several years earlier, the County, in their infinite wisdom, decided to lease it to our Township.

While we could've gotten more money for the farm on the open market, Bob and I wanted it to remain a farm. We felt selling to the Town offered the best chance of that happening. Fair Chance Farm had been a wonderful home for our animals and us for 26 years. It was also home to my folks' cremains and granite burial markers. Many of our horses, dogs, and cats were laid to rest throughout the property. I certainly didn't want anything disturbing their resting places. Our tentative plan was to sell the farm to the Town as soon as we came to terms. One of the terms would be that we could remain living there until we were ready to move the following spring.

By August, Randy was still showing signs of problems in his stifles, so we brought him to the referral clinic for radiographs of his neck and stifles. The clinic's x-ray equipment was much more powerful than our portable machine. Despite the more powerful equipment, we saw no evidence of joint damage in Randy's stifles. His cervical x-rays were clean too, so he wasn't suffering from any anomalies in his neck. While I was relieved not to see damage in either his stifles or neck, I was no farther along trying to understand his problem. Randy was three years old, and I should have been enjoying that powerful, huge trot of his. Instead he spent his days grazing, while we hoped that time and Mother Nature were healing him. We'd done everything we'd known to do – without much success.

Shadow and Licorice were beginning to show some aging, but they were 12½ years old, so it was to be expected. I knew the past few years of stress from my folks' cancers and transitions, Squiggles' three less-than-perfect foalings, Dash's surgeries and transition, and Randy's stifle issues didn't help matters. Even though I continually told my canine caretakers not to absorb my stress and anxiety, I knew they did. They felt responsible for caring for Bob and me. I so hoped they'd make the move to North Carolina, but only time would tell. They were the best farm help I had ever had – always on time and never complained.

I'd been having some nagging thoughts about Squigs over the summer – her energy seemed a little flat. She wasn't happy without a foal to look after, but there wasn't anything I could do about that. Once an individual's soul purpose has been attained, the need to remain in physical form diminishes. I worried that Squiggles might be considering returning to Spirit. It wasn't anything she communicated to me, it was just a *feeling*. Obviously, this wasn't a feeling I liked. I still wasn't over the loss of Dash or my folks. After a few weeks I mentioned it to Bob, saying, "Don't be surprised if Squiggles leaves in the near future." Bob questioned me further, but all I could tell him was, "I have a feeling, but I have no idea when or how."

My negotiations with the Town were progressing. By summer's end I felt quite confident that we would come to terms. I suggested to Bob that we throw a "thank-you" cookout on the farm for all our friends and clients. So invitations were sent out for our "Thanks for the Memories" party in mid-October. Four days before our party, Squiggles was very lame in the pasture, showing signs of the dreaded laminitis, or founder. This was the same hoof ailment that her brother Junior developed to teach me about the power of healing that can be obtained via shamanic journey.

The moment I saw Squiggles try to walk, I knew she was leaving. All my thoughts and fears of the previous few months were being proven true. Once again, my intuition was right-on. I hated being right, especially about this dear soul. I *hated* it! I ran for Bob and told him that Squiggles had foundered. Bob filled her with injectable pain-killers in order to make her comfortable, then ran blood tests. I wanted Squiggles pain-free for sure, but I knew this founder wasn't meant to be healed like her brother's had been. She had created this particular disease in order to return Home. I had learned all about creating illnesses that result in transition ten years earlier from Because Of Love. Now I was witness to it all over again with my greatest Master Teacher: Squiggles The Special.

I explained all this to Bob, but he *needed* to treat her. I understood his reluctance to put her down – somewhat. I knew he had to be sure before he could take that ultimate step. As long as Squiggles was willing to give him some time to accept her wish, I wouldn't push it. But I couldn't watch her live in pain for too long. I had no doubt why this had happened and how it had happened. In order to help convince Bob, I had a conversation with Squiggles while Bob took care of some farm calls.

Hi Squigs. *Hi.* What's going on with you? *It's really hard for me to move around.* I know. Why? *I'm not sure.* Are you wanting to go back to Spirit? *Well, it would be okay with me, but I'm not sure it is with Bob.* We both love you very much, you know. *I do, and I love you and the life you've given me here. I really don't want to live anywhere else. You said we were all moving next year, right?* Yes, we are. I've been worried you would decide to leave now that you've achieved your soul purpose here on this plane. *I know you have and you are right, but I also feel that you don't want to let me go, in your heart, even though you understand things on a higher plane.* You're right. It's very hard to say goodbye to someone who has been your child and taught you so much. I'm trying to put *you* ahead of my feelings. *Bob needs to understand what you do, but he doesn't really accept the knowledge.* I know, he loves you so much and will miss you too.

You both have been instrumental in my achieving immense soul growth that I couldn't achieve in the past. I know you will take wonderful care of the boys. I have no worries there. Don't punish yourself over Dash. He had his own agenda and it had nothing to do with you or me. I really miss being pregnant, but I know you had my best interest at heart, so don't feel bad. I really loved my time as a mother and will never forget it. Together we've brought wonderful souls into this world. And it took all three of us. I will never forget you.

Whatever you decide about this I'm okay with. I know you won't put me through unnecessary treatment just to make yourselves feel better. What you did for my brother was such a gift. He hadn't been happy for a bit. I'm not like he was. I'm happy looking at my boys every day. I just really don't want to live anywhere where I won't see you every day. What's the point? I've done it all. My life is fulfilled thanks to you both. Whenever you're ready, I'm ready. I love you! And, we you. I've never learned so much from another. You've been a grand Teacher, and I can't thank you enough for allowing us to be your "parents." Come back anytime. We'll miss you! I can't tell you when we'll be ready, but you'll know probably before we do. *You're right!*

I was overrun with emotions and wet from uncontrollable tears as we ended our conversation. Never before had Squiggles' lesson of forgiveness been more powerful. She was willing to accept living in pain to allow Bob the necessary time to accept her decision. She was more amazing than even *I* imagined. I'd had several conversations with her about our upcoming move, never thinking it would play into her decision to transition. Our mountain property was steep and inappropriate for keeping horses, so they would be boarded elsewhere. The whole concept of moving was to rid myself of the heavy work that caring for horses involved. I was humbled that Squiggles thought that highly of me, that not seeing me each day would matter so much to her. Learning that fueled my tears even more.

I shared our communication with Bob when he returned home. It took him another day to truly absorb the essence of her message. When he finally did, we gave Squiggles the last great gift we could – a peaceful transition. I cleared her with SRT prior to euthanizing her in order to facilitate the release of her soul from her body and ease its transition back to spirit form. Just as with her first-born, Dash, six months earlier, I guided Squiggles' head gently to the ground as her soul released from her body. Overwrought with grief, despite knowing this was exactly what she wanted, I was unable to feel those spectacular feelings of her exhilaration, flying free in ultimate joy.

I had two days to get control of my emotions while I prepared for our farewell cookout. My heart was shattered into a zillion pieces from the loss of this special soul who'd shared the last 18 years with me. As I struggled to make everything perfect for our friends and clients, hundreds of memories of Squiggles flashed through my mind, both happy and sad. I had undoubtedly learned more from her than any other being in my life, bar none.

The farm was palpably different without her marvelous energy. I was so proud of all she'd accomplished, and I understood her wish to go Home, but it didn't make it any easier to accept. My life would never be the same without her in it. I tried to focus on the two sons she'd left in my care. Randy's future was very suspect, but I had high hopes that Stormy would live a long and happy life with me. I believed there was a reason that I *followed my heart* and Stormy came to us. I *had* to!

And then there were two. Twelve months earlier, I could never have imagined that I'd be heading to North Carolina with two horses instead of four. It was inconceivable to me. I simply couldn't imagine my life without Squiggles to share it with.

Chapter 31

∞

Farewell to Fair Chance

For the first time in my life, I hired a caterer to handle the cookout. Our last big cookout was in the mid-'90s when we hosted a reunion of all of the people who rode together, at the barn of my childhood showing days. My family did everything – it was just the *Kaiser* way. It had been a fantastic event, but the memories of all the work it entailed were still vivid. Without my folks, I knew I couldn't do it myself – and Bob didn't cook. It was another of those serendipitous occurrences. Having lost Squiggles a mere two days before the party, I would *never* have been able to handle it. It was going to be hard enough just setting up the chairs and tables under the tent.

A gorgeous fall day greeted everyone as they arrived at our farm. We had an amazing turnout, which spoke volumes about what our clients thought of Bob (and me). I felt throwing this party would give them an opportunity to show Bob how much he meant to them, and their attendance didn't disappoint. We also wanted to thank them for their loyalty over the 30-plus years that Bob had practiced in the area.

As I said earlier, anyone who had met Squiggles always wanted to see her when they came to visit. I worried about this for the two days between her departure and the party. I tried to prepare myself for it. Just as I'd anticipated, I fielded lots of requests to see the horses, especially Squiggles. When I explained about Squiggles' recent transition, each person was truly saddened and expressed genuine concern for me. I coped well except with my closest friends. With them, I lost it and had to walk away, wipe the tears, and regroup. It was like pouring salt on an open wound.

Shadow and Licorice were thrilled with all the people, attention, and *food!* I placed signs all around asking that they *not* be fed any treats. I figured they scoff up enough food that was dropped on the ground. I'd been feeding them a raw-food diet since they were four years old – no people food. I knew too many extras would cause digestive disturbances galore. I watched as people tried to respect the signs despite the excessive begging going on by the two Labrador brothers.

I had put together a poster board presentation of our mountain property, with numerous pictures surrounding the house designs. Bob held court, explaining to anyone who wanted to listen all about our future home in the High Country of North Carolina. I could hear the excitement in our friends' voices as they viewed the gorgeous mountain scenery and floor plan we'd worked on all winter with the Deltec (round house) designer.

While we were busy thanking our friends and clients with our delicious catered cookout, many folks arrived with thank-you gifts for us, which was totally unexpected. It just never occurred to me that they would bring gifts, or I would have said no. But I decided they needed to express their gratitude for the great service we'd provided for so many years. It was very humbling when someone approached us with a thoughtful gift.

Given my tenuous emotional state, I lost it when my dear friend Melissa, who'd worked for us years earlier, handed me a box to open. Melissa and her husband, Ed, were very talented crafters. Melissa was the best barn help I'd ever had (besides Shadow and Licorice). I lost her when she left to have their first daughter, which I truly regretted. But life goes on.

Inside the box was a beautiful wooden plaque on which Ed had carved an image of my first Yellow Lab, Gentle Ben, and a poem from a card I'd sent one Christmas. I burst into tears as I read it. Remembering Ben, who I'd lost 12 years earlier, and Squigs, who I'd lost two days ago, was too much for my fragile emotions. This was a treasure that would have a prominent place in our new dream home in the mountains. Melissa hugged me, and we cried together for all the dear animal-friends we'd each lost over the years. The poem read:

> When God had made the earth and sky,
> The flowers and the trees.

He then made all the animals,
The fish, the birds, and bees.

And when at last He'd finished,
Not one was quite the same.
He said, "I'll walk this world of mine,
And give each one a name."

And so He traveled far and wide
And everywhere He went,
A little creature followed him
Until it's strength was spent.

When all were named upon the Earth
And in the sky and sea.
The little creature said, "Dear Lord,
There's not one left for me."

Kindly the Father said to him,
"I've left you to the end.
I've turned my own name from back to front
And called you dog, my friend."

Everyone had a wonderful time. Our "Thanks for the Memories" soirée had been a resounding success. I was exhausted by day's end and so grateful that I'd had the wisdom to have it catered. The food was delicious, plentiful, and more varied than I could have prepared. Not being responsible for the food gave me time to spend with our guests, although I never felt I had enough time to spend with everyone. I received so many compliments about the afternoon and our plans for the future, while everyone expressed how sorry they were to see us leave.

By December, we had a firm agreement with the Town, allowing us to remain on the farm until May 1st – our 27th wedding anniversary. We closed on the 18th of December and began packing 30 years' worth of stuff. We made numerous trips over the winter to the Carolina property, moving just about everything you could imagine, including Bob's operating table (don't ask).

We would load my horse trailer and another trailer we had bought (to dump manure) and drive to the property. We'd unload the trailers into the steel building that had been built over the summer. We stayed the night with the fellow who had put in the roads and prepared the house site. Ernie had horses, so we were kindred spirits and new friends. The next day, we'd drive the ten hours back to the farm and return to the business of running a farm, hospital, and vet office. Luckily I had found a wonderful gal to take care of the farm and animals while we were gone. Of course, Shadow and Licorice weren't too happy, but at their ages all that travel was not good for them. All the packing and driving was exhausting, but also exciting as we looked toward our future.

When my folks passed, my brother and niece took whatever they needed, but the farm-house was still filled to the brim with many treasures collected over their long lives together. My mom had amazing taste in linens, crystal, dishware, and furniture – always the best of everything. While they were beautiful, they weren't what I needed or wanted in our mountain house. Not knowing what else to do, I hired a local estate auction company to help me sell all but the most special mementos, which would make the trip south with me.

The auction was set for the weekend before Easter. It turned out to be *the* most difficult day of my life. I guess I had been naïve to think that people would recognize the quality of the items before them and bid accordingly. As the day progressed, I felt like not only were my parents' treasures being stolen, but my parents were being disrespected. Prior to the auction, I had invited my close friends to come to the farm and pick something they'd like to have to remind them of us and my folks. Had I known what a disaster the auction was going to be, I would've just given it all away to friends.

Several times throughout the day, a friend or client would come to share with me what they'd bought; I still cherish those moments. I was so pleased when a client excitedly shared that she'd purchased the Strauss Crystal chandelier that had hung over the dining table for 24 years. I thought about all the holiday meals that had been illuminated by that chandelier. I was thrilled that someone I knew would be enjoying it in the future.

I was demoralized by day's end. Bob's family had come to help support us and they and my friends were busy trying to cheer me up. Nothing was helping. The only positive result of the day was that we got rid of most all of it. To me it was a huge failure – something I'd never do again. I felt it had been a huge mistake, or as I call them, an opportunity for learning. As long as we learn from them, then there is value. I definitely learned from this one!

As our departure date drew nearer, the downside of moving crept into my reality – not having my horses right outside my door and not having easy access to my friends. Knowing my body couldn't handle much more farm work and that it was time to give my communication and healing skills the priority they deserved, helped me deal with the negative aspects of moving. We had enjoyed numerous Broadway plays over the past year, recognizing that after our move we'd be limited to the local University in the mountains for cultural events.

I made arrangements with the gal who ran the barn in North Carolina to ship Randy and Stormy in her large horse trailer. Due to Randy's stifle problem and both having limited trailering experience, I felt my two-horse trailer wasn't the best for the long trip to Greensboro. My friend's trailer would allow them each a large stall without having to tie their heads. We moved the horses on April 1st, a month before our departure. Randy and Stormy travelled great. They were on the trailer for 12 long hours. Bob and I were following with one of our trailers filled with horse-related equipment that we were bringing down for my friend's farm. Her trailer got a flat tire an hour from the farm in Greensboro, but luckily she had everything necessary for Bob to change the tire.

After we got the horses safely into their new stalls, I finally relaxed somewhat. Randy and Stormy settled in well. After such a long trip, I needed to be sure they were fine in the morning. I had explained to them before we left what was happening. I knew they weren't happy that I was leaving them, but I assured them that my friend would take excellent care of them. I was exhausted from the long trip, but more from worry about my neophyte, equine travelers. I'd shipped thousands of miles over my horse-show career and breeding mares, but those horses were all experienced shippers and I never gave it a second thought. Moving my "babies," albeit two- and three-year-olds, was filled with anxiety and emotional stress for me.

The next morning, the boys appeared to have no adverse effects from the 12-hour trip. As I said goodbye to each one, it finally hit me that I was leaving them so far from me. My horses had been with me every day for the past 27 years, 24/7. We'd decided to take two days to travel home, so we could spend time that morning with Randy and Stormy making sure they were all right. As we drove away from my friend's barn and my two "grandsons," my tears started. I never anticipated the emotions that welled up within me. I spent the next two days crying on and off as we headed back to a horseless Fair Chance Farm. The reality of my decision to move to the mountains struck home, and struck hard.

The farm didn't feel the same without Randy and Stormy (and Squiggles). It felt eerie, like a ghost farm. It was apparent that the energies of its inhabitants were tremendous contributors to the peaceful, serene atmosphere that Fair Chance used to possess. My missing horses left an empty feel to my distinctive home in New Jersey. Often in the past, clients or friends would stop by and marvel at the amazing energy on the farm, commenting on how exceptionally peaceful and calming it was. I'd stop whatever chore I was engrossed in; take a minute to feel my surroundings, smile, and say, "It is! I just wish it didn't take so much of my time, so I could enjoy it too."

Living on the farm minus our horses was bizarre. I was exceptionally sensitive to energies, or lack of them, due to my gift of being an empathetic healer, so it bothered me more than anyone. I missed my horses more than I'd ever have thought. It was the first time in 40 years that my horses weren't within an hour of me, and for the past 27 years just outside my door. The dogs and cats didn't know what had happened to Randy and Stormy, so I took some time with each of them to explain. Shadow and Licorice already knew about our move, but I hadn't shared the news with Bandit, Butch, Lucky, and Crystal – my barn-cat crew extraordinaire.

The last month on our farm was spent packing and visiting with all those friends that we were leaving behind. I couldn't believe there were still tons to pack since we'd moved so much over the winter. It seemed endless. Bob was a pack rat, and we had numerous buildings to store stuff in, and almost 30 years together for collecting. Bob still did some vet work, mostly chiropractic adjustments, which didn't require any equipment.

I was so happy that Shadow and Licorice were still with us. They would turn 13 years old a few months after we arrived in the mountains. Ben had transitioned during his 13th year, but I was hoping all the years of their homemade diet would allow them to stay much longer. I'm never ready to say good-bye and especially not after all of my recent losses. I looked forward to spending many hours with them on our 54-acre mountaintop property. I knew they would love it as much as I did. All they really wanted was to be with us, regardless of where.

One of the local feed stores that I frequented was selling dog crates that had been used in their grooming business. I bought three of them to add to the one I already had to house the four cats during the move. Despite the fact that Butch and Bandit were siblings, they really weren't too tolerant of one another; none of my cats were. Cats just possess a different mentality than dogs. You know – dogs are from Mars, cats are from Venus. The crates would ride to North Carolina in my horse trailer with one cat in each for safe-keeping. The day before we left I had a long conversation with each cat, explaining about the property, highlighting the plentiful wildlife – bobcats, bears, and even cougars. I especially emphasized the need to stay close to the steel building.

Besides informing the dogs and cats about our long ride, I walked all over the farm that last day taking a video of remembrance. I communicated with many of the plants and trees as well as the land itself, thanking them for sharing the past 27 years with us. So many memories flooded my awareness as I walked through the barn, through all the pastures, past everyone's resting places, and through both the houses we'd lived in. I was overcome with emotions and cried like a baby during most of the video. While I knew my choice to leave Fair Chance Farm was the "right" choice for me, it still hurt. My last day ended with the cats being secured in their crates in my horse trailer to be sure no one was left behind.

Early the next morning, we met three of my gal pals at our local Perkins restaurant for "the last breakfast." I'd be returning in July to join them for a Josh Groban (my favorite vocalist) concert, which made this farewell slightly less emotional – *slightly*. We met the moving truck back at the farm and began loading what *we* hadn't moved, mainly the big pieces of furniture and all our clothes. I could tell Shadow and Licorice were concerned about the movers despite my heads-up the day before. Once the movers left, we got ourselves organized and finished loading the large trailer that Bob would pull with his truck. When all was ready, I hooked to my horse trailer with its precious feline cargo and loaded Shadow and Licorice in my car.

Our little caravan pulled out of Fair Chance Farm for the last time on May 1st, 2004 – our 27th wedding anniversary. It had been quite a marriage and life since we were wed in Annabelle Taylor Hall at Cornell University. It was the end of an era that had been wondrous, but I was excited to begin the next chapter in my life, nestled on the side of Three Top Mountain in Creston, North Carolina. The last thing I shared with Fair Chance Farm were my tears as I pulled out of the driveway heading towards my new life.

Chapter 32

∞

Short-Lived Dream

*D*espite having gotten up early, we got away from the farm later than we'd hoped. To complicate matters, we hit the worst traffic ever as we headed out of Jersey. Hauling trailers in stop-and-go traffic is nerve-wracking and exhausting. As I sat in traffic, I realized there was no way we would make it to our new property in one day. Luckily, I travel with a motel directory in my car, so I called Bob on our two-way radio to tell him I was reserving a room for us in Northern Virginia. He agreed.

I was very concerned about Shadow and Licorice. They had never stayed overnight in a motel, or anywhere other than our farm for that matter. I struggled to control my emotions, so I didn't compound their anxiety. The four cats were tucked away in the horse trailer wondering what in heaven was going on. I was never more thankful for my skills as a communicator. I had a quick chat with all six of them about our latest plan.

Shadow and Licorice were quite anxious in the room, but settled down quicker than I did. Luckily, I found a room with a refrigerator for their homemade, fresh diet. Knowing they were very comfortable being in my car, they came with us to dinner. Neither one was used to being walked on a leash to do their business. They'd lived free on the farm all their lives. The only times they were on leashes were when we went to see their friend, Dr. Gary, for vet work, and at the beach.

The cats were wide-eyed when I crawled around outside each of their crates to feed them. I didn't dare try to clean litter trays for fear one would escape and be lost forever. I had a restless sleep, but we all survived. This was the first time in all the trips we'd made to the property that we'd had any delays. Of course, it would happen when we had our animal-family in tow – go figure.

We arrived on the mountain no worse for the wear. The dogs were so happy to get out of the car. The year before, we had purchased a camper to live in while our house was being built. It had been on the farm for six months, so the dogs were very familiar with it. The property was a long way from the nearest road, so I had no concerns about traffic. I knew any wildlife that was around would disappear as soon as they heard us, and especially the dogs. My biggest fear with wildlife was with our cats. They were the perfect meal for the carnivores that shared the 54 acres with us.

My plan with the cats was to leave them in their crates for a day or two inside the steel building, which was filled with our belongings. I hate cages or caged animals, so the next day I opened the crates, keeping the doors to the steel building closed. The cats took off to find special hiding places. I wasn't worried though, because the cat food was being eaten. The second full day we were there, after reminding each cat about the dangers that lurked in the woods, I threw caution to the wind and opened the overhead doors to the steel building. It took another day or two before I saw a cat outside the building. I think I had frightened them to death with my warnings of things that go "bump in the woods." Shadow and Licorice were in heaven. They had tons of areas to explore with their fabulous Labrador noses. Their eyesight and hearing were failing, but those noses were still as sensitive as ever.

My new job was building a house – or at least, overseeing the project. If anyone had ever told me I'd be so involved with a house, I would've told them, "No way!" I loved my mountain property even though we still couldn't see the views very well. As I walked Shadow and Licorice along old logging roads that crisscrossed the acreage, I truly felt as if my soul had come home. Following those two old Labrador butts along the trail the old road formed, I felt grateful that my dear friends had made the move and appeared to be as thrilled with our new home as I was.

The cats seemed to be in their glory, discovering all sorts of hiding and hunting places close to the steel building – their new home. Bob pulled out, heading back to Jersey, just as the furniture truck drove in.

He said there was more on the farm he needed to bring. I just couldn't imagine what else we possibly needed, but there was no dissuading him. I couldn't make the 126-mile drive to Greensboro to see Randy and Stormy until Bob returned from Jersey.

As soon as Bob got back, I flew to visit my horses. This was the longest I'd ever not seen a horse of mine. I was so thankful I could communicate with them whenever I wanted. It helped all three of us cope with the month-plus since we'd seen one another. The horses had settled in very well, and my friend was taking good care of them. Randy was still dealing with his stifle issue. Stormy was continuing to grow; handsome as ever. I could tell that my horse show friend and her mother were really impressed with Storm.

My friend and I spoke about Randy. Living with him in her barn, she saw what I'd been talking about with his hind legs. She recommended that I have him evaluated by her lameness guru about four hours away in Virginia. I told her I'd discuss it with Bob and let her know. We'd already had him examined by several excellent vets, so I wasn't sure what good it would do. It was so difficult to be so far from Randy, not knowing if he was getting worse or not. I stayed the night and spent more time with my boys in the morning before heading back to the mountain to await the arrival of all the house parts that would begin transforming our house design into the real deal. It was an enormous task, but with our general contractor's assistance, we got the thousands of house parts up to the site without a hitch. The construction of the house moved along quite well, thanks to a great crew.

I mentioned the lameness guru in Virginia, Reynolds Cowles, to Bob. He knew Reynolds and thought highly of him. My friend got an appointment for Randy. She came with me when I trailered him to Virginia.

Using Reynolds' digital x-ray equipment, we were finally able to see the damage in both of Randy's stifle joints. To have this much damage in a horse that had never been ridden was devastating. As each new x-ray appeared, my heart broke further. From what I saw, Randy would never be sound. I started to walk out of the room fighting back my tears, but Reynolds stopped me. "I don't think he's hopeless. Randy's young enough that he should be able to remodel his stifle joints given time." I had nothing but time. Reynolds discussed the radiographs with Bob, and they decided to inject Randy's stifles with a combination of agents to quiet inflammation and promote healing.

My heart knew it wouldn't matter. Nothing over the past two years had helped, including my spiritual healing techniques, which meant Randy's soul didn't want its physical form to be healed. I'd been denying what my heart knew was truth. I'd been avoiding another disastrous outcome with a being I dearly loved. I just couldn't let go of him, not Randy. I was open to anything that might relieve his discomfort and delay the inevitable. Reynolds asked me to call in a month with a progress report.

The trip back to my friend's farm was uneventful. As I drove out of the farm, I prayed my feelings about Randy's treatment would be wrong. I'd spent 27 years providing nursing care and intense observation for our clients' horses. Now I couldn't do that for a horse that meant the world to me. I came back in a few days, and then as often as I could over the next two months. What I found was really no improvement. In fact he was worse. Based on my own shoulder injections and my pharmaceutical education, I knew obvious improvement should occur quickly. It just wasn't meant to be.

Every day I made sure I laid eyes on each of the four cats. They seemed very comfortable using the steel building as their home base. My computer was in the small office in the building, which I think it made it feel more like our barn to them – minus the equine aroma of course. One day, I didn't see Lucky, so I sent out a telepathic plea that he please show himself, so I could stop worrying. The next morning, I noticed Lucky resting in the building. I thanked him as I continued on to the computer. Several hours later, I found Lucky lying in the rain outside the camper. My heart stopped. He felt like a limp rag as I huddled him close to my body.

Just before we moved Licorice had developed a slight case of Geriatric Vestibular Syndrome, which had affected Rainbow, the cat, years earlier. He needed a follow-up blood count shortly after we had arrived in North Carolina. The lovely people who we'd bought the property from referred us to their small-animal vet, so we knew where to take Lucky. But of course this happened on a weekend, so I heard a voice machine directing me to another vet in the area.

I rushed Lucky to the new vet. I already knew that he wasn't going to make it – I just knew. Lucky was admitted to the vet hospital. I waited for the blood results, which weren't encouraging. I asked her to do whatever was necessary to keep him supported, but I didn't want to do any heroics. Lucky died the next morning. The vet diagnosed poison, guessing antifreeze. How ironic that I'd worried about the wildlife threat on the mountain, but it was an inorganic predator that cost Lucky his life. Possibly one of the construction crew's cars or trucks was leaking. I kept an eagle-eye on my remaining three cats and two dogs. Fortunately, none of them got into whatever Lucky had.

Lucky had been my mother's companion, and had comforted her following my father's death. I found him numerous times sitting on top of my mom's cremains under her tree, which generated awe within me. Lucky had been so supportive, and now he was gone. I was having a hard time letting go of him. I had no one to share my grief with, since Bob had flown to New Mexico to visit the place he was donating our operating table to.

Over time, I realized that Lucky was ready to go. The person he had come to help in this life was gone. His job was done and done well. When Bob returned, we tried to bury Lucky. Our rocky mountain wouldn't let us dig a grave. Lucky didn't want to be on the mountain, which I really didn't understand at the time, but would in the not too distant future.

Now that Bob was back, I needed to check on Randy and Stormy. I missed having my horses with me, but I didn't have a choice for now. Randy really hadn't improved at all. I needed to call Reynolds, but I drove back to the mountain to face different concerns. Bob had made some comments before I left that worried me. He was depressed about how much the house was costing. I told him that we were too deep into it now to stop. If we had to put it on the market later, so be it. The value was there. Bob had been acting weird since winter, but I figured it was the stress of retiring and moving.

The night after I got back from checking on the horses, I heard words emerge from Bob's mouth that I will remember until the day I transition. *"I never wanted this house. I never wanted to be here. This is all your dream and I feel like I'm just along for the ride."* These words began my "dark night of the soul," which lasted the best part of three years. One minute I would be focused on getting the house completed enough to be protected from the weather; and the next minute I would be an emotional, crying wreck. My fantastic dream had now turned into my worst nightmare.

I was in a place I had never been to before in my life, and I was there alone. I was 600 miles from my home, my friends, and my support. I was devastated and very afraid. I was exhausted physically, mentally, emotionally – and especially, spiritually. I felt isolated, abandoned, and betrayed. My life was out of control. I was one sad and confused soul. I felt so alone, except for my dear dogs and cats. I wanted to simply stay in bed and cry, but I couldn't. I had animals that needed me.

A year after those fateful words, I began writing a journal to discover and comprehend what had happened and why. I wrote for 14 months and then edited for another 16 months. The result was my book, *Letting Go: An Ordinary Woman's Extraordinary Journey of Healing & Transformation*, which friends urged me to publish in order to help others dealing with intense challenges. While this was the direst time of my life, it also was a time of tremendous personal growth and transformation. *Letting Go* recounts how I learned from – and let go of – the pain that I was shrouded in following my husband's betrayal.

Master Teachers is about the selfless animals who have shared their lives with me, taught me, loved and supported me. The circumstances of my life provide the back-drop for their tales, so some of what befell us after our move to North Carolina has to be retold, but only as it pertains to those dear souls that lifted me up and helped me heal from this bleakest of times. Without their support, lessons, and love, I would never have made such a miraculous recovery. How these dear souls facilitated my healing from my divorce, and continue to love and teach me today, forms the remainder of this book. I encourage anyone who is dealing with life's difficulties and pain to get their hands on *Letting Go* in order to shorten their own healing journeys. Enough about my human drama – back to the tales.

Chapter 33

And Then There Was One

*A*fter Bob's announcement, I fell into a dark place that I called the Abyss. It was scary in the Abyss, but I wasn't there alone. Shadow and Licorice, Bandit, Butch, and Crystal, and Randy and Stormy were there with me. Without them, I might never have extricated myself. There were numerous times, given my belief in reincarnation, that it seemed easier to transition and return at a later date. But who would take care of my dear animals?

All my years of caring for my animals were paid back a hundred times over with the love, affection, and support I felt from each of them during this dreadful time. I was lost on a mountain where I had thought I'd live out the rest of my years. Shadow, Licorice, and I walked the loop of roads that circled the dream house and steel building four or five times a day just to get us out of the camper for some exercise. The mountain that had touched my soul so deeply now felt like a prison. It would *never* be my home.

The unfinished dream house was put on the market to be sold. I struggled to deal with the life that was crumbling around me. I knew I had to find a house to live in before winter. A family of two dogs and three cats precluded renting, so I began a search for a house to purchase. I tried desperately to grab onto one positive thing in each day, but it was so hard. I knew better than most, the effects that divorce can have on the animals in the family. I'd helped countless clients in similar situations. Shadow and Licorice were already aged. They didn't need the added stress from me.

I communicated with them daily about not taking on my negative energy. But they knew better than I how incapable I was of dealing with my negativity. Their presence in my life coerced me into working on my own pain so it wouldn't shorten their lives. They were my rocks, and eventually they saved me from the depths of the Abyss.

The energy on the mountain improved significantly when Bob left, thankfully. He was driving his operating table to the Navaho reservation in New Mexico that he was donating it to. During his trip, Shadow became very ill. Having run a vet hospital for so many years, I'm usually not an alarmist. I'd been treating Shadow for a diarrhea problem for a few days, which appeared to be resolving. Early one morning, he threw up blood. Fear gripped me, and I panicked.

I rushed Shadow to the vet and they took him from me. I was overcome with emotions, because I didn't realize I'd have to leave him. When I got teary, they immediately took me to him. I couldn't have another soul taken from me, even just for a few hours. I regrouped and communicated to him that he had to stay. Luckily, the vet felt he would be fine after a round of antibiotics. Shadow had picked up digestive bacteria that were prevalent in the area. I was only without him for a few hours – that much I could handle. Shadow showed me that I was still capable of taking care of myself and my family, whether I believed it or not.

However, I was riddled with guilt. I knew that on a spiritual level my animals were absorbing my negative energy. I had dealt with this type of problem in my animal-healing practice many times. Our animals are continually trying to help us deal with our challenges. Years earlier in a consultation session, I was "told" that companion animals come to answer cries for help from human souls on earth. Shadow, Licorice, Butchie, Bandit, Crystal, Randy, and Stormy were all proof positive. They were here for me when my soul was crying its loudest. I had another long discussion with my animal family about not taking on my negative energy. At the same time, I knew that discussion was pointless – they were here to take care of me, just as I was for them.

My teacher from New York City, who had helped me awaken my telepathic skills, once told me that I would go through a tunnel and emerge from the other side a different person. I would need to do this in order to come into the full power of my abilities in this life. Her explanation of the tunnel made it sound like an awful thing. My life was great at the time, so I just smiled and let it go. It was one of those significant bits of information which, back then, seemed so innocuous. A decade and a half later, with the assistance of my animal family, I crept from my dark Abyss into a Tunnel of learning and powerful transformation that would last for several years.

After Bob returned, I headed to Randy and Stormy. I was supposed to have called Reynolds with a report on Randy's progress, but there wasn't anything good to say. Instead of a month, it turned into more than two months. I kept trying to give Randy more time, because the alternative was unacceptable to me. I wasn't ready to let Randy go and I was terrified of what his loss might do to me. My fragile emotions were taking their toll on all of us.

Bob had gone off the mountain for the weekend. I waited for his return so we could call Reynolds together. By Tuesday, I gave up waiting and called myself. Reynolds was very sorry. He'd thought it was worth a shot, but with no positive change, more injections wouldn't help – which I already knew. This meant the end of the line for Randy. I began to cry, knowing what I had to do. Why this dear soul? Why was this happening to me? Like I was the one getting ready to leave.

I was shattered all over again, but I had to make the best decision for Randy. I've had to decide for all of my animal friends, but normally at the end of a full life. Randy was only three years old. I thought we'd have many years together. But this was about what *Randy's* soul wanted. I had to keep my promise. I had to let go. I communicated with Randy, who assured me that he wanted to go. He was glad to have helped Squiggles achieve her soul's purpose, but it was time for him to leave. My soul ached from the pain of losing Dash and Lucky, my broken marriage, and now this. I *had* to let go. Randy was ready, and I had no right to keep him here. I had to say good-bye once more to Ben/Rainbow/Randy. I could only hope that he might choose to join me again in a happier time.

Many times animals have expressed to me their confusion during euthanasia consultations. They simply don't understand the intense sadness their person feels regarding their impending transition. Animals understand reincarnation. They perceive death as a beginning rather than an end. To them it is the start of a new, and inevitable, cycle of Spirit. Their teaching dissolved my fear of death and showed me the continuity of Spirit.

I was trying to embrace this lesson with dear Randy – without much success. To me, it has always appeared a conundrum. Our animals hold on in order to teach us. We have to let go in order to learn. The more we can't let go, the harder they hold on. When we finally let go, they let go – and hopefully, the lessons are embraced.

My expertise doesn't make losing a dear animal-friend any easier or hurt any less. My experiences allow me to recognize it sooner than most, which hopefully saves my friends from unnecessary suffering. I've always felt euthanasia is the last great gift we can give our animal friend(s). It's something that I never take lightly, I *hate* to have to do, and is always difficult, regardless of whose animal it is.

It's amazing what animals are willing to go through. They stay in order to teach us how to say good-bye and let go. I've witnessed animals endure almost no quality of life for years, until their person was ready to accept their fate and release them. I have vowed to my animals that I will never allow them to suffer for me – never!

When you make the final decision to send someone Home, you need to do it *yesterday*. Knowing what lies ahead is excruciatingly painful. Bob was away again, so I asked my friend to make an appointment with her vet. I had to wait 'til the following week, which was agonizing for me. While I waited, Bob reappeared. I told him about the conversation with Reynolds, and my appointment to euthanize Randy. He listened, nodded, and walked away. I was stunned. I fully expected him to tell me he would put Randy down. Randy was showing me the new paradigm of my life – *Bob doesn't care!*

I drove to my friend's farm to meet a stranger to do the most difficult thing any animal loving person will ever do. A *stranger!* I waited half an hour for the vet, which gave me time to say goodbye to Randy, and explain to his younger brother what was happening. I expected my friend to be there, but she never showed. I have never felt so *alone* in all my life. I tried as hard as I could to send Randy off willingly, but I broke down into torrents of tears as the vet injected the poison. It didn't matter that Randy wanted to go. I didn't want him to. I couldn't let go.

His soul was out in a flash. Randy was free of the physical body that was so impressive, yet gave him so much trouble. I thanked the vet and drove my broken heart back to the mountain in a flood of tears. Bob never made one comment when I returned. Randy's parting lesson for me was that *I'm on my own.* I know it's not the spiritually evolved thing to say, but I don't think I will ever be able to forgive Bob for my ordeal that day. It was a hard lesson that required extraordinary pain in order for me to truly embrace it, but thanks to Randy, I did. I would never forget that enormous stride as he floated across our big pasture – a memory for a lifetime.

And then there was one.

Chapter 34

∞

Follow Your Heart

*A*s I struggled to accept my shrinking animal family, I continued to search for a house for us to live in. I couldn't believe that only eleven months earlier I'd been looking for a barn in the area to board *four* horses, now I was left with just one. My heart was broken, which made looking for real estate that much more difficult.

The needs of my animals dictated the houses that I might consider. Shadow and Licorice were steadily aging, and the stress of losing Randy didn't help. I needed a house that didn't have stairs to climb to enter it. Many of the houses in the mountains have lots of steps up to the living level. Butch, Bandit, and Crystal were outdoor cats, so I couldn't be near any heavily traveled roads.

Eventually I settled on a new log house that was up a gravel road away from traffic and surrounded by woods. There was only one step onto the wrap-around porch from the driveway and three steps into what would become a fenced yard for Shadow and Licorice. As soon as I closed on the log house and was able to move in, my next mission would be to find a place for Stormy. I needed him back in my life, and he needed me.

The Universe took pity on me and found Stormy's new home in a most unexpected way. Part of the appeal of the log house was that the builder was willing to use some of the bath fixtures that I'd chosen for the dream-turned-nightmare house. Using these fixtures required new countertops. The contractor that I hired for the countertops had a wife who rode horses. He noticed all the photos of my horses and asked if I still had one.

I explained that Stormy was stabled in Greensboro, since I'd been unable to find a local barn when I had looked the summer before we moved. I told him about the perfect farm I'd found back then, but it was closing to the public that fall. He knew it, and told me that he'd been past it recently and saw their sign advertising for boarding. I called immediately. The young gal, Kim, remembered me from our visit the summer before. I told her things had changed since we'd last spoken – I only had one horse and no vet-husband.

The answer to my problem of a home for Stormy is a perfect example of universal orchestration and co-creating. My thoughts were focused on an appropriate barn in the area. I had no way of knowing the owners of the *perfect* barn had reconsidered their decision about boarding others' horses. I didn't place any restrictions or limitations on what I wanted, so the Universe sent a messenger in the guise of my countertop person. I think the Universe and my Guides and Teachers knew how much Stormy and I needed one another.

Four months after Bob's caustic words, I brought my much-needed equine healer home. Leaving the barn in Greensboro was an unpleasant and hurtful event. My friend, who judged me for my decision to euthanize Randy, became quite nasty when I happily shared that I'd located a wonderful barn for Stormy in the mountains. She now joined the ever-growing list of losses I was accumulating. I needed my entire animal-family if I was going to survive alone in the woods of the High Country of North Carolina.

I drove the 126 miles to collect Stormy and all his "luggage." Horses require an inordinate amount of equipment. This was the first time he'd been on the trailer alone and I was worried, so I gave him a light tranquilizer injection. Truth be told, *I* probably needed it more than he did. Stormy shipped wonderfully to his new home. I arrived at the farm exhausted from worrying about Stormy's inexperience with traveling.

The next day, I went to check on how Stormy was settling in. It was so wonderful to arrive in half an hour rather than two. He was out in his own huge, grassy pasture. When I called him, he whinnied and galloped over. He was genuinely happy to see me. I started to cry, because someone cared for me, and I so needed that. I had missed being with my horses so much. They are an integral part of me and always will be.

Now I had my last one back in my daily life. My salvation had arrived, because I had *followed my heart* back on my farm when he was conceived and again when I brought him home to the mountains. This was the first positive thing that had happened to me in four months, except for buying a house. Stormy was so much more important to my healing, my recovery, and my sanity. He was my angel with four legs, who would give my life some sense of purpose again.

Two months after Stormy arrived in the mountains, an old friend in New Jersey emailed this poem that embodies the significance of Stormy – and all my horses – to my life.

"In The Heart of A Horse"

When your day seems out of balance and so many things go wrong. . .

When people fight around you and the day drags on so long. . .

When parents act like children, in-laws make you think "Divorce". . .

Go out into your pasture. . .

and wrap your arms around your horse.

His gentle breath enfolds you, and he watches with those eyes.

He may not have a PhD, but he is, oh so wise!

His head rests on your shoulder.

You embrace him oh so tight.

He puts your world in balance, and makes it seem all right.

Your tears they soon stop flowing.

The tension is now eased.

The garbage has been lifted, and you're quiet and at peace.

So when you need the balance from circumstances in your day. . .

The best therapy that you can seek. . .

is out there eating hay!

The unknown author had obviously spent time with horses. I just burst into tears, when I read the poem. It was truly synchronistic. It spoke the truth about how much all of my horses have meant to me over the years, and how much they've enriched me.

The farm was simply beautiful and absolutely perfect. Kim, his daily caregiver, was very capable. She was a younger version of me. I couldn't have asked for anything better. I had absolutely no concerns for his well-being. I'd be a mere half-hour away if anything serious came up.

The downside of having horses in the mountains is the lack of veterinary service. For me, it wasn't too much of a concern. I had all those years of experience. What I didn't have was a veterinary license. For all of the worrying and stressing that I did in all other areas of my life, I did none regarding Stormy. I knew I could handle anything that might come along. If not, he'd ship to wherever to deal with whatever. I wouldn't let any negative thoughts create an unhealthy reality for Stormy.

It was interesting, because my thoughts were still out of control in the rest of my life, but not where Stormy was concerned. I found it intriguing that I had all the confidence in the world with him, but absolutely none with my Self. I had spent my life caring for and loving horses. It had been my true joy. I was very good at what I did, and it showed in my self-confidence and knowing around them. Through my experience with Stormy, it became painfully apparent that I had spent a life focused totally away from me. I had been completely unaware of it until that moment. This would prove to be one of my biggest lessons as I clawed my way out of the Abyss, into the Tunnel, and eventually out of the Tunnel.

I trained Stormy about four days a week. He was only two, and didn't need too much exercise. He was wonderful and seemed to enjoy the attention. I felt like I had purpose to my life again. I have a wonderful rapport with horses, which is rooted in my deep respect and love for them. Working with Stormy boosted my deflated self-esteem, which had taken a severe beating over the past six months.

While at the farm, I was fully in the moment, feeling the joy I used to. There is something so serene and peaceful about anywhere horses are. To look out over the pristine pastures and see Stormy grazing in his huge, grassy field touched my heart. Follow Your Heart was reawakening my heart, albeit slowly. Being at the farm, bathed in the energy that I'd spent so much of my life in, was nourishing to my soul.

One of *the* most spiritual times for me had been the nights in my old barn, when I'd just listen to the sounds in total darkness. I'd hear the horses munching hay, moving around the stalls, snorting hay dust out of their nostrils, breathing. Those sounds and the stillness bought me as close to Being, to Presence, to my Essence, as anything. They were magical, healing, mystical times that touched my heart deeply. With the arrival of Stormy, I hoped to recover some of that. It was imperative I resurrect those feelings in order to heal my heart, and ultimately, my soul.

Stormy's presence in the mountains was crucial to my escape from the Abyss and entry into my Tunnel of personal growth and transformation. The time spent at the perfect farm with Stormy renewed my spirit. Shadow and Licorice joined me most days, and I could see the positive effect on them as well. They'd spent their entire lives around horses, so being back on a horse farm put a spring back in their step as well. Training Stormy, my four-legged angel, allowed me to focus on my one true passion – horses. Training young horses can be both frustrating and rewarding. Given the chaos surrounding the rest of my life, I found more satisfaction working with Stormy than anywhere else.

As a three-year-old, Stormy began to exhibit some resistance to our training routine, which wasn't unexpected by me. I had begun numerous youngsters, so I anticipated the various stages encountered during their education. Stormy really started to test his boundaries by displaying an iron will. I knew his father, Inspiration, had a very strong will. Knowing offspring inherit more than just physical attributes from their parents, I tried to finesse Stormy through what I described as his teenager phase.

Stormy was bored with the routine in the ring. My conundrum was to keep his mind busy and challenged while working lightly to prevent any injury to his young body – it's a fine line between the two. It was my responsibility to deal with these challenges with patience, yet firmness. I had to be mentally and emotionally stronger. Part of the wonder of training horses revolves around how you accomplish that. What works well with one doesn't necessarily work with another, which is why horses are never boring. Stormy and I had embarked on a new phase of our relationship.

Stormy's challenges kept me present in the moment and away from the pain outside the safety of the farm.

As a species, horses are one of the most willing participants in our lives. I knew Stormy wanted to be cooperative. I attributed his resistance to simply being a baby. Little did I know the powerful lesson he was trying to teach his grandmother. My challenge of encouraging Stormy to accept his boundaries without confrontation continued for months. Being more intelligent, I needed to finesse his cooperation. In the end, I realized what a joke that was. Who was recognizing the lessons being offered? Certainly not me.

Stormy's strong will and resistance was truly testing my patience and my expertise. I needed to get some insights and guidance from the spiritual realms, so I scheduled a session with my friend Gregory Possman. I had met Gregory a year after I moved into my log house. He is a gifted spiritual advisor and trance channel who helped me enormously during my "dark night of the soul." Many of the lessons revealed during these channelings are chronicled in *Letting Go*. The information and guidance received from numerous spiritual entities that "speak" through Gregory were integral to my healing. Having such a talented resource a mile from my home was another of those universal *coincidences*.

With Gregory's assistance, I was finally shown the *real* reason for Stormy's uncooperative and unpleasant behavior. Just as I'd been totally clueless about my husband's plans to leave me, I had completely missed the deep meaning behind Stormy's battles with me. Gregory channeled Archangel Michael, who described my conflict with the Universe and my soul with respect to my issue of getting what I wanted vs. getting what I needed. When he equated my thoughts of *I don't like it, I don't want it, I want out of here*, to that of a rebellious teenager, a spotlight shined on Stormy! Michael laughed and admired the efficiency of the Universe as I acknowledged my "*aha!* moment." All was always in perfection. Stormy had been training *me* – or trying to. While I was doing what I loved, Stormy was trying to teach a lesson I didn't want to learn! You'd better have a sense of humor to survive the earth plane.

Once again, this animal communicator had been so in the dark. I had learned from so many of my own and my client's animals just how integral our animals are to our lives. Even I, who knew how much Stormy was contributing to my recovery, was blown away by the awareness I'd just received. So *now* who was the stubborn student? I agreed that it was most definitely *moi!*

Michael encouraged me to acknowledge and then surrender to my soul's creations. He challenged me to seek out joy, to become accountable and responsible for my happiness, and to respect my Self and my soul. It was imperative that I was honest with myself about *who* was the creator of my drama. Stormy had been reflecting my own strong, stubborn will and resistance to my soul right back to me. His level of objection was an indicator of my own resistance to surrendering to my soul's creations.

Just because I'd had an epiphany during this session, my equine "teenager" didn't miraculously improve. Clearly, I was still not accountable for my role in creating the most horrific time in my life. Several weeks later, Stormy was a delight to work with – exceptionally cooperative. The following day with Stormy was a carbon copy. It was late October, a year since Stormy's return to my life, and I finally had a happy and agreeable horse to ride. What more could I ask for? We rode all around the gorgeous farm enjoying the beauty of the season and each other's company. No tedious training, just the pure joy of Nature. The summer of our discontent had ended.

It had been 16 months since Bob's confession. I had been divorced for 10 months and finally felt happiness within me – something I hadn't been sure I'd ever feel again. My animal angels, and most especially Professor Stormy, facilitated the return of joy to my life. Stormy and I weren't totally through with our squabbles, which meant I still had issues to reconcile with my soul. I was blessed with so many fabulous teachers supporting, guiding, and being patient with me.

The importance of my Master Teachers is huge. I received a poem from a horse friend that expresses the value of horses to those who suffer from this "dis-ease." Stormy's powerful role, which allowed me to recognize such a crucial component of my own healing, is epitomized by this poem.

"It's Just a Horse"

From time to time, people tell me, "lighten up, it's just a horse,"
or, "that's a lot of money for just a horse."
They don't understand the distance traveled, the time spent, or
the costs involved for "just a horse."
Some of my proudest moments have come about with "just a horse."
Many hours have passed and my only company was "just a horse,"
but I did not once feel slighted.
Some of my saddest moments have been brought about by
"just a horse," and in those days of darkness,
the gentle touch of "just a horse" gave me comfort and reason
to overcome the day.
If you, too, think it's "just a horse," then you will probably
understand phrases like "just a friend," "just a sunrise," or
"just a promise."
"Just a horse" brings into my life the very essence of friendship,
trust, and pure unbridled joy.
"Just a horse" brings out the compassion and patience
that make me a better person.
Because of "just a horse" I will rise early, take long walks,
and look longingly to the future.
So for me and folks like me, it's not "just a horse"
but an embodiment of all the hopes and dreams of the future,
the fond memories of the past,
and the pure joy of the moment.
"Just a horse" brings out what's good in me and diverts
my thoughts away from myself and the worries of the day.
I hope that someday they can understand that it's not "just a horse"

but the thing that gives me humanity and keeps me from being
"just a woman."
So the next time you hear the phrase "just a horse" just smile,
because they "just" don't understand.
anonymous

You may want to look closer at your relationships with your own animal friends. You might be overlooking one of your greatest allies. Perhaps one of these wonderful teachers is waiting to enter your life.

Chapter 35

∞

Leaning on Labradors

Shortly after Stormy arrived in the mountains, Shadow developed a urinary infection. Thanks to my growing confidence that was nourished by Stormy's presence in my life, I was able to handle Shadow's illness without panic. He had suffered a urinary infection on the farm in New Jersey, so I knew as soon as I saw his symptoms what it was. A quick visit to the local vet and a urinalysis confirmed my suspicions. A round of antibiotics and some vibrational remedies had Shadow back to normal quickly.

Shadow was definitely aging faster than his brother, Licorice, but that wasn't surprising. Shadow and I were soul-mates through and through. Despite my pleas not to take on my negativity, I knew he was. It's what many of our animals come to do for us. While I regretted it, I felt no guilt, for guilt is a negative emotion, which would just add to the problem. I accepted that Shadow was here to do whatever was necessary to help me heal and recover, as was all of my animal-family. The answer is to learn from your pain and let it go as soon as possible so they don't absorb it, which was why I'd started to journal about my experiences.

While I was experiencing the summer of my discontent with my equine partner, Shadow slumped to the floor in the bathroom one evening. Torrents of tears began. *No, you can't leave me. I can't let go yet. Please!* I was terrified of losing him. Shadow stood up, saying, *What's your problem? I'm not going anywhere.* I regained my composure, assessed the situation, and ran to the phone hoping to catch the vet, who'd already left for the July 4th weekend. Shadow looked fine, so I told the receptionist I'd just watch him closely.

When Shadow fell, all I could think of was a heart attack or stroke. My first Lab, Ben, had suffered from seizures in his advancing age, but this wasn't a seizure. It came and went fast, but was quite dramatic in its effect on him. I watched Shadow like a hawk for the rest of the night. I tried to prepare for whatever might be coming, but you can never be prepared for trauma that affects so important and true a friend.

The next afternoon as we returned from Stormy, Shadow slumped to the floor inside the door. I rushed to break his fall from in front of him. I watched his eyes darting back and forth very rapidly. This episode lasted a slight bit longer than the previous one, but after it passed he was fine again. I called the covering vet's office, who referred me to yet another vet I didn't know . . . so I called my vet-friend Gary in New Jersey. In less than an hour he was on the phone with me.

After describing Shadow's symptoms, Gary diagnosed Geriatric Vestibular Syndrome. As soon as I heard it, I *relaxed*. I had dealt with it with Rainbow and Licorice. My emotions returned from the edge of disaster with Gary's diagnosis. We discussed treatment needed until the local vet returned on Tuesday from the holiday weekend. Gary put me at ease instantly, because I'd known him forever and had all the faith in the world in his expertise. I was relieved that Shadow would recover just like Licorice and Rainbow had.

Shadow seemed totally normal the rest of that afternoon and evening. I heard him stirring around 3 a.m. and started to get up. (He'd needed to relieve himself during the night for months.) When he didn't follow me, I looked back. What I saw woke me abruptly from my sleepy state. Shadow couldn't get up! His eyes were flashing back and forth terribly. I helped him stand, but he couldn't walk. I half carried him outside where he immediately tinkled.

My heart almost stopped with what I'd just experienced. Shadow went back to sleep, but I couldn't. Fear and worry consumed me. Licorice and Rainbow had never been like this. Maybe it wasn't Vestibular Syndrome. I couldn't see his regular vet for another two days. Over the next hour and a half, while I obsessed, Shadow vomited and pooped in his bed.

I was on the phone to Gary as soon as I thought it wasn't too early to call. He explained that it still could be GVS and that Licorice and Rainbow had suffered very mild forms. Shadow's symptoms appeared to be a moderate case to Gary. Moderate? Gary gave me some suggestions to help with his symptoms. I was relieved when Shadow ate a small meal and was able to drink.

I had to go into town to get medicines Gary recommended for his nausea. The thought of subjecting Shadow to a ride in the car was worrisome, but I couldn't leave him alone since he might fall and injure himself. Licorice couldn't drive, so it was up to me. Getting Shadow into the car was no easy trick with my bad back. The adrenaline from my fear for my dear friend allowed me the strength to lift him into the car. Licorice joined him and off we went. It was a quick trip to the store for whatever I thought I needed for the next few days. Shadow seemed indifferent, so I continued to the barn for some meds that Kim was lending me. The trip was uneventful for Shadow, but I was a wreck.

The critical nature of Shadow's condition made him my number-one priority. I reverted back to my days of caring for critically ill horses. I felt quite certain Shadow wasn't dying, but his condition required my undivided attention, 24/7. I began medical journaling, so I'd have crucial information for Gary and the local vet. Poor Shadow's eyes never stopped flashing for days. I imagined what that must have made him feel like. His world had to be spinning, spinning, spinning. No wonder he was vomiting.

By Monday, the 4th of July, Shadow's appetite dropped off to nothing, which I understood, but didn't like. He tried to take a small biscuit, but couldn't chew. I knew he had to eat, so I got him in the car and went to the store for several different food options. He was such a pathetic-looking fellow with those darting eyes. It just broke my heart. I cleared Shadow with SRT and prepared remedies for him, but still felt powerless.

Shadow couldn't stand or walk on his own, so it was up to me to get him outside. I stayed by his side, ready to assist in any way I could. I used a large towel under his chest to steady him. I saw the humiliation in his eyes each time we started to venture outside, but he always allowed me to help him. All the lifting caused me a great deal of back pain, but I had no choice. I knew my pain couldn't compare to what Shadow felt.

Things had been quiet, fireworks-wise, for my first Carolina Fourth of July. Shadow needed to go out around 9 p.m. Since all was quiet, I put Licorice in their yard and returned to help Shadow out the front, where there were no stairs. I no sooner got outside with Shadow and *boom!* The silence was broken by sounds of fireworks – loud explosions. Licorice was so *terrified* that I thought he'd break through the fencing. I hated to do it, but I had to lay Shadow down and rush to Licorice. By the time I reached him, he'd urinated all over the porch and was trembling from head to toe.

I tried to calm Licorice as we retreated into the house, while Shadow patiently waited for my help. After he tinkled, we joined a petrified Licorice inside. I felt so guilty. I was supposed to prevent these things from happening. Licorice's emotions were fried – as were mine. I knew from my years of animal healing that this had triggered past life memories of similar terrors.

The next morning I cleared myself and then Licorice with SRT. It had always proven very effective for my clients' animals' firework and thunder issues. An added benefit was that I had to clear myself before I could work with another soul. I had needed healing too, but it was my love for Licorice that motivated me to do the healing work for both of us. He, like his brother, was a fabulous teacher. I often wondered what their opinion was of their slow student.

I made up vibrational remedies for Licorice to lessen his new fears of fireworks, thunderstorms, gunshots, etc. – all sudden loud noises. Ideally, a half-hour prior to an exposure to the fear is best, but one doesn't always have advance notice. The night before, when I returned to the house with Shadow, Licorice was salivating, trembling, and inconsolable. The more I tried to calm him, the worse he shook. It was horrible. I'd heard about these symptoms from clients, but I'd never experienced them in any of my own dogs. After the SRT, Licorice was still worried and slightly anxious, but there was no salivating, trembling, or trying to hide.

If I had advance warning of a storm, the remedies would make him almost normal. If I didn't get a heads-up, I could watch the remedies slowly lessen his apprehension as they circulated throughout his body.

Licorice provided me a window into the wonderful world of spiritual and vibrational healing, and for that I was an extremely grateful student.

I worried that Licorice's fireworks assault might have been a result of my need to clear my own negative energy. I hoped not, but I couldn't discount the possibility. If that were the case, it was important for me to recognize the lesson and honor what Licorice experienced in order to gift me with my lesson of taking care of Self. I didn't want anyone to suffer in order for me to learn.

As I sat with Shadow, waiting to assist him, my mind pondered the timing of his ailment. Its appearance took my focus off a disaster that I'd been confronted with, and the resulting depression. Shadow's illness pulled me out of my unhappiness and into an intensely focused critical-care mode. Energetically speaking, I was sure some of the underlying causes of Shadow's sickness were the negative emotions I'd subjected us to. I had contributed to his GVS as well. I was sure of it. If I didn't process my negative experiences, I'd create illness within my own body. This I knew was truth.

Being available to help Shadow allowed me the time to think about the lesson he offered me. We both needed to release the negative energy. I vowed to learn the necessary lessons, accept them, and then let go of the negative energy contained within them. I was responsible for my dearest friend's situation. I understood it, accepted it, and released any guilt within my realization. As I stated before, guilt is just more negative energy. To harbor guilt would defeat Shadow's purpose.

Finally, we got to the local vet. She examined Shadow and agreed with Gary's diagnosis and treatment. She drew blood and gave me additional medications for him. I was happy to relinquish Shadow's treatment plan to her. His eyes were still flashing, but slightly slower. He was such a great patient. The blood results showed a slow thyroid, so I picked up meds to correct that. As long as we were out in the car, I ran by the barn to see Stormy. I hoped it would pick up the dogs' spirits to go somewhere they truly loved. Shadow, especially, hated being in the house too much. I was pleasantly surprised that Shadow required less help at the barn. He was almost able to walk. I figured it had to do with adrenaline, but I thought that was a wonderful sign of progress. His appetite was still not great, but he had started to be able to chew some small, soft treats.

Things were moving towards normalcy. He had a long way to go, but I hung onto any semblance of positive signs. Shadow's need for help prevented me from doing much else. I came across a very apropos section in Eckhart Tolle's *Stillness Speaks*. Tolle writes:

> "The playfulness and joy of a dog, its unconditional love and
> readiness to celebrate life at any moment often contrast sharply
> with the inner state of the dog's owner – depressed, anxious,
> burdened by problems, lost in thought,
> not present in the only place and only time there is;
> Here and Now. One wonders: living with this person,
> how does the dog manage to remain so sane, so joyous?"

This thought-provoking query was a birds-eye-view into the purposeful lives of our wonderful canine and feline companions. I'd counseled others about their secret mission many times. Here I sat, confronted by my own demons and the resultant effect on one of my dearest friends. Shadow needed me and in the intensity of the moment, I didn't even see the powerful lesson he was offering me – to battle just as hard for my Self and soul. I was grateful for Shadow's unconditional love and assistance in coping with the tremendous stress I was subjected to.

During the first weeks of Shadow's GVS, he had symptoms of too much thyroid medication. The over dosage wreaked havoc with our sleep pattern. Some nights Shadow wanted to go out every half-hour. The first time he'd tinkle. The following times he'd roam around acting confused. I had called the vet about checking his dosage sooner, but she said we had to wait.

After a few more sleepless nights, I called Gary. Gary felt I didn't have to wait that long. My skill as an animal communicator resides in my ability to hear and feel what the animals are saying and experiencing. I called the local vet and told her I *knew* it was too much. Shadow needed to be retested now! My intuition about my dog was spot on. Big surprise! With a reduced dose, Shadow's strange behavior vanished. I chided myself for not standing up for what I knew to be true. Once more, Shadow was teaching me to say no, to have faith in my knowing, and to trust my Self. Shadow – my ever-patient and selfless teacher.

Shadow continued to get stronger and return to his normal self. All the while, he tried to teach me to love my Self as much as I loved him. I'd do anything for everyone else but me. I knew for the sake of my animal family's health and well-being, I needed to start to recognize and accept his lesson. I had worked with many people who'd do anything for their animals and nothing for themselves. They'd call me to help their animal, but really the people needed the help more. The love for their animals awarded them the healing that their own soul was crying out for. I was the wounded healer now with my soul crying out to get me to pay attention.

I was grateful that Shadow was returning to his old self. He was about 80 percent normal – no head-tilt, but more unsteady than before. Rather than weakness, it was legitimate ataxia (unsteadiness resulting from some nervous system disorders), which pointed towards a residual neurological component. I gave thanks for each day he and Licorice gave to me.

What mattered most was Shadow's continued recovery and future well-being. I didn't even want to think about life without Shadow and Licorice. I simply couldn't go there. Shadow was steadily improving. I'll never know if he was planning his retreat and I stopped him with my plea to stay. Whatever the motivation, it seemed like he was granting me more time. As long as they each had quality of life, I wanted them with me. I reiterated my vow to let go at the first sign that either wished to go. My promise to my friends!

Chapter 36

∞

A Promise Kept

My scare with Shadow rattled me. Seeing aging animals every day kind of dilutes their deterioration. Shadow's bout with Geriatric Vestibular Disease brought his and his brother's advancing ages to the forefront. They turned 14 the following month, making them the oldest Labs I'd ever had. They knew how much I needed them, which was why they were still rambling around. Licorice and Shadow were staying until I could cope with more good-byes. I prayed I'd be ready whenever I saw *that* look in their eyes telling me it was time to go Home.

Despite some residual ataxia from the GVS, Shadow recovered quite well. Licorice's thunderstorm and firework issues had been dealt with, and his remedies stood by the ready just in case. Both were never far from me unless the weather was too warm for them to join me at the barn while I trained Stormy. They loved going to the defunct mountain property to check on it and do whatever was required there. We'd walk, albeit slowly, all around the property. I apologized profusely to them often about it not being their home. They didn't care. They resided in the present moment – which was, and is, one of the most powerful lessons they and Stormy taught me.

I received an email from an old client-friend, Kathy, who had moved to Virginia several years before we moved to the Carolina mountains. She was a vet tech, trained dogs, and occasionally bred Labradors. Kathy was planning to breed one of her females to a stud dog in Arkansas who she really thought highly of. She was looking for prospective buyers for the litter. I'd always thought that I'd get my next Labs from Kathy when the time came.

Although my boys were aging, I didn't think I'd be ready for pups when Kathy's female, Dini, would be whelping (giving birth). I told Kathy as much, but I'd like to be kept in mind for another litter. As luck would have it, Kathy elected to do artificial insemination rather than breed naturally due to the high costs of fuel after Katrina hit New Orleans. I knew Kathy was disappointed when she reported that Dini was not pregnant, but I smiled at the serendipitous event. I had no idea when Shadow and Licorice would tell me when it was time for each to go Home, but my feeling was that it might coincide with Dini's next breeding in Arkansas in possibly six months.

My dear Shadow was aging rapidly with worrisome signs starting in late fall – stairs became a real issue. Shadow *always* wanted to be wherever I was, but the stairs to the office were very strenuous for him. I'd assist him with a gentle push to make the climb. Coming down was far worse, because he was too weak to hold himself back. Eventually, I restricted him to once a day.

Shadow also fell tackling the three stairs into their yard. Wisely, he'd wait for help. He was humiliated by his decline, but accepted it with grace, which was something I was unsuccessful at – acceptance and surrender with grace. Shadow epitomized grace. As I tried to prepare myself for the inevitable, I prayed that I'd know when the time came. My confidence was on the rise since my divorce a year earlier, but self-doubt still plagued me.

 December's ice and snow proved challenging for us. While the snow wasn't deep, sleet and freezing rain turned my acre and the road into a glacier. The dog yard was abominable. Using my ice chopper, I broke up about one third of the yard hoping it would be safer for the boys. It helped Licorice, but seemed worse for Shadow. He couldn't cope with the clumpy snow due to his residual ataxia. I moved all the clumps to the sides making it manageable for Shadow.

The terrible conditions lasted for most of December. Shadow's feebleness kept him from walking up to where the car had to be parked. He obsessed each afternoon, walking around and glaring at me saying,

Let's do something. I had rugs all around, but he'd still slip if he tried to play. It was heart-wrenching. His mind was young, but his body wasn't. Shadow reminded me of someone else – talk about reflections!

My best-friend's husband lost his three-year struggle with melanoma cancer in late January. I had my pet sitter on alert. I felt Shadow would be okay to leave for the few days I needed to go to support my friend in Jersey. When I explained to him and Licorice where I was going, Shadow said, *You go. I'll be fine – don't worry!* I was banking on my intuition being accurate. I harbored no uncomfortable feelings about heading to New Jersey to be with my best friend and her family, who had just lost an amazing husband and father.

I was so grateful to Shadow for allowing me to head north. I knew it meant a lot to my friend, who'd been there for me since my Ex had abandoned me in the woods of North Carolina. I trusted that the Universe wouldn't let anything happen to them while I was gone on my mission of mercy. Shadow and Licorice were well cared for and happy to see me when I got back.

I knew Shadow's departure was inevitable, but I just hadn't seen or heard his request yet. I kept telling him I'd be all right if he needed to leave. After all, he'd been by my side for well over 14 years. He'd been selfless and I owed him nothing less. I'd promised that I would *never* allow anyone to suffer on my behalf. He seemed to have survived my absence quite well, so I felt good about my decision to go to New Jersey.

I wrote for a bit and then headed to the mountain property. Coming downstairs, Shadow's hind end seemed *very* bad. I put them in their yard to tinkle before we left. I heard a noise. Shadow had fallen on the porch stairs. He couldn't seem to hold his weight up. Our eyes locked, *I can't stay any longer. It's time. I have to go.*

I burst into tears. I'd been dreading this moment for months, years actually. I remembered hoping they'd make the move to the mountain. I decided to go to the mountain property. I knew the vet's hours were long enough to give Shadow one last visit to a place he truly loved. I battled my emotions so as not to alarm my boys. I rationalized that visiting the mountain would give me time to be sure. With *that* look, I'd received the knowing I'd been anticipating. What I needed now was the courage to make the call.

My heart wanted to create a lasting, happy memory. I wanted Shadow to be joyful once more for all the years of joy he'd given me. I *needed* this last happy memory to cling to. The importance of memories was a lesson I learned from my folks' transitions. I made the fateful call from the unfinished house looking out over the spectacular view. I believe the incredible power from the mountain itself gave me the strength to call.

The vet could see us in a little over an hour. I explained to my dear companions and "sons" what was happening. I knew Shadow knew, but I wanted to be sure Licorice had an opportunity to tell his brother whatever before they separated for the first time in 14½ years. I drove back to our house an emotional mess before heading to initiate my final act of love for Shadow.

I walked the boys outside the clinic until they were ready for us. Putting Licorice in the car, my heart broke at the thought of *the* best brothers ever parting. I wasn't sure how Licorice would deal with his loss, since they'd been inseparable since birth. Shadow's choice was made and that was all that really mattered. I sat with Shadow in my lap for almost a half hour while the sedative took hold. This was the longest, most excruciating half hour of my life. I was saying good-bye to *the* dearest and most loyal friend I had. Shadow deserved an easy transition.

My mind flooded with images of our years together. He was there for every foaling, every horse we lost, and every one we saved. He helped me feed, turn out, ride, muck stalls, and do office work. As he lay in my lap, I remembered the years I spent sitting on the floor with him in my lap watching TV. Bob used to laugh when Shadow would stare me down to the floor where he'd sleep in my lap for hours. Now he was back in that lap for the very last time. Despite the sedation, he was still trying to console me. *Don't cry. This is what I want. It's time. You're ready to let me go. Please be happy for me!* I understood this better than anyone, given my years of experience in the animal communication business. I was trying to be happy for him in spite of my complete and utter anguish.

I worried about Licorice all alone in the car as the sedative finally relaxed Shadow. For me it had seemed like an eternity! As the vet administered the euthanasia solution, I completely lost it. Shadow made a blood-curdling cry that ended in almost a howl. I hugged him harder telling him I'd be all right. It was okay to go. It was a horrifying sound that I will *never* forget. The vet told me that dogs with brain tumors make that cry. A brain lesion explained why Shadow never fully recovered from the vestibular syndrome. I was glad I hadn't known before. I may have euthanized him prematurely based on radiographs rather than his request. Once Licorice joined Shadow in Spirit, I'd return their ashes to Fair Chance Farm – their real home.

I was very experienced assisting animals in transition after 30 years of marriage to a horse vet. Much of my communication and healing work is involved with euthanasia, so I am privy to knowledge the average person isn't. I've been telepathically connected to many animals as their souls released from their physical bodies. Our language has no words that can adequately convey the level of joy, exhilaration, and freedom that I feel as the soul releases from the physical body.

Despite this, I'm so grief-stricken that I've *never* felt that unbridled joy and exhilaration from my own animals. My heart knows they're experiencing it, which offers me some slight sense of peace. I sent Shadow into the Light a month to the day before my 55th birthday. I told him to look for Gramp – no one loved dogs more than my dad. I find comfort knowing they're together with all those that I've lost over the years. My dad loved Shadow The Perfect, almost as much as me.

I gave Licorice a huge hug, and just cried. He looked so alone and bewildered as we drove away. My heart was broken yet again. Now, we had to face going home without dearest Shadow. I worked very hard to control my grief for his sake, because Licorice was grieving his brother's loss as well. In all the years, they'd never had the slightest disagreement. I simply could *not* have walked into that log house without Sweet Licorice. As agonizing as losing Randy was, Shadow's loss was even more heart-wrenching. I felt empty. As much as I loved Licorice and appreciated his being there, Shadow's passing left me feeling utterly lost and alone. Shadow and I had been *one.*

A few days later, I got a thank-you card from my friend Michelle, whose husband had transitioned in Jersey a mere 12 days before Shadow. When I called to thank her, I told her Shadow deserved the thanks. I never would've gone if I thought he was so close to leaving. Waiting for my return was his last gift to me. I truly believe he knew how much Michelle needed me. Being the selfless soul that he was, he gave me the *gift of good-bye* – in New Jersey and North Carolina.

As I moved out of the intense emotions of the moment, I acknowledged that the universal orchestration was in perfection. I'd been worrying that something might happen out of regular vet hours and I'd have to use a vet I didn't know, or I'd be snowed in, or any of a million possible scenarios. Mostly I feared I wouldn't hear or see his request or my inability to let go would paralyze me. In reality, I had no trouble receiving Shadow's message. It came through loud and clear. My unconditional love for him gave me the courage to let go. Love is *the* most powerful of energies.

I couldn't ignore the timing of Shadow's readiness to return to Spirit and mine to join a spiritual trip planned by my friend Gregory and his wife. I'd been struggling with whether to book the trip due to the dogs' advancing ages. We are *all* connected. Like the ripples on a pond from a pebble, our thoughts and decisions affect everything and everyone. I believe the closer an individual is to us, the faster and more significant the consequences. This universal view is the foundation behind synchronicity. Our decisions appeared almost simultaneous. Once I chose to go on a trip that would result in the culmination of my healing journey, Shadow knew his job was done. He realized I'd learned, grown, and was almost healed, so I'd be okay. Being my soul mate, Shadow would *never* have transitioned until he was sure I could survive it.

Licorice and I went back to the mountain the next day to begin the dreaded firsts. The first time I looked in the rearview mirror and only saw a black dog brought tears to my eyes. The missing energy was palpable. We walked around experiencing the mountain property minus Shadow. Licorice was checking things out, but without the usual joy in his demeanor. He was grieving as well. Anyone who thinks animals don't have souls or feel emotions has never truly spent any time with them. Just being around Licorice confronted by his obvious pain would convince them.

We didn't stay long, because it was too hard. My raw emotions over Shadow's loss brought unresolved pain from my divorce and my lost mountain home racing back from wherever I'd been hiding them. Even in Spirit, Shadow was helping me to acknowledge this. He was ever the teacher and devoted helper, regardless of where he resided. Licorice and I headed back to the log house to continue our grieving process. My mission of learning to let go of Shadow required all my attention and strength. I needed to embrace the grace that Professor Shadow had taught me all his life. While I had released him physically, I would *never* forget the memories we shared and the lessons Shadow taught. My gloomy Black Lab and I tried to get accustomed to life without our friend and brother. I tried to lessen Licorice's stress, but it was impossible to stop my tears.

Several days after Shadow's transition, we had the deepest snow of the winter, about ten inches. I almost smiled – pleased that Shadow didn't have to cope with it. It had been so difficult watching him struggle, having known the dog that used to fly around our big paddock chasing down every frisbee thrown. Where did the years go? They'd simply evaporated. As much as I hated losing him, I was grateful that he transitioned before this heavy snow.

The vet office called to say Shadow's ashes had arrived, but it was still snowing. I hated that Shadow's ashes were sitting on a shelf all alone. It took another 48 hours until I was plowed out. I made a beeline to retrieve my Retriever's ashes. I knew they weren't Shadow, but I had a tremendous *need* to have his remains in my possession, to wait to be returned to his farm with Licorice's. I needed to guarantee that the body that housed such an extraordinary soul was honored. I placed Shadow's ashes on the fireplace next to a favorite David Dalton photograph of him – Shadow The Perfect.

Chapter 37

∞

Cats to the Rescue

L icorice and I consoled one another after Shadow's departure. Now I worried about Licorice being alone in a few months, when I departed for my spiritual adventure. Of course, my wonderful pet sitter would be with him, but he'd *never* been without me *and* Shadow. Of course, he still had three old cat-friends, who I hoped would bring him some comfort. All of my dogs and cats had gotten along, but I wasn't sure how much support they might be for Licorice. Not being a true cat-lover, I was surprised by how much they had helped when Bob left me. Butch and Bandit were old soul-friends from the past, one a dog and the other a horse, so it didn't surprise me that I found solace with them. The real surprise turned out to be my first-time friend, Crystal – healer extraordinaire.

Being barn cats, my cats were much more comfortable living outside. One of the things that attracted me to the log house was a large crawl space that would allow the cats a warm place to live in the winter months. I set it up with beds, a litter pan, and food. Feeding the cats in the crawl space worked fine in winter, but once the smaller wildlife awoke from their winter's sleep, it ceased to be a feeding station. Too many possums and raccoons were taking turns eating with the cats. During the warmer weather, feeding was a nuisance. I had to take their food in and out from the porch, mostly at their discretion – you know, cats have *staff*.

Butch had become somewhat of a house cat during the days in my folks' house. Bandit was so anxious in the house, she'd stay a moment and then slink to the door to escape. One winter I made her stay inside because of the harsh weather. She spent the entire time upstairs either on top or underneath one of the guest beds. Her litter pan ended up in the shower. Crystal was exceptionally shy, sometimes even with me. She used to glare at Bob and then run like she didn't recognize him. Maybe I should have paid more attention to that! In the cold weather on the farm, she began staying in the house some nights. Her purr was both mesmerizing and relaxing. I always felt better after being bathed in her purr. It was quite healing for me.

When I moved into the log house, Crystal slept with me *every* night for the first *year*. Her presence made my king-size bed a little less empty. I marveled at her response to her needy person. She altered her own desires to support me in my worst time. I took it as a good sign when Crystal stopped coming in at night. It showed me that I was growing stronger and my little healer cat felt I could handle sleeping alone. She still came inside many nights and watched TV with Shadow, Licorice, and me. Shadow would give me the evil eye. I could hear him grumbling about why that damn cat was on the love seat and he wasn't. I missed those funny looks of disgust so much now.

As I sat with Licorice, I couldn't help but contemplate what Shadow had taught me about trust, loyalty, forgiveness, selflessness, devotion, and the most essential lesson of all, unconditional love. Living fully in the moment was simply the way he lived, which allowed Shadow to love unconditionally. It dawned on me that to love without condition you have to live in the Now! Shadow was a shining example of the ideal. I vowed to honor Shadow by striving to express unconditional love to myself and others, both animal and human.

I couldn't help but notice the contrast between Shadow's passing and Ben's, years earlier. When I lost Ben, I couldn't look at anything that reminded me of him. With Shadow, I looked at pictures of him around the house and found peace in them. Why? I'd learned much during the years between their two deaths. Mostly, I believe it was because Ben's death was unexpected, and I was unable to accept and surrender to it. Although he was 13½ years old, Ben hadn't been visibly declining like Shadow. He became ill and transitioned a day or two later. I wasn't prepared when

I saw the look and heard that first telepathic communication. Shadow's aging allowed me to process some of the emotions that lay ahead for me. It was similar with my folks, who I knew were leaving soon. Shadow and my folks allowed me the time I needed to accept the inevitable and be ready to let go.

My greatest supporter, Licorice, definitely felt a need to watch over me. He stuck to me like glue. Shadow must have alerted him to how needy I'd be. He became my new shadow. It was really cute and made me smile a little, but I was having fits with all the firsts. The first time I stepped out of the bathtub and didn't have to step over Shadow. The first time I prepared home-made dog food for *one*. I cried nonstop when I washed the dog beds and stored the extras. The worst was the empty space where Shadow slept. The vacant corner next to me just broke my heart, so I relocated Lic's bed there. He obliged and settled down in it, knowing I needed him to sleep there.

It is a great comfort knowing that Shadow led a wonderful long life, mostly running free on our farm in New Jersey. We took care of one another in the good times and the hard times. Our love for each other never waned. I was grateful he stayed as long as he did. I am proud to be the person he chose to share this life experience with. I know we are each better souls for having lived with and learned from one another.

I was pleasantly surprised to see all the cats spending time with Licorice. While he wasn't overtly affectionate with them, I could sense an easing of his sadness. The cats stayed around the porches more than usual, keeping an eye on both Licorice and me. I was greatly appreciative of their concern for both of us. I knew Butchie was missing Shadow. They seemed to have the closest relationship. I always thought it was because they were the same color – Butchie thought he was a little brother.

I was worried about Butchie because he'd been losing weight and getting into fights with some critter in the neighborhood. He had been to the vet's multiple times for antibiotics and wound care. Each time he had to be crated in the crawl space with a collar on to prevent him from pulling out drains that were placed in the abscesses from his bite injuries. Those injuries were almost as hard on me as Butch. I'd have to sit in the crawl space after I removed his collar, so he could eat. I couldn't trust him to leave his injuries alone despite many requests to do so. After his third trip to the vet for fighting, I told Butchie he'd used up all his hospital expenses. I simply couldn't keep running to the vet each time, so he needed cease and desist. Of course, I'd do whatever was necessary, but Butch Cassidy didn't know that. I sought motivation to encourage him to walk away – something that's hard for even a neutered male cat to do.

The fights stopped after my hollow threat to Butch. However, several weeks later he was *very* wobbly as came to greet me. My heart seized up. I couldn't handle another good-bye this soon! My first thought was Geriatric Vestibular Syndrome, but there was no rapid eye movement. I called his vet, who was closing shortly and referred me to another practice; but they were overbooked. I asked them if I could leave Butch, who *had* to be seen. The gal agreed.

Later, the vet called asking if Butch could have come in contact with pesticide. I doubted it, but couldn't be sure since they were outdoor cats. The blood tests were all normal. When I mentioned my first thought upon seeing Butch's symptoms, the vet informed me that there was another type of GVS that didn't display the rapid eye motion. He was leaning towards that diagnosis and wanted to keep Butch for observation.

When I checked the next morning Butchie was eating, drinking, and grooming himself. And (I was sure) purring, since he *always* sounded like an engine. The following day when Butch came home, the vet told me, "He's a great cat." I agreed that he was a *great* cat. All my animals were great. I was amazed, confused, and grateful for Butch's apparent complete recovery, given that he'd received no treatment during his stay. Butch's forays to the vet clinics stopped for a while.

Despite my fragile emotions after Shadow's loss, I had handled Butchie's mystery crisis quite well. Either Butch wanted to see if he'd really used up his hospitalization, or he wanted me to know that I was stronger than I thought. I figured it was probably 50-50. Butch, Bandit, and Crystal continued to rub all over Licorice in an obvious attempt to ease his sorrow. Just watching their behavior made me so grateful that they were a part of our family.

Butch and Crystal would spend time in the house, but Bandit just couldn't overcome her dislike of four walls. She'd stay briefly to get some attention, which she dearly craved. While she battled her feline claustrophobia, *I* couldn't take the constant drooling while I stroked her. Bandit would get so excited she'd create of pool of cat-spit in my lap. Her feline life was definitely different from her equine life as my first foal Mr. Watch It. We'd come a long way together, as did Butch and I, who'd been my old collie, Velvet, when I lived at the Jersey shore. While I'd acquired the cats to patrol our barn to keep it free from rodents, they'd assumed a much greater role for Licorice and me as we adjusted to life without our missing soul-mate and brother. Their presence was invaluable to both of us. Though small in stature, they were consummate teachers.

Chapter 38

∞

Synchronicity

Licorice and I celebrated my first birthday without Shadow, which went better than expected. Licorice loved being at the farm, as did I. Time spent with Stormy did wonders to heal the hole left in my heart by my missing friend. I purchased a July concert ticket in New Jersey as my birthday gift to myself. It would guarantee another visit with my friends, who'd all been enormously supportive since Shadow's passing. My friend Michelle planned to fly down to visit for a few days and drive to Jersey with me.

A couple of weeks after my birthday, Kathy informed me that Dini was in heat, so she'd be heading to Arkansas soon. Given that Shadow was gone and Licorice would soon follow, I believed this breeding would be a success. Kathy emailed to report that Dini had been bred the last day of March, which would produce pups late in May if all went as planned. As soon as I read her news about the breeding, I sent out an intention to the Universe for two puppies from Dini's litter: Black and Yellow. That was my only requirement, and then I forgot about it. I trusted the Universe to guide those souls that were waiting to join me to the prefect body for each.

Six weeks after Shadow's departure, Licorice had some trouble coming down the stairs, and I wondered if this was the start. The next day he hesitated again coming down from the office, but it wasn't a weakness issue like his brother. My heart sank. Was it starting? I helped him down like I'd done often with Shadow, but Licorice wasn't as cooperative. By the third morning, he showed frank lameness in his left foreleg. I started some analgesic tablets left over from an earlier problem, and he improved. We'd had more snow, sleet, and ice, so I thought perhaps he had slipped when I wasn't looking. As long as the meds kept him sound, so be it.

Two weeks after Licorice's front leg issue, he acted very strange. I couldn't ascertain if it was pain or stress, but his hind end seemed much weaker. I couldn't lose Licorice just yet. I wasn't ready. I started to cry with the thought of another good-bye. You'd think after all of the good-byes suffered in the past six years, I'd be a pro. I called his vet for an appointment. After half an hour, Licorice relaxed, so I told the vet I'd watch him and call back if he changed. Luckily, he didn't. To this day, I have no idea what it was. Maybe he was thinking about leaving, but my meltdown convinced him I wasn't ready to be left just yet.

I wanted to be sure Licorice was comfortable and well before I left on my spiritual adventure to Sedona and Mt. Shasta in a little over a month. My worry about leaving Licorice was diffused somewhat by the news from Kathy that Dini was, in fact, pregnant. I'd known all along that she was. The timing was just too coincidental, and since there are no coincidences... I *knew* my next pair of Labrador teachers were on their way. What I didn't know was whether or not Licorice would be welcoming them into our family; my intuition was leaning towards *not*.

Ironically, it was Butch rather than Licorice who complicated things a mere five days before my departure, when I found him with a nasty hole on the top of his head behind his ear. Off to the vet we went! I didn't have time for this. The last thing I wanted to do was leave my pet sitter with a patient to treat. He couldn't have picked a worse time. They cleaned the abscess (another bite) and put Butchie on antibiotics. Thankfully, he didn't require stitches, a drain, or a collar. I added topical comfrey salve to promote healing. My pet sitter could deal with this.

We had a run to the barn the day before my trip, with lots of treats for Stormy. I wanted Licorice to have the opportunity to ramble around the perfect farm before he became housebound for almost two weeks. He was more tolerant of staying home than his brother had been, but still, all this was a first for him – and me. I was about to embark on the trip that I'd decided to take on the same morning Shadow chose to leave. I truly believe that my decision was the catalyst behind his decision to go. The only bad news was, I was leaving Licorice for the first time, but I *knew* he'd be just fine. I held off getting the suitcase out as long as possible. I didn't want to unnerve Licorice. We had a chat about my trip. I also knew he had lessons of his own to learn about being without me.

My trip to Sedona, Mt. Shasta, and Lassen Park was filled with experiences beyond my wildest dreams and is chronicled in my book, *Letting Go*, so I won't belabor the details here. While in Mt. Shasta, I received a voicemail from Kathy heralding the arrival of the anxiously awaited litter of new souls. There were eight pups, but the last-born was struggling. I'd had a call the day before regarding an old friend, who'd lost his battle with liver cancer. I couldn't help but compare the loss of an old friend with this one heralding the arrival of two new ones – the circle of life in less than 24 hours, sadness transmuted to joy. I *knew* there were two souls in the litter who'd come to be my new Master Teachers. I possessed a *very* strong feeling that one of my dearest soul friends was returning again. Time would reveal if my intuition was true.

As I began my trip back home, I called to inform my pet sitter I was starting back. I asked how Licorice was, even though I'd been communicating with him throughout the trip. She said that he'd been acting really lively and barking at her for the past two days. I smiled and told her that I'd been communicating with him about coming home for that long. Even after almost 20 years, I continue to be amazed hearing unsolicited validation of telepathic animal communication. You'd think I'd get used to it, but it's a wonderment – magic!

Licorice was so excited when I got back to the house. He appeared to survive my absence very well, which confirmed my decision to go on a trip that proved to be the culmination of my healing journey as retold in *Letting Go*. Kathy had emailed more detail about Dini's litter, which included four yellow males, two black females, and two black males – all had lived! There were three people who would be choosing ahead of me. Four was the perfect number for my wish of one of each color. Isn't the Universe amazing? Sex didn't matter to me.

Kathy sent pictures almost every day, which really helped ease my impatience. I was so grateful that Licorice had stayed this long. I couldn't have handled his brother's loss without Licorice's companionship and teaching. As anxious as I was for the new pups to arrive, I couldn't think about losing another dear friend. Licorice seemed fine, but decisions can happen in an instant. I promised to honor whatever decision he made, whenever.

Knowing when the pups were born allowed me to calculate when they would be able to join my family. Incredibly, their weaning would fall exactly when Michelle's visit and my trip to New Jersey for the concert was planned. Even I, who had experienced universal timing and synchronicity, was blown away by this. To have so many unrelated events flow perfectly together was even too much for me. This was universal orchestration at its finest. The only question that remained unanswered was whether or not Licorice would choose to be an "uncle."

Shortly after the pups' one-month birthday, my curiosity about which two puppies would be my new teachers was getting to me. I asked Kathy if the three people ahead of me had picked yet. I was shocked when she corrected me saying there were *five* ahead of me! How'd that happen? Four was no longer the perfect number. Kathy guessed she'd forgotten to count herself. Well, that was one person not two. She wouldn't pick until the pups were eight weeks old. If the females had good conformation they were spoken for; but brothers worked for me. My friends were *very* concerned. I reassured everyone that my intention had always been for one of each color, so that's what I'd created. My heart was telling me to trust – don't fret. I truly believed that the appropriate souls would find one another.

From Kathy's photos, I was becoming attracted to the yellow male with the green collar. The concern was whether there'd be a black pup left for me. My strong feeling about the return of my dearest soul-friend Ben/Rainbow/Randy included the belief that he would be in a yellow body. My friends didn't have the same faith that I did about the situation. Kathy startled me again when she mentioned that she'd *never* sold two puppies to one person before. It was just something she didn't do. She knew I had raised two great puppies in Shadow and Licorice, so she left it up to me. I wanted two – everyone needs a friend.

Licorice and I sat together anticipating Fourth of July fireworks. When

I checked to be sure it was all clear before letting Licorice out, I noticed that Butch's head was swollen. I brought Butch in for a closer look. As I held him, an abscess burst open, spewing bloody, smelly pus everywhere. I put him in the sink and rubbed the area to express the pus out. I found two holes (more bites). The entire time, he just kept purring. I ran to the vet's office in the morning for oral antibiotics.

Butchie and I had another discussion regarding fighting. He'd better stop fighting or *else!* The last time we had this same chat he was good for about eight months. Butchie had had a few problems back on the farm, but nothing like this. He really looked older than Bandit, although they were siblings. I couldn't send him back to Spirit unless I was sure he wanted that, and I wasn't. I just kept flushing his wound twice a day, applying the topical antibiotics, and dosing him with the orals.

I was struggling with some information that I had received during a channeling session with my friend Gregory after I returned from my trip. The topic of Licorice and the puppies came up. I was informed that Licorice would still be with me when the puppies came home. I wanted that to be true, but my heart kept telling me something different. I focused on Licorice staying longer as Michelle's visit and my subsequent trip to New Jersey approached, but my nagging thoughts plagued me.

I left Licorice home for a few hours to meet friends of Gregory's who were visiting from Long Island. I got home to find Licorice trapped under a glass-top table. I didn't know for how long, but I felt so guilty for leaving him alone. I had an appointment the next afternoon, so I brought Licorice and kept the car's air conditioner on. Licorice was perfectly content in the car. The next day I was ordained into the Universal Brotherhood Movement by Gregory, his wife Sandie, and my new friend George – all UB ministers. The ceremony was performed on the deck of the Deltec, gazing at the million-dollar view. For me, this was the ideal location to express my commitment to my future healing work. This mountain property had been the catalyst behind my miraculous journey of trauma, learning, growth, and healing.

My ordination was a public dedication to the healing work that I'd failed to make a priority in my earlier life. I had no idea where my path would lead, but I was determined to follow it in joy and happiness. It was fitting that Gregory and Sandie performed the ceremony, because without them I wouldn't have been ready to make such a commitment. The lessons I'd been shown through Gregory's sessions, the experiences we shared on our trip together – but more importantly the friendship they had given me – were integral to my healing. I was blessed to have them in my life.

However, my greatest blessing was Licorice, who'd been with me for every minute of my two-year struggle from the depths of my trauma. He lay inside the Deltec waiting for me as usual. Licorice was happy on the mountain and usually seemed five years younger there, but not that day.

The puppies weren't due home for a couple of weeks. Were my intuitive thoughts about Licorice not wanting to be an "uncle" coming true? My heart turned from the joy of my ordination to concern about another possible good-bye.

My car needed rear brakes before I left for New Jersey. I had no option but to leave Licorice home alone while I took the car in for service. I explained to him where I was going and hoped that would lessen any distress. It took *forever*. They kept telling me it would be ready soon. Sitting there, knowing how much Licorice didn't want to be alone and how stressed he'd been lately, was agonizing for me. Two-and-a-half hours later, I flew home to hear Licorice barking. His voice was hoarse and filled with anguish. I *felt* his pain. I rushed inside to find him caught under the chair next to the door. The seat was covered with spots of saliva. He'd been trapped for some time. He was distraught but so happy to see me.

I *knew* what he wanted when he looked into my eyes. My heart broke with the meaning of his plea. I was consumed with guilt although I'd done nothing wrong. I calmed Licorice and told him I understood what he wanted. I would help him go Home, so he could find Shadow. The tears just poured out of me. My heart knew it was Licorice's wish, but it also broke with the pain of another good-bye. I was overwhelmed with sadness, grief, and pain all over again.

From my years of communication consultations with animals about to transition, I knew they were happy, looked forward to the return to Spirit, and considered it the beginning of a new cycle. Only we humans look at it as an end. I didn't want to cause Licorice anymore stress than he'd suffered all morning. I vowed to make our remaining hours together the best I could. I owed him nothing less. He'd been by my side for almost fifteen years. Along with Shadow, he supported me through the most horrific events of the past two-plus years. His devotion had been unwavering.

Without Licorice and Shadow, I wouldn't have made it. Licorice knew that I was healed enough to survive his departure. It was as though my ordination signaled that he could go. He also knew from our discussions that I had new teachers on the way. Sometimes I hate having such accurate intuition. I *knew* he didn't want to be an "uncle," which was his parting lesson: Believe what's in your own heart regardless of where conflicting information comes from. You know best.

The vet had an appointment available two-and-a-half hours later. Licorice seemed much better, and I understood why. He knew his waiting time was almost over. I had brief thoughts that maybe he wasn't ready to leave, but understood from my years of consultations that once an animal knows that its wish to go Home has been realized, they become very upbeat, appear younger, and almost normal. I always warned clients not to misinterpret their friend's behavior. I spent the afternoon telling myself the same thing over and over and over.

I devoted my time to Licorice, struggling with my emotions as I remembered our years together. We had mostly happy times. He'd surely been a Master Teacher. I only hoped that I'd taught him what he needed to learn. We headed to our destiny with every ounce of self-control that I could muster. I sat on the vet's floor with Licorice's gray head in my lap stroking him and crying. It was impossible to keep my tears in check. Licorice was sedate so quickly that I thought he might have transitioned with just the sedative. His reaction to it was in stark contrast to Shadow's. I prayed that he wouldn't wail like his brother had. I could still hear that sound and always would.

The vet returned and injected the solution. His spirit was on its way Home before very much of it had entered his vein. It was the easiest transition I'd ever seen, which was Licorice's final gift to me. He was *so* ready to go Home. I tried to feel his exuberance and exhilaration as he returned to Spirit, but grief blocked me once again. I was relieved it was over, but consumed with sadness that I'd lost yet another of my family. My promise was kept, my last gift given, and my heart broken one more time. Now they were both gone. I returned to the house and felt *totally* alone. The silent house felt dead, which intensified my sorrow.

The stillness of the house was unsettling in my fragile emotional state. I just couldn't stop crying. Licorice's passing marked the end of an era that had been rewarding and filled with purpose. I was happy for Licorice and grateful for the time he'd given me since Shadow had left – almost five and a half months. I needed every minute of it to recover from Shadow's loss, complete my healing journey, and emerge from the dark night of my soul. His willingness to stay was a priceless gift. In return, I honored his choice, heard his request, surrendered to it, and then let go.

As I tried to get to sleep, all I could hear was *nothing*, which was excruciating. I used to hear breathing next to me – now, nothing. I used to hear Shadow and then Licorice repositioning themselves in their beds right next to me – now, nothing. For more than two years, I had to clean up Licorice's poop accidents – now, nothing. For the last year, I'd had to let Shadow out to tinkle multiple times through the night – now, nothing. I would give anything to have to wake up to take care of those chores again – *anything!*

Chapter 39

∞

Two Old Friends

I woke the next morning exhausted. I wasn't sure how long I'd slept, but it hadn't been long enough. The silence was *deafening*. I headed directly to the barn to my four-legged angel who'd gotten me through so much pain these past two years. I needed Stormy to force me into the moment and out of my pain. Stormy could sense the sadness in my heart and was a joy to ride. Animals are so much more sensitive to *our* emotions than we are to *theirs*. My time on his back was already starting to heal the hole in my heart left by my dear Licorice.

I kept reiterating the advantages of Licorice's decision to leave, trying to convince myself it was a good thing. I knew it was positive for him. I was trying to make it positive for me, but I wasn't succeeding. Mother Nature came to my rescue with a messenger in the form of the worst thunderstorm since moving to North Carolina. For an hour-and-a-half I was subjected to booming thunder and lightning. Her message was akin to the deepest snowstorm of the winter just after Shadow's death. I lay there listening to the fury of the thunder, thinking Licorice would've been panicked despite his SRT clearings and remedies. This storm had *me* trembling and salivating. Finally, with all my heart I accepted the positive act that Licorice's passing was. I gave thanks for events always being in perfection even though we don't always see it at the time. I thanked Mother Nature for helping me finally accept Licorice's choice and let go completely, which I hadn't until the storm's lesson was taught. I slept well and awoke with a lighter heart.

Michelle's visit meant I only had two-and-a-half days alone in the house. Obviously, my soul – creator of my experiences – and Licorice realized I couldn't cope with anything longer than that. I marveled at the universal orchestration of what seemed to be unrelated events in my life that were in reality a miraculous creation by the Universe and my soul. I had purchased tickets for a concert in New Jersey early in the winter necessitating a trip back there in July. In an effort to help Michelle process the loss of her husband (just before losing Shadow), she planned a visit to North Carolina, so that she could ride back to New Jersey with me. Michelle arrived only two days after Licorice transitioned. The puppies' birth meant they could join me on my return from New Jersey – a mere two weeks after Licorice's exit. Simply astounding! Most importantly Licorice's ashes would be home before I left, granting my wish to spread both dogs' ashes in the big paddock where we used to play Frisbee every late afternoon – another promise kept.

Shadow and Licorice had worked our farm by my side for most of their lives. It was the only place they belonged. Shadow's ashes had been waiting for more than five months. My grief over Licorice's loss was balanced by the wonderfully positive events ahead: time with Michelle in North Carolina, meeting my new pups, returning Shadow and Licorice to their true home, seeing my dear friends in New Jersey, enjoying a concert, and filling my silent house with my newest teachers. I was flooded with gratitude as I anticipated picking up Michelle. The silence in the house would disappear. My soul and Licorice were so wise, because I wouldn't have lasted another day.

At the airport, Michelle and I hugged each other trying to absorb one another's pain and sadness. Since we didn't have another passenger – one who couldn't handle the heat of Charlotte – we had total freedom to do whatever and go wherever. It was a freedom I hadn't experienced in years. I wanted Michelle to experience a session with Gregory, which was scheduled for the next morning, so we headed to bed around midnight. It was so nice to have another being in the house to drown out the silence.

A portion of our session concerned the personalities of the two puppies who were waiting to join my family, but I wasn't told which traits went with which pup. I didn't need to ask about the two colors, because I had already learned what a powerful creator I am. I received confirmation that Ben/Rainbow/Randy was returning. Of course, I wasn't told which puppy's body he was entering; that was for me to recognize. That didn't worry me – we had a love bond that stretched across eternity. During lunch, I got a call that Licorice's ashes were back. We retrieved them and placed the treasured container next to Shadow's. I'd always been able to bury my animals on the farm, so this would be another first for me.

After dinner, I called Kathy to confirm our plans for the following day. I hoped the people ahead of me had made their choices by now. They had, and there was a black pup left – the red-collared one. My heart beamed with joy. My faith hadn't let me down, nor had my soul. I'd be getting what I had intended from the start – Black and Yellow pups. I had manifested destiny. Kathy also shared that the green-collared one was available. "He's going to be a hellion," she said. He sounded like he matched Archangel Michael's description of one pup. I told her I wouldn't really know until I met his soul, but I'd been attracted to his picture. I simply couldn't wait until tomorrow.

I had to admit that I'd asked myself early on if I really wanted to be obligated to two more souls. The freedom Michelle and I had experienced over these past four days was something I hadn't felt since college. I'd been a caretaker of dogs, cats, and horses for 30-plus years. I didn't entertain those thoughts for very long however. My vivid memory of the dead house washed away any hesitation. I knew I couldn't live without dogs in my life. It was my reality and my Truth. I was sure these were new Master Teachers coming into my life. I intuited that we had important things to teach one another. Michelle had female Chocolate and Yellow Labs home waiting for her. I think she was almost as anxious as I was to meet the pups. We were making a happy forever memory together – the only kind to create.

There was a buzz of anticipation in the house as we prepared to leave for Kathy's. I finally gave myself permission to focus on the puppies now that my excruciating wait was almost over. In a few hours I could answer everyone's questions of which two. We found Kathy's house fairly easily. She led us to the whelping area. My eyes were wide with expectation. I'd been waiting for this moment for forever. All eight were leaning against the board that held them in. I was so focused on meeting puppies, feeling energies, recognizing old friends, that I'd left my camera in the car, or I would have gotten an adorable picture of Dini's family.

We carried them outside and let them loose. They were in perpetual motion – each cuter than the next. The black pup was a given, so I grabbed him as he went flying by and got my first black kiss. I focused on the three available yellow pups, mostly the green-collared one who was zooming all over the place. I tried to stop him to see if I recognized an old friend, but he was focused elsewhere. He was cute, but there wasn't a connection. Interesting!

All of a sudden, I noticed one yellow pup sitting *quietly* while staring at me. When our eyes locked, my heart melted. I'd found dearest Ben/ Rainbow/Randy. The smile spread across my face, into my heart, and to every cell of my being. There was *no* doubt. He'd found me just like he had when he reincarnated as Rainbow. He sat by me now in the identical way he sat by me then. He wore a black collar and had a cowlick the length of his nose. I showed Michelle and she asked, "Did you see his nose?" I laughed. Her two-year-old Yellow Lab was the first dog I'd ever seen with a cowlick the length of its muzzle. I knew she was getting blown away by the coincidences the Universe was throwing at her during her visit. This was by far the coolest.

I was in puppy heaven. We played with them for a while, but I didn't want to monopolize Kathy's afternoon and we still had several more hours to drive. Michelle took pictures of me holding my two new teachers. My smile was huge and had appeared within moments of meeting them. I hated to put them down, but we had to get going. As we left, I acknowledged another private coincidence. My new brothers wore red and black – the exact colors Shadow and Licorice had worn. I recognized my old friend as soon as I looked into those eyes and *saw* his soul. I thought about the cherished ashes that I was bringing to the farm and the circle of life. My jeans were covered with dirt from the pups' feet, but I didn't care. I'd been waiting so long to feel their joyful exhilaration.

Even though I was exhausted from the roller coaster of emotions of the past five days, I couldn't wait till morning to find out who the black pup was. I quieted my mind and asked if I knew the soul in the black body? *You are old friends. You have been in many, many lifetimes together, but not yet in this one.* Okay. That fit with not consciously recognizing him. Having learned that our companion animals come to answer our soul's cries for help, I knew these two dear souls had been hearing my shrieks for quite some time. I'd never before experienced such deep pain. I couldn't wait to get reacquainted with my new, old friend in the black body and with Ben/Rainbow/Randy in the yellow one.

I didn't ask about names, because the names that I'd chosen months earlier were *perfect* – two of my favorite places on Earth: Hana and Saba. Saba is a volcanic island near St. Maarten, so I named the black pup Simply Saba. The yellow pup was Heavenly Hana – a spectacular area on Maui. My newest teachers had come to assist in my healing, so being named after remarkable places that emitted amazing healing energy seemed perfect. I did tell the pups what I'd like to name them. They loved their names. Then I fell into a deep, contented sleep.

As we drove toward New Jersey, I pondered the return of Ben/Rainbow/Randy. Before moving, a chiropractic client of Bob's, who knew nothing about horses, offered Randy a home for life if we decided to euthanize him. Back then, I still hoped he might heal. Many people fear dying as the end of existence, but my Master Teachers had taught me otherwise. When you accept that dying is merely a change of form, it doesn't carry the same finality. It was a kind offer, but I told my husband no. If Randy wasn't meant to live a long, pain-free life, I believed his soul would return in a new body. His euthanasia had been the single most difficult thing I'd done in North Carolina.

Being reunited with this special soul that had been housed in that big, gorgeous, yet unsound equine body reassured me that I'd made the right decision for Randy. I felt vindicated by his return in the yellow pup lovingly nicknamed Hana-Banana. To have a soul return to share its life with you four times is extremely humbling. This soul's return taught me even more about the purpose of Randy's short life – to teach Squiggles that she could produce live offspring, plain and simple. If I hadn't made the choice to send Randy Home, I wouldn't be anticipating sharing, learning, and growing for the next 12–15 years with him now. Everything happens for a reason and for our best and highest good. Everything!

Our first stop in New Jersey was to return Shadow and Licorice to the only real home they'd known. Michelle and I headed out into the big pasture with my friends' ashes. I hoped putting their ashes in the place we'd spent so many hours playing would bring me some closure. It did bring some peace to my heart knowing they were home. As we sprinkled their ashes in the breeze, all my grief and pain erupted like a dormant volcano. I'd experienced a seesaw of emotions these past two days, which reminded me of Khalil Gibran's words on joy and sorrow from *The Prophet*.

"Your joy is your sorrow unmasked.
And the selfsame well from which your laughter rises
was oftentimes filled with your tears.
The deeper that sorrow carves into your being,
the more joy you can contain.
When you are joyous, look deep into your heart and you shall find it is
only that which has given you sorrow that is giving you joy.
When you are sorrowful look again in your heart,
and you shall see that in truth you are weeping for
that which has been your delight.
Verily you are suspended like scales between your sorrow and your joy."

I had just survived it – the pinnacle of happiness and joy with the puppies in Virginia, and the depths of grief and sorrow on the farm sprinkling cremains and at Michelle's husband's grave. Little did I know my animal family was about to be reduced in size yet again.

On my way to meet friends for breakfast, my cell phone rang. It was Sandie, who was looking in on the cats for me. Butch's face was swollen from another battle, which he'd obviously lost. My heart sank. Her description allowed me to make the decision I'd been struggling with for months. I hated to ask, but would she take him to the vet to be put down. I would call the vet and make the arrangements. I'd never euthanized an animal without being with them, so this was an agonizing decision. But Butchie hadn't left me much choice. His needs were my biggest consideration. After I set it up, I communicated with Butch to tell him what was happening. *I'm ready. Don't cry! I'll go find Sandie.*

I was teary when I sat down with my friends. Michelle asked what was wrong. When I explained, she was wide-eyed because as we left the log house, Butchie had appeared to say good-bye. I scratched him, told him I'd be away, and he *had* to behave himself. I told him two new puppies were coming back with me. As we drove out, I told Michelle that he'd be the next one to leave me. I just *knew* it. I hadn't thought this soon, but I had expected it. Like I said, decisions happen in an instant.

Sandie called again. She and Butch were headed to the vet's. I couldn't thank her enough. The tears flowed again. Butch knew I couldn't handle another good-bye so soon. I hated not being with him, but it was out of my control. He would be Home soon with Shadow and Licorice. My powerful intuition kept me from being totally devastated by sudden losses, which was a gift rather than a curse. I was so thankful Butch had come to say good-bye before we left. I had *no* idea it would be our final good-bye, but I know Butchie did.

I had a wonderful time in New Jersey despite the sadness surrounding Shadow's, Licorice's, and Butch's transitions. On the return trip, as I headed towards my new puppies, my anxiety started building. Two pups were a huge responsibility. Was I up to raising two puppies alone? Could I do this? My self-confidence was taking a hit. I kept focused on those two little faces that I'd seen at Kathy's. I used my wonderful memories of life with Shadow and Licorice, and the awful feeling of the dead house to combat any second thoughts. I knew these two souls were destined to be my Master Teachers, so I drove towards Virginia with a full heart.

I met Kathy and some of her friends for dinner. We talked about Ben, Shadow, and Licorice, who she'd known back in New Jersey. I told her about the soul in each pup. I'd been amazed years ago when I'd discovered that Shadow and Licorice were related to Ben. She asked who Ben's sire was. She thought he was in Dini's pedigree. I'd been wondering if there might be a chance, since Kathy had lived in New Jersey for most of her life, too. I smiled at the possibility of all my Labs being related and the synchronicity of this litter's arrival in my life – it would be perfection. I thought about Licorice and couldn't believe he'd only left two weeks ago. I thought about Butch and the orchestration of his departure. No turning back now. My new teachers were ready, willing, and waiting, and so was I!

Chapter 40

∞

Best Friends

I headed towards Kathy's, knowing that these two dear souls were answering my soul's pleas for help. They would heal the holes in my heart and allow me to love without condition and without fear of being hurt. The puppies would fill my life with joy and erase the pain that remained in my heart. I vowed to give these pups the *best* possible home and to keep them healthy, happy, and safe. All I needed back from them were manners and *love*.

Kathy had everything ready: paperwork, a blanket, familiar toys, marrowbones for the trip, and collars and leashes for each. What else but red and black! Best of all, Dini's pedigree contained Ben's sire. It gave me such a sense of continuity and perfection. The five Labs that chose to be with me were all related. My heart was so full. It was as though Ben, Shadow, and Licorice were still around. Ben's soul was, but genetics linked Shadow and Licorice as well. It was the icing on the cake.

Every cell in my body vibrated in pure joy and happiness. I couldn't stop smiling. I marveled at how well Kathy bid them farewell. She was a unique gal, who I'd be forever grateful to for my new family. For the next hour and a half, I was battered with constant yelling from Hana. He wasn't crying as if he missed his mother and siblings. He was having a temper tantrum. Saba was being a perfect gentleman. I called Perkins to tell Michelle because Archangel Michael had forewarned about a *screamer*. I wanted to make Michelle aware of the veracity of his information. She had no trouble hearing Hana!

We arrived home a little worn from Hana's complaining. I realized that just two weeks earlier I'd sent dear Sweet Licorice Home. I glanced at the fireplace from time to time to where the two boxes had waited. All that was left were the David Dalton photos of them. The house was no longer silent or calm. It had been fifteen years since I'd raised pups and I hoped I was up to it. Anytime I began to doubt my decision, I looked into those adorable faces, my heart melted, and I knew we'd be fine.

My schedule had the flexibility to handle the intense supervision puppies required. I figured there would be whining the first few nights, which was typical with new pups leaving their litter behind. I put the pups together in a crate in front of the fireplace, which would provide space between us at night. As expected, the whining started up right away. This time it was a plaintive whine. I assumed it was Hana. To my surprise it was little black Saba. He sounded so pitiful, but I stayed put so they didn't learn that they could whine to get what they wanted. Luckily, he gave it up after about ten minutes – much less determined than Hana.

I let them out several times through the night, which I'd anticipated. It was no different from the early morning needs of my elderly pair. With pups, I could look forward to the age when they could last until morning. It wouldn't be that long and I was in love. Welcome to the first night of the rest of your life, animal lover! All in all, we were off to a good start.

Puppies are intense – full out play or sound asleep. While the experts felt two puppies were only for the rare person, I wouldn't have had it any other way. I don't consider myself rare. I considered myself twice blessed with the unconditional love of *two* dogs. I had an insatiable need to be loved and looked at with adoring eyes.

We had an appointment at the vet's for a simple physical. I knew they were healthy, but I wanted to create a happy visit to set the tone for future visits. The pups passed with flying colors. Everyone came in to see them. Already they were working their wonders on their circle of influence. We continued to the perfect farm, so Kim, who cared for Stormy, could meet my new family. I'd been showing her pictures for weeks. They showered Kim with unbridled joy. Labradors are people dogs, plain and simple. I've always found it fascinating that dogs bred for hunting are so enamored with people.

Life revolved around keeping an eagle eye on the pups for signs of needing to go out. I knew the usual times to be sure they were outside. Housebreaking is the biggest chore to start. The intense attention is exhausting, but necessary. Accidents happen – it comes with the territory – but having hardwood floors made clean-up much easier. The pups were smart as whips, learning their names in one day.

Unfortunately, I came down with an illness that hit me like flu and lasted for several weeks. It was a bad time to get sick, with two new puppies to chase after. I started my usual herbs to boost my immune system. I rested whenever the puppies rested. Lying on the loveseat, I acknowledged the wisdom behind the timing of Licorice's transition. While the pups had been good for their age, they were way too busy for Licorice. I silently thanked Licorice for choosing to go when he did – always in perfection.

While I struggled to get well, some much-needed rain didn't make my forays outside any easier. Hana was very good about doing what he needed to. Saba, the dog that loved leaping around the river at the perfect farm, didn't like the rain. Each time I'd have to accompany him. He'd sit by my feet under the umbrella. The trick was to outwait him, which works if you're healthy and patient.

After having waited in the rain for too long, I picked Saba up and yelled at him. Instantly, I felt tremendous remorse. His adoring eyes questioned my meltdown. I was filled with shame. There was no excuse for losing my temper. Saba was just a baby. Now I felt worse emotionally than physically. Guilt overwhelmed me. Being terribly ill was no excuse.

An hour later, sweet Saba came over and lay down on my foot. My tears flowed. All of my self-loathing disappeared. His lesson of forgiveness was so powerful. My heart just melted with his teaching – this tiny little creature that forgave my indiscretion so quickly. If only we people had that same degree of forgiveness, the world would be at peace. Saba's gesture allowed me to let go of most of my guilt and transmute my negativity into love – proving himself as a true Master Teacher despite his young age.

As my health improved, I began to enjoy my new puppies and learn their powerful lessons. Their presence in my life was in perfect timing to help me to let go of whatever residual negativity I still clung to. It was impossible to be unhappy around them. They look at life from one perspective only, which is play. The simplest thing becomes a toy. Their happiness, joyful exuberance, and life-loving, blissful nature provided powerful lessons for the woman who'd allowed life's obligations and responsibilities to bury those childlike traits.

I knew these special souls would help me regain my happiness, my joy, and my passion for life. Despite their young age, they were already teaching me valuable lessons about living life to the fullest, which was something I really needed to master. My soul had brought me two more Master Teachers just when I needed them the most. Heavenly Hana is definitely the mischievous one. Simply Saba has a very calming personality. They are a perfect combination.

Initially Saba wanted contact with me, while Hana was content to lie by himself with his eyes riveted on us. These traits reminded me of my departed friends. Shadow needed contact and Licorice was more to himself. Many times they would do things that brought me to tears. The similarities to my missing brothers allowed me to release emotions I'd thought I had let go of. The healing that Hana and Saba had given me in the short time that we'd been together was astonishing. They looked at me with adoring eyes, which melted my wounded heart. When either of them put their head on top of my foot, I was filled with a warm, loving sensation. My self-esteem soared. My love for them was so intense that it almost hurt. They were teaching me that I was still worthy of being loved and that I was still capable of loving.

Loving animals had never been an issue for me, because I had never been betrayed or deceived by them. I had never lost trust in them. These two Master Teachers taught me as pups that I was able to "love like you've never been hurt before." The love expressed in their eyes was like a powerful laser straight into my heart. Along with dear Stormy, Saba and Hana brought joy back into my life.

When the pups were about nine months old, Saba injured his hind leg during an out-of-control session of play in their yard. They played harder than any dogs I'd ever had. There was never anything aggressive in nature, just rough-and-tumble. I'd been worrying that someone might get hurt, but they didn't – until one afternoon. I heard a yelp and they stopped. My dear Saba Baby was holding his right hind leg up. Immediately, I ran to them to keep them from starting up again. I escorted Saba into the house to keep him from doing any more harm to himself.

The next morning, Saba would bear weight on his leg, but he was very lame. I called his vet, but I couldn't get an appointment. I reiterated how lame my puppy was, but the receptionist wouldn't budge. So I called the vet who'd taken care of Butch for me and got an appointment right away. As it turned out, I wasn't pleased with that vet's examination of Saba or his diagnosis of a torn ligament requiring surgery. Guilt swept through me. I'd broken my puppy and he wasn't even a year old yet! He prescribed some analgesics for Saba. I told him I'd have to think about his recommendation. Surgery just didn't *feel* right to me.

I was distraught with the vet's findings. I called Gary, my small-animal vet in New Jersey. He called back within the hour and soon had me calmed down and less emotional. Based on my description of Saba, he didn't think it was a surgical case, but he wanted me to see my local vet. Next, I called Kathy, who was a vet tech as well as the breeder of Hana and Saba. Saba was sleeping under the computer desk while I spoke with Kathy. She asked me to manipulate his hind leg, which I did, huddled under the desk. We discussed his lack of pain when I manipulated his leg, and she verified that Saba had not torn his ACL.

I called my regular vet the next day. I got tough by refusing to argue with the receptionist. I told her my pup needed to be seen and I wanted to talk with the *vet*. My vet knows my background and knows that when I say I have a problem – *I have a problem!* The vet told me to come right over. I might have to wait a little, but she would see Saba. Tons of anxiety dissipated with her words.

We didn't have to wait long at all. The vet did a lameness exam on Saba outside, much like Bob would do for a horse. The other vet had me hold Saba down on his side on the exam room floor. Saba fought to get free, making the examination stressful for all of us. This was more to our liking. My vet disagreed completely with the diagnosis and recommendation of surgery. She gave me some more analgesics and instructions to keep Saba from running or playing for four to five weeks.

Needless to say, it was a challenge to keep Saba quiet with Hana wanting to engage in play constantly. The easiest way was to have them outside separately. Of course, Saba's limitation required that *I* become Hana's playmate. It was a long recovery, but it went without a hitch. I added vibrational remedies and color therapy to the treatment regime, knowing how well they promote healing. Being able to communicate with the pups really helped them understand the odd arrangement. Saba felt better pretty quickly, which made keeping him restricted even more challenging. Without the ability to explain why to him, I doubt he would have been as cooperative.

Saba's injury taught me powerful lessons about believing in my knowingness, especially when it comes to my own animals. When this first happened I was still recovering from the huge hit my self-confidence had taken from my husband's betrayal and abandonment. Saba knew better than I what a powerful healer I was, and he taught me to trust my abilities again. Thankfully, I must have learned my lesson well, because there haven't been any more illnesses or injuries to test that.

Bandit and Crystal taught the pups to respect them from the start, which was a good thing as the ten-pound puppies eventually grew into 80-pound Labs. Watching my dogs and cats treat one another with respect and love made me wish that people could do the same. Even though Crystal was timid with people, she didn't shy away from the dogs at all. She truly loved Shadow and Licorice and has formed similar relationships with Hana and Saba. Bandit has always been a dog lover. She rubs on their legs and walks underneath them, showering them with love and affection. Other cats – well, she tolerates them.

Hana and Saba are five years old now. They have assisted with and witnessed my complete healing and emergence from the Abyss and Tunnel. My computer desk is crowded as they lie under it, helping me write for hours on end. When they think I've been working too long, one or both will climb onto my chair, begging me to play. After a few minutes of floor play, they let me go back to work. Somehow they know when I'm communicating, doing SRT clearings, color therapy, or making up remedies, because they lie quietly near me downstairs without interrupting.

I was concerned when they first joined me that perhaps I'd favor Hana due to his *four* successive lives with me. Not to worry. The connection to

Saba flourished quickly. I love him as deeply as I do his brother. In fact, I think we've been together in *more* lives, based on my powerful feelings for him. Saba is *extremely* sensitive and gets *very* upset if I raise my voice – mostly at Hana.

Writing these tales has been much more difficult and emotional than I ever expected. Obviously, I hadn't processed my losses when they occurred, but the obligations of my farm didn't allow much time for anything extra. Often I've been typing and crying simultaneously. Saba absolutely cannot tolerate my tears. He launches himself into my lap, trying to kiss me, saying, *Don't cry. Be happy!* Saba forces me to release my sadness, stop my tears, and smile at him. He provides a powerful mirror into my soul.

I think Ben/Rainbow/Randy/Hana has finally incarnated into the life he's been dreaming of. Not only does he live in the house with me, which he couldn't do when he was Ben (due to my husband's allergies), but he and Saba sleep *on the bed*. Hana has retained his devil-catcher status, but age has tempered it somewhat. He is definitely my protector. If I didn't know whose soul had returned, I'd think it was Shadow. Every night Hana whines at me until I join him and Saba on their beds in front of the loveseat to watch TV. I smile, knowing that *Ben* finally has the life he couldn't have back on the farm – firmly planted in my lap, receiving all the love he can absorb.

Rather than similarities to Ben, I've noticed opposites. Hana is the barker of the two. Ben barked only about six times in 13-plus years, mostly at the hot air balloons that flew over the farm. Ben was not overtly affectionate. Hana loves with all his heart and soul. I look into those adoring eyes and explain that I've always loved him even when he couldn't live in the house with us. I always felt bad for Ben, but it was either have a dog that lived in the barn or none at all. Then, as now, I couldn't survive without a dog by my side. Who would teach me about unconditional love, the present moment, playing, etc.?

Saba and Hana's lifestyle is so different from Shadow's and Licorice's on our farm. They have a small yard off the side of the log house rather than a six-acre farm. They have to be leashed more of the time rather than be free. They do roam free on the mountain property while I'm tending to it. We hike together – sometimes off-leash when no one is around. They love to be with me and hate having to stay home when it's too hot. We go *everywhere* together, except on vacation. I can't imagine life without them. I pray they'll stay for at least as long as their predecessors – another 10 years.

Saba and Hana have taught me profound lessons about my Self: how to trust again, how to love again without condition, how to stay in the present moment and make the most of each one, how to live in joy, how to take life less seriously, and my most challenging, how to forgive and let go. My soul cried out and the best teachers I could ever want have appeared. I tell them every day, "You're my best friends!" They were powerful teachers as pups and have matured into two of my greatest Master Teachers – right alongside Squiggles and Stormy.

Chapter 41

∞

My Equine Therapist

Stormy's training had become fun after I became accountable for being a co-creator of my husband's betrayal and our divorce. Once I reached that point, Stormy no longer needed to reflect this lesson to me. I gave myself tons of credit for exerting patience and tolerance with him during his testy time, which had rewarded me with such a happy and willing four-year-old. Finding solace working with Stormy helped me cope with my losses, both recent and past.

One spring afternoon, I decided to give Stormy a break from ring work with a walkabout around the farm. He was being really good for the first time out of the ring since we stopped for winter. All of a sudden, a bird flew up in front of him, he spooked and flew sideways, and I hit the ground. My biggest worry wasn't about myself, but Stormy being loose on 33 acres. I wasn't angry, because he'd merely responded naturally to the bird "attack." Horses are fright/flight creatures – safety lies in running away.

I walked toward Storm, telling him telepathically it was okay and not to worry. He looked confused asking, *What are you doing down there?* It was pretty comical. I mounted and finished our walkabout, so he didn't learn he could dump me to end the ride. We were completely relaxed as if nothing had happened. I guess I needed to fall to learn that despite my advancing age, I still knew how to fall without getting hurt. The episode taught Stormy that he wouldn't get punished for doing something natural, even though the result was me falling off.

Time spent with Stormy was better than any therapist. He enabled me to release whatever frustrations life was dishing out. Things that had been so challenging for him last summer just didn't bother him anymore. Working through issues with youngsters, using patience and tolerance, reaps welcome rewards, which is what I most treasured in starting young horses. The progress made through willing cooperation molded our partnership more deeply. I laughed inwardly at the knowledge of my soul's pleasure in working with the increasingly cooperative person that I'd become, always recognizing Stormy's attitude as a reflection of my own.

Being a four-year-old, Stormy was ready to learn to jump. Once I recovered from the mystery illness that hit me when Hana and Saba joined the family, I was strong enough to get back to riding. Stormy felt wonderful! My heart was filled with gratitude for my beautiful horse, and my two new puppies. Many times while I rode, I looked at the perfect farm that surrounded me and pondered how fortunate I was despite what had transpired the previous two years since I had left *my* beautiful farm in New Jersey.

After about a week and a half, I felt it was time to introduce Stormy to some small jumps. I couldn't remember the last time I'd jumped, but he was definitely ready to tackle something more challenging. I just hoped I was, too. Stormy's acceptance of this step-up in his training was so promising. His wonderful willingness encouraged me that I'd released much of *my* own stubborn resentment, anger, and pain. Had I not, Stormy would've reflected that to me; instead he was a delight. I hoped my soul felt the same about me! Stormy's cooperation confirmed that I'd made the right decisions with my method of training. Each horse is unique – no different than we humans – so each requires specific modes of training. He had been challenging last year during a time when I was fighting for my own survival. It was comforting to know I'd chosen properly.

Driving home after his first jumping session, I realized it had taken *eight years* to reach this moment. I'd bred his mother, dearest Squiggles, for the first time eight years ago. Through disasters with his two brothers, Dash and Randy, I'd suffered so much pain and disappointment, but eventually learned the lessons they had come to teach. The fun and joy

Stormy offered me after just a few jumps began to wash away the painful memories of my losses.

Stormy continued to amaze me with his calm approach to something completely new for him – jumping. While he was teaching me how I needed to approach something completely new for me, I was anticipating resurrecting my animal healing practice. There was some trepidation about rejoining the workforce, but Stormy was showing me how. I had only done communications for myself, friends, and family since my folks were each diagnosed with cancer eight years earlier. Thanks to my animal-family, especially Stormy, my self-confidence was on the rise.

I was ecstatic that Stormy enjoyed jumping so much. I can't enjoy something if my partner doesn't. Now there's a lesson for the ages! So I was thrilled that he loved his new job. I hadn't had this much fun in a very long time. With all the pain and heartbreak surrounding the losses of his brothers, I looked forward to lots of joy with Stormy in order to return to a place of balance and harmony. I will never be able to repay him for his contribution to my happiness and healing.

My sanctuary on the perfect farm began to change just after 2007 began. The farm owners called to offer me Kim's job, because she was moving south with her fiancé. My heart stopped when I heard the news. I felt as though I'd just lost a trusted employee – flashbacks to Fair Chance Farm and one of the major factors leading to our decision to sell. I thanked the farm owner for the offer, but my future was elsewhere. I'd learned all I could from running our own place. I wasn't going to make the same mistake. My communication and healing work would become the priority in my life.

Kim was replaced by a wonderful couple slightly older than me. When I met them I couldn't figure out why they wanted to manage the perfect farm. It was a tremendous amount of work even for a younger couple. Their daughter managed a large horse facility in a neighboring town, so this job would bring them closer to her and their granddaughter. They took great care of the horses and kept the farm looking picture perfect. But the effort required took its toll and they left after six months. I certainly couldn't blame then, but I was very sorry to see them leave. We had become good friends.

The next gal had a wonderful résumé on paper, but when her horses arrived the lack of care they displayed concerned me. She lasted five weeks and left without a word, so the owner ended up cleaning the barn while they searched for a replacement. I was reminded of all the labor issues I had had back on my farm and smiled within, knowing it wasn't my responsibility anymore. Labor in the horse business is the biggest problem – always was and always will be. Whenever I found a good person, I did everything to keep them happy and working for me. I'd begin to feel like I was working for them. I was so glad that portion of my life was complete.

The young man they next hired was a disaster. I worried about Stormy every day – something I hadn't done until now. I drove to the farm each day, weather permitting, to make sure Stormy was alright. Snow kept me away for a couple of days. In that time Stormy had gotten a cut on his hind leg probably from the fence board. I noticed his swollen leg as soon as I approached him in the field. Based on my experience with horses' injuries, this was an old cut that the young man totally missed. I tended to Stormy's injury, which was deep enough that it would have benefited from some sutures, but it was too late now. Ideally, cuts should be sutured within the first six hours, but for sure within 24 hours. Stormy's wound would have to heal on its own. I had the appropriate medications, but it would take longer due to the worker's negligence.

I walked Hana and Saba around the perfect farm while I tried to calm down. I couldn't leave Stormy here any longer. While it broke my heart to be leaving the place that had been such a huge component of my healing, Stormy's safety was paramount. I called my friend, who'd taken such good care of him for the six months after Kim left. "Do you think your daughter has an empty stall at her place?" She gave me her daughter, Collette's, phone numbers. I called and left messages on all her phones. Collette called back fairly quickly and ended my misery telling me she'd *make* room for Stormy. Moving was delayed two days because of snow – winter in the mountains. We arrived in Blowing Rock five days into 2008.

Life on the perfect farm provided a safe haven while I recovered and healed from my divorce. It offered a sanctuary from the challenges and frustrations of my dark night of the soul, which compromised the first three-and-a-half years in North Carolina. For that, I would be eternally grateful. So, the one constant in life – *change* – reared its ugly head again.

Animals don't handle change well, especially horses. At least this change was one of my own choosing, which would allow *me* to surrender and accept it. Stormy's well-being was at the root of my decision. Apparently, the Universe and my soul knew I was healed enough to cope with a change of home for my largest Master Teacher. I just kept reiterating my belief that everything happens for a reason, in our best interest, and always in perfect timing.

Chapter 42

∞

Payback

Stormy settled in at his new barn very well. Winter allowed him time to get used to a bigger, more active location. In reality, it was just what he needed. Some of the issues I'd had with Stormy revolved around loss of attention. The perfect farm was very quiet, so any little disturbance required Stormy's attention. Blowing Rock Stables was home to several horse shows in the summer months. They also rented stalls to campers who brought horses to ride out in Moses Cone Park, which bordered the property. It was *busy*.

With horses, it's better to have too much happening around them than just a little. When it's so busy there's too much for them to focus on, so they give up trying to take it all in. This was exactly what happened with Stormy. It was the perfect time (big surprise) for us to be at this type of horse facility. It was challenging initially to keep Stormy's mind focused on just what was happening in the arena. Stormy assumed the role of "social director," always needing to check on all the horses that were coming and going from the park. Over time, he got less and less concerned.

Collette was the director of the complex. She was a younger version of me. We became fast friends. She knew my background from her mom and was quick to ask advice on just about anything. I was thrilled to offer whatever help I could. Over-confident people won't ask for help, which always worried me. Collette's willingness to seek help reassured me. It was obvious how much she loved horses; she fell madly in love with Stormy. Who wouldn't?

As I was leaving for vacation in Maui, Collette asked if I wanted her to trail-ride Stormy while I was away. I told her he'd never been on one, but to do whatever she felt like with him. I was just grateful to have him worked. Leaving Stormy in such expert hands allowed me to go on vacation without worrying about my biggest angel.

When I returned, Collette said she'd taken Stormy out in the park several times. He'd been pretty worried to start, but got better each time. We trail-rode together, so I achieved something that I'd always wanted to do once we moved to the mountains – trail-ride on Stormy. He was anxious, but then so was I. Collette and I discussed numerous things that seemed to really bother him: stumps, fallen trees, stone formations, stone walls, the lake, and trail signs. He was actually *afraid* of these things. I could *feel* his fear (rapid, pounding heartbeat) and knew what I needed to do.

Collette knew I could talk to animals, but she didn't really know about the healing work I did. I told her I needed to clear him with SRT for all his fears on the trail. I didn't explain further. I'd just let Stormy teach her about the power of SRT. So, I did both Basic and Specific SRT clearings for Stormy. I rode in the arena for a few days while the clearing was being completed by the spiritual beings that work with me. I was anxious to get on the trail again, so I could assess his improvement.

Collette and I went back out on the trails, and Stormy taught both of us how powerful this process is for clearing away past life negative influences. It was as though I was sitting on a different horse. While he was still wary of the signs, logs, rocks, etc., he was no longer fearful. There was no change in his heartbeat. Even I was blown away by his relaxed behavior on the trail. I knew it would only get better with more time on the trails. Unlike many of the gals who rode exclusively on the trails, I had a horse in training, and trail-riding was relief from the intensity of the ring work. It wasn't an everyday experience for us. I needed Stormy to enjoy our time on the trails if it was going to do what I intended it to.

Collette and I trained Stormy together. It was wonderful to have such an experienced, lovely rider available. While I jumped Stormy most times, Collette would also jump him, so I could see his progress. It was so helpful to be able to watch him jump. I knew what he felt like – fabulous. But, I needed to be able to see him as well, which Collette let happen. It was the perfect partnership. She was invaluable to his becoming the wonderful jumper that he is. Stormy is the nicest horse I've ever sat on with the most powerful, easy jumping style. He is everything I'd hoped for when I bred Squiggles to Inspiration so many years ago. I felt blessed, knowing that breeding horses is like rolling the dice – rarely do you get what you hope for. In this case, I got more than I hoped for.

Collette and I trained Stormy for three seasons at Blowing Rock. They were the *best years* I'd had in the mountains. When my horses are healthy and going well, life is good. Those three years were payback for all the years I hadn't been able to ride on Fair Chance Farm due to the unending responsibilities of an equine hospital, vet office, and breeding farm. Part of my decision to sell the farm had to do with my *need* to get back in the saddle before my bad back, knee, hip, and shoulder prevented it. Now that I was older, I appreciated my time on the back of a good horse even more – and I had a *great* horse. Stormy was responsible for bringing my passion back to life. Nowhere was I more joyful than over a fence with him underneath me.

The second spring brought more sadness to my life when dear Bandit developed congestive heart failure. She was 16 and had lived a wonderful life, mostly on her farm in New Jersey. I alerted the vet's office about her condition before I brought her and Crystal for their yearly vaccinations. I knew she wouldn't be coming home with us. The vet agreed with my diagnosis. In fact, Bandit's blood pressure was so low it made it difficult for the vet to administer the euthanasia solution.

I wasn't sure how Bandit's loss would affect Crystal, who was only 12. Bandit had always been around. They didn't appear to be great friends, but none of my cats ever did. It was obvious that Crystal missed Bandit. She began to spend much more time in the house with Hana, Saba, and me. Six weeks after Bandit left, Crystal disappeared. On the last day of May, I put her out for the night and never saw her again. I waited a day before I sent out a telepathic plea for her to come home – nothing. I tried to connect with her – nothing.

I'll never know exactly what happened, but I believe Crystal may have been killed by coyotes that reside in the mountains, or one of the many loose dogs. I missed her terribly. She'd been such a support to me when I first moved into the log house. I would never forget her concern for me and the healing purr she emitted. My time at the barn with Stormy helped to assuage the losses of Bandit and Crystal over such a short time. Our family had been reduced from six to four in a matter of weeks. While I loved all my barn cats, I wouldn't be adding any more felines to my family. Saba, Hana, and Stormy are in charge of me now.

By the third summer, we were jumping decent-sized fences, which suited me more. I saw the distances better (guiding the horse to the proper place to leave the ground). I was thrilled that Storm seemed to love to jump as much as I did, which made our schooling sessions pure delight. Things were going great until one day Stormy did something before each of two fences that abruptly tossed me over his head onto the ground. When you've ridden as long as I, you know when you've reached the point where it's easier to fall than try to stay on. I hadn't fallen since the bird attack at the perfect farm – and never twice in one day.

Stormy was a prince. He slowed as he felt me fall in front of him and waited next to me. Collette rushed over totally surprised. No one was more surprised than I. Even more so when I jumped several more fences just fine and then *bam*, again on the ground! Collette pleaded with me to stop, but I wouldn't. I was taught as a young rider never to stop with a fall or a refusal. So, I jumped two more fences and then stopped.

Luckily, my body seemed to handle my falls fairly well. I could tell Stormy was confused and felt bad. I didn't blame him for anything. He was a wonderfully willing horse. I was concerned about *him*. Something had obviously caused him to make that perplexing move at the base of the fence. Despite that, he still jumped it, which is what catapulted me out of the saddle – his sheer power. There was no quit in Stormy or me.

While grazing him after we both settled down, I asked what happened. *I don't know. I couldn't push off the ground when I wanted to. I'm so sorry. Are you alright?* I assured him I was fine and not to fret over it.

We had another two perfect schooling sessions with no glitches. He jumped tremendously. Even though we were jumping three feet, nine inches, he hadn't yet made an effort over a fence. He was just amazing. Sadly, I hit the ground during our third school. I knew Stormy was concerned, but Collette was *really* worried that I'd get hurt. I just didn't understand what was happening, which disturbed me. Two weeks of horse shows were about to start, so we would be relegated to mostly trail riding anyway.

I'd been observing some odd movement in Stormy's hind legs for years. I was always fearful of stifle issues due to Randy's stifle problems, but Stormy's symptoms never progressed. They mostly appeared when he was cross-tied in the barn. Cross ties control horses while they're being groomed (brushed) and tacked-up (saddled and bridled). A cross tie attaches to each side of the horse's halter and to the wall of the barn to keep them from wandering off. Stormy was never lame, moved beautifully, backed normally while I was on him, and jumped like a deer, so I practiced what my Ex and I used to call "skillful neglect." Now, I was wondering if this odd motion in his hind legs had something to do with my hitting the ground three times.

Once the shows were over we got back to training and jumping. I was concerned that we would both be a little nervous. Stormy was fine (always living in the present moment), and I relaxed after a few fences. Unfortunately, too much weed-whacking and mowing on the Creston property, combined with my three falls, caused my weak back to become acutely painful. Riding was out of the question for a while.

Collette was joining me for the first week of my Maui vacation. I was providing the resort as a thank you for all the help she'd given me with Stormy. She had made the three years in Blowing Rock memorable for Stormy and me. It was the least I could do for her. I was worried that my back wouldn't hold up for the long flights to Maui. I prescribed rest, SRT, remedies, color therapy, magnets, and analgesics for myself. An old friend and fellow healer learned from Facebook that I was suffering and offered an unfamiliar-to-me healing technique – Spiritual Restructuring, developed by the founder of the Spiritual Response Association. Almost immediately, I felt improvement. It didn't eliminate all my pain, but enough so that I felt I'd make it to Maui. His expression of concern and quick response meant even more to me.

The healing energy of Maui, and especially Hana (the town not the dog), is something that has to be felt to be understood. I knew Maui could heal me if I could get there. Arriving with my back and knee no worse than when I left home was a relief. After soaking up Maui energy for five days, Collette and I headed to Hana for an overnight. I wanted to share a magnificent Hana waterfall with Collette. I hoped I could handle the hike, which under normal circumstances was quite easy.

My bruised body handled the hike to the falls better than I expected. I sat by the falls and asked to communicate with the Guardian of the Falls, with whom I'd spoken two years earlier. A feminine energy surrounded me, welcoming me back. *Ukahulu* remembered me because not many humans speak with her. I asked if I might receive some healing for my injured back and knee. She was *so* pleased by my request.

I sat for 20 minutes with my feet and legs in the pool beneath her 400-foot waterfall – the word phenomenal doesn't do it justice. As Collette and I prepared to leave, I thanked *Ukahulu* for her healing. She wished me well and would look forward to my next visit. We started back down the Pipiwai Trail through a magnificent bamboo forest. Listening to Nature's symphony as the trade winds "played" the bamboo, my knee seized up. It felt like an odd cramp. After a short while, it passed. It occurred numerous times while walking on the manmade boardwalk through the bamboo, which was the *easy* section of the hike.

My concern about reaching the car grew stronger – hiking down is always harder on the knees. We had another hour to hike over uneven terrain. In answer to my ever-increasing concern, I heard (in my head) someone say, *Flow colors.* Good idea, I thought. I'm not sure whose voice I heard, but it definitely came from the bamboo forest. I began color therapy just as I would for a client. I flowed the master healers, silver and turquoise, throughout my body and energy bodies. Once I began the colors, my knee never had another episode. I was pretty impressed and thanked my wounded body for the lesson.

My left-brained, analytical side was trying to assess if this odd symptom was a consequence of the waterfall's energy, since I'd never experienced anything like it before. It wasn't important that I understand it mentally. Intuitively, I *knew* the two were related. I left Hana with a renewed spirit and a curiosity about what, if any, improvement might result from my time with *Ukahulu*, the generous Guardian of Waimoku Falls.

My knee was significantly better the next morning. A little over 24 hours after my immersion in the waterfall's pool, I noticed a change in my lower back. During the second night, I slept in positions I hadn't been capable of for more than three weeks. My entire body continued to improve over the next few days. What *I* hadn't been able to do using all the healing modalities I work with (plus one of another healer), this Spirit of Nature accomplished in a relatively brief encounter. I am forever grateful for my ability to communicate with Nature's healers and especially to *Ukahulu* for her kindness. My lesson: keep an open heart, ask, surrender, and *believe in miracles!*

Collette made the first week on Maui so special. I showed her as many of my favorite spots as I could fit in a week's time. I was so grateful for her company and her part in creating some fabulous memories. She headed home as I readied myself to meet up with my dear New Jersey friends, Gary and Kit, in a few days' time. Our trips hadn't been planned to coincide, but the Universe orchestrated that for us. It was delightful spending time with them on Maui. I hadn't seen them in three years – since my visit to New Jersey when I brought Saba and Hana home.

Vacationing on Maui is all about Mother Nature for me. The natural beauty of Maui is unsurpassed, both flora and fauna. Its crystal-clear water and colorful fish are spectacular for snorkeling, whether off a beach or a boat. I had booked two snorkel trips to Honolua Bay – a favorite spot with an amazing reef – one with Collette and the other with Gary and Kit. Before leaving on the first trip, I communicated with the over-soul of the local dolphins requesting they join me if possible. I *needed* to feel their joyful, healing energy.

As Collette and I approached the bay, we saw a large number of spinner dolphins in the distance. Numerous dolphins showed us how they got their name by spinning above the water all around us. I communicated my thanks as their joy filled their human audience. Even the crew was blown away, meaning this wasn't an everyday occurrence. We snorkeled among fabulous coral and hundreds of fish, moving to another location after lunch. Unbelievably, the spinners were still with us. Our second snorkel trip also included them. The energy they imparted to the water was overwhelming. It just doesn't get any better.

Unusually high surf the second week kept Gary, Kit, and me away from Honolua Bay – a lesson in *flexibility*. Again, I sent out a similar request to the dolphins. We headed in the exact opposite direction to a reef where turtles entertained us. While not as clear as the first trip, the water was still amazing and the fish as colorful. As we headed home, a *huge* pod of dolphins surrounded us. More spinners were dancing – including babies that were learning to spin. Remembering me from the week before, the crew said, "Wow, you're really good luck!" I just smiled with excitement and continued shooting pictures, hoping some would turn out. I shared with the captain what I do and about my requests to the dolphins. He'd been doing this for *20-plus* years and said they might see dolphins every 50 to 100 trips. To see hundreds twice within a week was *extraordinary*. I confessed, "It doesn't always work." These dancing dolphins knew better than I how much I was going to need their healing energy. I, however, was clueless.

Collette called me before I left Maui to see how the rest of my trip went. I told her about the dolphins on the second snorkel trip. I was headed back in the morning. She asked me to call her when I got in. Even though the flights went well, I'd been travelling for 17 hours and was exhausted when I left her a message saying I'd call her the next day. Hana and Saba were thrilled to have me home. We all sat on the floor together for the first time in weeks.

Collette called – she needed to tell me something before I picked up my mail at the post office. The barn would be closing for the winter. I had 45 days to find a suitable home for Stormy in an area that is *severely* horse-facility-challenged. My relaxation and sense of renewal from two weeks of Maui's healing energy evaporated in a heartbeat.

Given my recent falls while jumping and the barn-closing disaster, the pursuit that generated the most joy in my life was under *attack*. My therapy, my sanctuary, was creating stress and anxiety – the two things it was meant to relieve. I knew something much deeper had to be involved. Obviously, I wasn't getting it (because I didn't want to), so I set up a session with Gregory, my dear friend and gifted trance channel.

Chapter 43

∞

Paralyzing News

I arrived at Gregory's house for my session just as I had for many previous ones. For the first time, a collective of *my* Guides and Teachers channeled through Gregory. Their message was blunt and to the point, followed by an apology for being so direct – but they felt it was the only way to be sure I understood the message I'd been *missing*. I was told in no uncertain terms that if I continued to jump, I would have a tragic fall that would break my back and restrict me to a wheelchair for the rest of my life! Kind of like a patient who's just heard they have cancer, I didn't hear much after that. Luckily, Gregory records his sessions. Of course, it was *my* choice what I did with the information. They couldn't interfere with my free will, but they hoped I'd make the wisest choice.

My head was spinning as I headed home. I'd *never* expected anything this serious. I had a choice, but really what choice did I have? To be wheelchair bound would be a fool's choice. I'd just been told I could never again do the one thing that had always brought me such *joy*. I felt like I'd been hit in the stomach with a bat. I cried and cried and cried for days. Jumping horses had been my passion for 50-plus years – the one constant in my life.

I only shared my devastating message with a few close friends, including Collette. I could hardly get the words out before I would start crying. The next time I saw Stormy, I hugged him and cried, telling him I didn't want him to *ever* feel like he'd hurt me. I'd been told that I could probably jump a couple more times without incident. The thought of *never* experiencing that feeling of freedom and power again was agonizing. I *had* to take the chance to jump one last time. I *needed* to. I hoped by doing so I'd be able to accept my sentence of "life without jumping." I had no doubts about the veracity of the message or the method by which it came to me. I knew others probably did, but that was their issue.

Stormy hadn't been worked in more than a month due to my back pain and vacation. I worked him until the last chance I had to jump before the barn closed. Collette and I felt he'd be fine jumping through a gymnastic (series of three jumps sequentially rising in height). Stormy's trouble had only occurred at single fences. I wondered if I'd be tense, given the information I had received. I wasn't because I *believed* that I'd be protected so that I could say good-bye to *joy* without incident, so that I could create a final lasting memory.

Stormy was great for not having jumped in so long. We jumped through the gymnastic several times. Collette raised the last oxer (spread fence) each time. I tried to burn the memory into my being – that fantastic feeling of Stormy over the big oxer – to hold onto for the rest of time. He is the absolute *best* horse I've ever jumped, and there've been many.

I could've jumped forever, but knowing Storm wasn't fit enough I stopped. As soon as I did, *I lost it!* The tears streamed down my face, as they are right now. Stormy and I walked around the upper half of the ring with Collette by our side, her hand on my leg telling me it would be all right. But, it *wouldn't!* My life's passion had just died and took joy along with it. The loss of my ability to jump was more heartbreaking than the loss of my husband to unexpected divorce six years earlier. I'd been married for half my life, but I'd been jumping for my entire life, and jumping had *never* disappointed me.

I fought away the tears as I headed back to the barn. I didn't want to upset Stormy any more than I already had. I didn't want anyone else to know what I'd just said good-bye to either. I was reeling from the roller coaster of emotions, plus it was private and personal. I had surrendered to the message from my soul, my Guides and Teachers, the Universe, but I was a long way from accepting it – a *very long* way.

I am grateful for my intuition that let me know something was amiss. I am grateful for the message, which allowed me to make an informed decision before it was too late. I knew many weren't so fortunate (including a friend and fellow jumper rider, who dove into a lake and spent the rest of his life training students and their horses from his wheelchair). I felt lucky and grateful one minute, and then devastated, angry, and *extremely* sad the next. Surrendering is way different than accepting. Without both, you won't truly heal.

While I tried to comprehend the loss of my one true joy in life, I was consumed with finding a new barn for Stormy. Collette made calls to everyone she knew in the area, without much luck. A wonderful group of ladies had gathered around Collette at the barn. We'd become a family, which is unique as boarding facilities go. We hated being torn apart, but that's exactly what was happening. For those who returned seasonally to Florida and South Carolina, the closing didn't have much effect. It was those of us who lived in the mountains year-round that felt the sting of the Board of Directors' decision to close for winter.

All the boarders began searching in earnest for homes for our horses. Each of us had our own set of needs and requirements. Most are pleasure-trail riders, while I'm training a jumper with trails worked into my program to balance the intensity in the ring. While we would've loved to stay together, that was unrealistic.

Quality of care is the most important factor for me. Distance traveled runs a close second. I'm a hands-on horsewoman, who lived for 27 years with my horses just outside my door. I need my horse to be an almost daily presence in my life or there's no reason having one. The demands on my time from my animal-communication clients and my writing necessitate having Stormy relatively close.

Processing my reactive, emotional response to the closing news allowed me to begin to focus on a positive resolution. I kept hearing myself telling clients and readers, "Everything happens for a reason and in our highest good." As we eliminated more and more possibilities from our list, I struggled to stay optimistic. Responding to the positive thoughts of my dear friends, family, and clients, the Universe presented a totally *unexpected* option.

A local horseman had decided to start a boarding facility on a spectacular 6,000-acre property 45 minutes from my home. Having considered this venture for several years, the closure of our barn was just the catalyst he needed to bring his dream into reality. The Ranch was an amazing place with tons of potential. It was a work in progress: grass pastures with clear, natural creeks running through them; a horseman's barn; riding arena; and miles of trails that lead to waterfalls, ponds, and long-range mountain views. It was like having a national park just for us. It was truly horse and Labrador heaven.

The day finally arrived for our move. I'd shipped horses all my life, giving me lots to compare to. Stormy had *very* limited experience, which added to *my* anxiety. Becoming my own client, I had a conversation with Stormy giving him all the details. Knowing animals feed off our energies, I surrounded both of us with healing light, which I use often with my clients, to calm and relax us. Stormy gave the trailer a little look and then walked calmly onto it. He stood patiently until we drove off – patience isn't one of his strong suits. We drove the hour to the Ranch without a hitch, no pun intended. I wasn't a bit anxious, which surprised even me.

I offloaded Stormy into his new stall with a view. He was wide-eyed looking at the huge, grassy pasture that awaited him. After a couple of hours, I turned him out in a smaller paddock, so he could get acquainted with The Ranch. While Stormy calmly explored, Hana & Saba helped me unload his luggage. I was astonished by the results of the communication and healing light. I was sure Stormy would come off the trailer sweaty, but he hadn't turned a hair (horseman's term meaning not nervous, i.e., relaxed). Driving home, I calculated that Stormy had only been shipped six times – hence my concern. My ability to communicate ahead of time and while driving eliminated any uncertainty in him. If he wasn't worried, I wasn't.

A week later, I had to reach into my bag of gifts again as I watched my well-trained, respectful horse have an *emotional meltdown.* It was upsetting, yet extremely educational, to experience. If I hadn't seen it with my own eyes, I wouldn't have believed it – both the meltdown and his recovery.

Stormy had embraced the role of herd leader – or as I termed it, "Fury, King of the Wind" – after being out on 200 acres with several horses for the week. Adding three new horses pushed him over the edge. His self-proclaimed position of protector turned my manageable horse into an out-of-control bundle of nerves. Having raised Stormy from a foal, I knew him. The horse before me in no way resembled mine. Stormy became so fractious that he bordered on dangerous. Having a horse's attention when you're handling them is crucial, especially one Stormy's size. In all my years with horses, I'd never seen such a radical change in behavior. While fascinating, I was concerned for both our safety.

Being an empath, I *felt* what Stormy felt. He was too far gone for communicating. Knowing what he was experiencing helped me diagnose the problem. His new routine had triggered memories of mustang lives – lifetimes of leadership. All those emotions were fueling the meltdown I was witnessing. Luckily, I had a very effective antidote for Stormy's "dis-ease": Spiritual Response Therapy. I cleared Stormy with SRT before heading to The Ranch. He'd been cleared before for other much less explosive issues, so I knew the healing work wouldn't take too long to complete, probably less than a day.

I found a slightly improved version of my horse when I arrived. At least, I didn't feel he was dangerous; I could hold his attention. After working Stormy in the arena, I decided he was manageable enough to join my friends on our inaugural trail ride. It was simply spectacular – both the Ranch's natural beauty and Stormy's transformation. Stormy's meltdown provided me with another peek into the healing power of the spiritual realms. I was even more thankful for the gifts I'd uncovered through my work with the animals. Helping one of my best friends deal with a potentially disastrous situation was so gratifying. It was payback for all the joy Stormy's brought into my life over the past eight-and-a-half years since I helped him enter the world.

Six weeks after Stormy's move to The Ranch, he injured his right hind leg badly. I noticed nothing unusual walking him in from his 200-acre pasture. He seemed fine while grooming and tacking, but when I began to trot I realized he was hurt as he collapsed underneath me. I jumped off immediately and went for a lunge line. I needed to see exactly how he was handling his right hind leg. Trotting with my weight definitely aggravated his lameness, which was now obvious even at a walk. There was no swelling or cuts anywhere, but the inside of his right hock felt warm, meaning inflammation. Intuitively, I *knew* it was a stifle injury. Given his level of lameness, I feared Stormy might have torn his patellar ligament.

All my years of caring for injured horses in New Jersey kicked in. I hosed the leg with cold water for 15 minutes. I applied green jelly (topical anti-inflammatory) to the inside of the hock and stifle area to further cool the leg and lessen inflammation. I started Butazolidin (oral painkiller) to treat his pain and inflammation. I was distraught! Luckily, a local vet was due out for another horse in the morning. I called his office asking him to add Stormy to his list.

When I got back home, I began the same healing work I would for my clients' animals. I cleared Stormy with SRT for anything that was contributing to this injury from past lives. I tested him for vibrational remedies, which I brought in the morning. Remedies are normally given two to three times daily. I could only dose him once a day, but I figured it was better than nothing. What did I have to lose? I added color therapy as well for Stormy, which consisted of twice daily sessions of "applying" (long-distance healing) whatever color I was *instructed* to administer into Stormy's body and energy bodies. Color therapy begins with lower vibrational colors and proceeds to higher vibrational colors as the healing progresses. The only thing I held off on was a shamanic journey.

I asked Stormy how he'd injured himself. I sensed his embarrassment as I heard, *I slipped.* As I heard his answer, I also *felt* what happened. Stormy was crossing one of the creeks. His left hind wouldn't support his weight, so he used his right hind to catch himself, which slipped on the rocks in the water. I felt the leg stretch away from his body in a way that a horse's leg should *not* go. I'd slipped a number of times on the rocks myself, but I don't weigh 1300 pounds.

The local vet suggested rest, Bute, and x-rays if he didn't improve within a couple of weeks. I wasn't waiting. I'd already decided to go to an equine hospital about an hour away. I wanted a *definitive* diagnosis. Fearing a ligament injury, I knew ultrasound was necessary to image soft tissue damage. As I drove back from the Ranch, I contacted the equine hospital. Stormy couldn't be seen until after the weekend. Until then, I continued with the cold showering, topical treatment, Bute, and my spiritual healing methods. I stopped the Bute 36 hours before our appointment, so the vet would get a clearer sense of Stormy's injury.

Collette and I drove to the equine hospital with high hopes of getting an accurate diagnosis of Stormy's injury. As severe as it was, I needed a treatment plan to insure a *complete* recovery for Stormy – my grandson. I needed Collette for moral support in case the news was bad. Collette had been to this vet before with good results. Well, if there's one thing I know, it's horse vets, having lived with one for almost 30 years. I would make my own assessment.

The hospital was *very* impressive looking. The vet asked to see Stormy move in a pen adjacent to his clinic. Collette trotted him in a circle while the vet and I watched. I didn't say a word as I watched a completely sound (not lame) horse. Collette changed directions; sound. The vet finally said, "He looks sound." I laughed and said, "Always the way." He then asked Collette to turn Stormy loose and chase him a little faster. His only comment, "Wow, look at that trot!" I smiled and replied, "Yea, he's pretty special!"

Knowing the vet got over-exaggerated descriptions of horses' symptoms all the time, I shared my background, followed by my assurance that this horse had been *severely* lame five days earlier. He said, "I believe you." He still thought we should radiograph his stifle, and I mentioned ultrasound as well. I described the odd hind leg behavior that Stormy had had for years, which was most obvious when cross-tied and backing up on cross-ties. "It sounds like Shivers" – a term I'd *never* heard before. The vet began a lameness exam. As soon as he saw how Stormy handled his hind legs, he said, "That's classic Shivers."

While his vet-techs radiographed Stormy's right stifle, the vet printed out pages of information for me about Shivers. The x-rays looked good, but I still wanted to ultrasound the joint as well. I had come for all the information he could offer me. There was no evidence of damaged soft tissue. All he found was some minor wear and tear in the stifle's cartilage. Given Stormy's age and level of work, the vet felt it was to be expected. Not only was I relieved that Stormy was okay, but I was thrilled to have found a fabulous equine vet, who wasn't too far away for any emergencies that I couldn't handle.

Even I was blown away by the level of healing that had occurred in a mere *five* days. Seeing the effects of SRT, remedies, and color therapy that hadn't been completed yet on Stormy's injury was a valuable lesson for me. I hear back all the time from my clients about the miraculous results from these unique forms of healing, but experiencing it myself is so much more powerful for this one-time pharmacist. I thanked Storm for being my professor extraordinaire... but enough already; I don't need any more proof. I believe!

The vet sent me home with instructions for another two weeks of rest for Stormy. He also told me that, with Shivers, Stormy should *not* be turned out in 200 acres with creeks. When we got back to the Ranch, I informed the nice fellow who ran the barn about the vet's opinion that Stormy needed a smaller, safer pasture. Stormy's continued rest gave him two weeks to fence a spot for him.

I went down every day and hand-grazed Stormy for at least 45 minutes, so he could get some grass. I couldn't imagine standing in a small dirt pen gazing at all that grass and not having access to it. At the end of two weeks, I got on Stormy and he felt fine. I had asked the fellow who ran the farm if he'd been thinking about fencing a paddock for Stormy. To which he replied, "Yup." No fencing ever appeared, so I had to do what was best for Stormy – move again.

We ended up at a barn where Stormy received excellent care, including a large grassy pasture to roam around in with several other horses. The bad news was the distance from my home – 75 miles each way – resulting in only seeing him twice a month due to the fuel costs. Given that I had lived with my horses on my own farm, this was *extremely* challenging for me. Matters got worse when the excellent vet that diagnosed Shivers in Stormy told me later over the phone that Stormy shouldn't *jump* because of it. Now we'd both been sentenced!

Financially, the vet's prognosis of no jumping for Stormy was a disaster. Being such an amazing jumper made him a valuable show prospect. To me he was invaluable, of course. But if I had to sell him, I hoped to recoup some of the costs of breeding, training, and caring for him. Personally, I wasn't sure if just riding without jumping would be enough for me – a horse trainer driven by a goal for my whole life.

I had tentatively planned to sell Stormy when he turned 10 years old, a very marketable age. I'd be 61 and figured it'd be time for me to accept my age. Mind you, that was only a year away. I kept trying to tell myself, "What's the big deal whether you do it now or next year?" I think it had to do with *choices* and perfect timing. In *my* opinion, this wasn't the perfect timing for this particular choice, but I couldn't risk digging in my heels and being stubborn.

Not being able to ride delayed my assessment of the situation. Since I wasn't ready to let him go just yet, Stormy came back to the local barn in mid-April. I would have to determine what's truly best for both of us before they closed again. Storm's a beautiful mover as well as a gifted jumper. His father was a Grand Prix level dressage horse and Grand Prix jumper. Maybe that's what lies ahead in Stormy's future. While I can appreciate dressage and even get teary watching elite horses and riders dancing together, it's not for me. Some dogs can't learn new tricks!

I haven't given up on Stormy's future in jumping, even though mine has been decided. I have stopped crying, but I haven't been happy since the day I left Maui and arrived home to the disintegration of the thing I hold most dear in my life. I simply didn't understand how this could be in my or Stormy's best interest, or what possible reason there was for these circumstances. I had hoped that when it was time for me to hang up my tack (saddle and bridle) for the last time, it would be on *my* own terms. These were anything but that. I know *my* fate has been sealed, but I'm not so sure about Storm's. I still have a few healing tricks I haven't tried yet. Perhaps some time on the back of my fabulous horse strolling in Mother Nature will help me process all that's happened and finally accept my fate.

Chapter 44

A 21st Century Shaman

Acceptance eluded me all winter. Surrender had me resigned to the fact that my jumping days were over. My inability to accept my fate had me taking down all the photos of me showing on Jolly Man back in the day. I just couldn't look at them. I did leave two photos of me on Stormy, one of which was the last jump we took together. Secretly, I hoped his fate was still up in the air – no pun intended. Well, maybe a little.

I just couldn't shake the haunting sadness that engulfed me. I felt imprisoned by my choice to heed the warning that I'd been given by those who were in charge of my spiritual health – my Guides and Teachers. Knowing how much writing *Letting Go* had helped me heal from my dark night of the soul, I decided it was time to write the book I'd always intended to write one day. In early February, I began *Master Teachers* with an added intention of hopefully gaining some further insights and understanding about the circumstances that were at the root of my current pain – the disappearance of joy and passion from my life.

Hana and Saba were great company all winter, but I really hated the distance that separated Stormy and me. Knowing that he was being well cared for made the situation slightly more acceptable. His safety and well-being was more important than my happiness. Winter brought us the second most snow since I'd moved seven years earlier, which would have kept me away from even the local barn. I tried to convince myself that it wasn't a big deal, but it was. I missed my horse, plain and simple.

As soon as the barn opened, Stormy came back home. Having him readily available made life more bearable for all of us. We eased back into work since neither of us had done anything since we had to leave the Ranch in early December. I was happy to be in the saddle again, but knowing I couldn't jump was killing me. The first few times I rode in the arena I got teary. Instead of being pleased to be on my wonderful horse, I was overcome with grief at my loss. It was as though I was grieving someone's death, which I was of sorts – the death of joy.

While I'd surrendered to my fate, I hadn't surrender to the notion that Stormy would never jump again. Years of working with spiritual healing methods with the animals had taught me that Spirit lies behind everything. If we can heal Spirit, we can heal the mental, emotional, and physical. I'd been waiting for Stormy's return to the mountains to begin my efforts to heal the spiritual energy behind his Shivers condition. It would take more than me to accomplish such a miracle, but I knew exactly where to go to find such extraordinary healers – "non-ordinary" reality.

After training Stormy for a month, I was ready to embark on a shamanic journey for healing on his behalf. I hadn't journeyed in almost eight years, so my confidence was shaky. Interestingly, I was engaged in writing about my earlier journeys for this book as I was considering journeying for Stormy. Oh, those coincidences. Reliving my earlier shamanic journeys allowed me to remember the amazing results I'd achieved.

I'd been dragging my feet a little, so the Universe provided the perfect push to get me started. I was on the phone with my friend and webmaster, George, who is also an accomplished shaman. I was explaining that I was going to journey, but I hadn't done one in such a long time, which concerned me. George said, "I just *heard* that you'll be better than before." I smiled at the synchronicity of our call.

I decided I should practice before I journeyed for a healing for Stormy. I thought for a while about what to journey for. All of a sudden I heard – *acceptance!* I smiled – still a slow student when it comes to my own needs. So I set my intention to journey to the Upper-world to gain some wisdom and guidance for acceptance of my inability to jump and my loss of joy in life.

I depart from my mountain property that I still have. I haven't come upon anyone yet. I've gone up two levels. Now going up a third. Not really seeing anyone on the third, but it just feels like I should stay here and look around.

Oh, I just heard a growl behind me. (Turning) It's my friend the cougar, who I haven't seen in years. Oh, she's greeting me. She's missed me as much as I've missed her. *Why haven't you been to visit in so long?* Telling her so much has happened that's kept me from journeying, but I'm going to start doing more now.

I'm really sad (crying). I can't jump anymore. I need some help! *I can feel the sadness in your heart. Walk with me.* This is a new area I've never been to before. At least, I don't remember it. It's very pretty, very natural – meadows. Kind of reminds me a little bit of the Teton Wilderness where the rivers run through the grassy areas. It's really quite lovely. I'm really not seeing anyone yet. *Be patient!* (Laugh) Not my forte.

I'm starting to see a little community. It's not really people. It's little beings – Nature Spirits and what-not. They're very light and ethereal-looking, very pretty. *Very* busy. There's such a contrast between them and the solid, powerful cougar that's leading me in here. They're not afraid of her. We're just wandering through lots of little beings. *Go ahead. I'll wait for you. I can't go any farther. You keep going.*

Walking, walking. Getting a little more wooded. I can hear some water running. I'll head towards the water. That always seems to be a good plan. There's a . . . I think I'm about to meet Blue Rain – one of my Guides that I've not ever met before. Out from under the waterfall this beautiful, beautiful . . . I don't know if you'd call it a . . . Fairy. I guess Nature Spirit works.

Are you Blue Rain? She curtseys and glides over and hugs me. It's the most wonderful feeling. (very emotional) *I know the sadness you're carrying. I want to help you get rid of it, because it does you no good.* I've tried to accept this, but jumping horses was the one thing that brought me joy. (more tears) It always brought me joy, and now I've lost that. *You've got it all wrong. Joy is ever-present. It's always surrounding you. It's just that you choose not to see it. You block it. You don't allow it to come to you because of the anger and resentment. There are so many places to look for joy, but you're just not looking. I understand how important jumping has always been for you, but it's time to move on and look for joy in other places. Come with me now.*

This is such a beautiful place. I only hope she can help me finally accept this. *I'm going to try as best I can. It's what I'm here to do for you. I've been with you for many, many years. You haven't been aware, but I've been with you. I'm so glad we've finally met.* So am I. Now we're going to a more open area away from the water. There's not any water here but it's still quite beautiful. Along the side of a type of mountain – not really. It's flat gray stone, like a wall of slate stone.

She's waved her arm like a wand, but she doesn't have a wand. She sent out this blue light towards the stone. Oh, now it's like a movie screen. I'm seeing scenes from last year when I was jumping (crying). He was *so* good! It's so much fun, and I'm never going to do that again. (very emotional) *You're looking at it in the wrong way. Look at it with gratitude. All of it is stored in your memories. You can remember how if felt, you can relive it, and enjoy it whenever you want. But you're not looking at it in joy; you're looking at it in pain. The picture is the same. It's the perspective that you look at it with. The memory is the same, but it's the perspective of how you look at the memory – whether you look at it in joy and be grateful that you've always been able to do it and how lucky you've been because many, many have not had the opportunity – or not.*

I do understand that. (sobbing) It's just that I'm having so much trouble accepting that I'll never physically do it again. She's trying to get me to relax. *If you're too emotional, you can't understand the lessons being offered. Maybe this will help the acceptance.* She changes the scene on the stone screen. I'm seeing me jumping again with Stormy. Oh my God! This is the accident! (hysterical) I can't move! Everybody's rushed into the ring, and I can't move. I can't feel anything. Where's Stormy? Is Stormy okay? I need to make sure he's okay. (*extreme* emotion) Collette says he's okay. Oh, the look on her face, she looks terrified.

Calm down. This is not the reality you chose. By the choice of not jumping again, you've saved everyone from the pain that choice would have created in more than just your life. (Sighing) She's showing more of it. I'm in a wheelchair. I can't do anything. I'm depressed. I'm in like a . . . I don't know . . . it's some kind of an assisted-living place. It's terrible. (sobbing) I can't take care of myself anymore. (*extreme* hysterics) I don't have my dogs anymore! It's awful. (weeping) She's taking me away.

That's not you're reality. It's the reality you could have been living, but because of the information you received from your Guides and Teachers, including me, you made the choice not to live that. There was no purpose for it. Just calm down! You need to understand, and be grateful, and be thankful that that is not your reality. You still have your dogs. You can still ride your horse. You can still live by yourself and take care of yourself and do everything. You have no limitation except for jumping. Is that so much to give up? It isn't.

Oh my God, that other life . . . I couldn't have . . . it would have been just horrible. (crying and sighing) I understand now. I think it's going to be much different for me now. To feel that experience was terrible. *I'm sorry for having you do that, but I didn't know any other way. We've been hoping you'd get over this, but you didn't seem to be able to. You just kept not processing it and ignoring – not accepting and being thankful and grateful for the choice you were given. You weren't being proud of the choice that you made. You need to move forward!*

I think I will be able to now, since I've felt that other life and it was just terrible. *Once you move through this and fully accept and realize that you are living the highest possible way for yourself then you can remember your memories, and remember the feelings in joy, and be grateful, and be happy that you were able to jump as much as you did in your life. You will be able to attract joy, because you won't be pushing it away by being resentful that you can't jump anymore. You have to acknowledge that it is* your *choice.*

I am so grateful to have been given the choice. I really can't thank her enough. I'm so glad that we've finally met. She's just an absolutely beautiful, beautiful being – shades of blues and hues of turquoise – many, many of my favorite colors. Her energy is just so – well, Guide-like. What can I say? I feel so protected with her, like I do with Dancing Hawk (another Spirit Guide). I can't thank her enough for sharing this with me. She's giving me a big, big hug that just . . . I can feel it healing, healing my broken heart that's broken because I've lost my reason for being. (weeping) But I can feel it healing. I think the understanding is allowing it to heal. My perspective is shifting and changing.

Now, you'll be able to attract joy. You need to look for joy everywhere, because it is everywhere around you. You've been pushing it away and not allowing yourself to attract joy. You need to begin to attract joy. There is so much, so much that you have before you to do – important work, work with the animals and beyond. You need to start to get out and interact with more people and look for new avenues of joy. There are so many available. You are surrounded with it, but you can't attract it until you stop saying the only thing that ever brought you joy was jumping, because that is not true! There is so much in your life that has brought you joy. My life has changed so much. (tears) I just don't know what to expect. *Expect it to be joyful and satisfying and productive and filled with love and purpose.* (sighing) *It's time for you to go. Your cat is back.* She is!

We just walk back the way that we came through all the little devas (nature spirits) and beings. There are just so many different varieties and types. I've just never been on an energetic level like this to envision them. I wish I could see them when I walk through the forest at home, but I'm just not able to. My pretty cougar is taking me back. *Good-bye!* Thank you. *Don't stay away so long.* I'll try not to. I just hadn't had the confidence to do this. You've helped me regain it. (emotional) I love you so much! *I'm always here for you. All of your power animals are. Never doubt. Always trust. Trust in your ability, and trust in everything that's available.* I'm so grateful! I'm heading back to the mountain property now. (Huge sigh) I'm back now.

I returned from "non-ordinary" reality totally drained by the experience. It was *the* most emotional shamanic journey I'd ever taken. Once my strength returned, I noticed a lightness that had been missing. The burden of my unresolved anger and resentment had been melted away by the intense emotions that erupted as I viewed Blue Rain's "movie" of what could have been. I felt like a new person almost immediately. My goal had been achieved. Acceptance of never jumping horses again was the treasure that accompanied me back from the Upper-world, and it was instantaneous. My confidence in my shamanic ability had been restored by my cougar, Mystic, and my dear Nature Spirit Guide, Blue Rain. I was forever in their debt. I couldn't wait to seek a healing for Stormy's condition of Shivers the next day.

Before I embarked on my shamanic journey for assistance with Stormy's condition, I knew to clear him with SRT. I removed any negative past life energies that were contributing to his odd neuromuscular syndrome, so they wouldn't negate any of the healing that I returned with from the gifted healers awaiting me in "non-ordinary" reality. Once I was done with his Basic and Specific SRT clearings, I got out my drumming tape and recorder and embarked on yet another incredible adventure.

I journey to the Lower-world for a healing for Stormy's condition Shivers. Going down through the water slide. I'm in an area that's sort of arid. It has big rock formations like Sedona. Red rocks. Lots of scrub brush Not a lot of green. Not my favorite scenery, but ... I'm just looking around to see if I see anyone who can help me with a healing for Stormy. It's really very quiet, very warm. I'm seeing some dust – something's moving in this direction pretty fast. Oh, it's Destiny, my big black stallion. *I'm so happy to see you. It's been much too long. I can't believe you've stayed away so long. Get on!*

I just fly up on this *huge* horse so easily. I wish I could do this in my reality, but everything is easier in "non-ordinary" reality. He wheels around, and we head away from the red rock formations, which really are quite spectacular. We head across a vast plain of desert-looking cactus and such things. I'm not quite sure where we're headed, but in the distance things do seem to get a little greener. We're in a little bit of a rocky area, climbing up. It's very shale-like, almost slippery, but he glides across all this. It's so unlike riding in my reality. Oh, now we've reached the top of a precipice that looks out over a huge Indian dwelling. It's very green. There's a river running through it, but then it gets arid as you get away from the water. I can see more red formations beyond it.

Now we're sliding down the other side of it, heading towards this kind of encampment that's got people and teepees and horses and campfires. It's really quite lovely. It's not a community that I've been to before, so this is a different Indian settlement. Now he's stopped in front of a teepee. *Go inside. Someone inside will be able to help you. I'll come back later when you're ready to return.* Thank you for your guidance!

I enter the teepee. There's a beautiful Indian woman inside. *Come in and sit down with me.* She's not old. Probably younger than I am – maybe in her 40s, very beautiful long black hair. *How can I help you?* My horse, Stormy, has a condition called Shivers that affects the placement of his hind legs, and it causes him some discomfort and prevents him from jumping, which he loves to do. I was hoping you might be able to give me something that could correct this and heal Stormy of this condition. *This is something I've never heard of before.* I smile. That's what everybody tells me when I talk with them about it.

You've been brought to me for a reason. I work often with the native plants of the area. There must be healing within my region that can help Stormy with this. I will call on Great Spirit to guide me to that which will heal Stormy's condition of Shivers. She gets out her pipe (peace) and prays to the Four Directions, to the Father Above, and the Mother Below. I'm sitting quietly until she's finished asking Great Spirit for assistance. I guess she's seen or heard or felt whatever her Guides needed to tell her, because now we're going outside.

What I need to use for your horse is further away, so we'll take ponies. We get on some Indian ponies. *Follow me and stay with me until we get to where I need to go.* Moving along the river then veering away from it. *There are several locations we need to visit to obtain what I need. This is a complicated healing that I've been told. We'll go to the farthest place first and stop at the others as we return.*

We're actually headed over towards some very steep rock formations. We're going up a very narrow winding trail. *I've been told to go to a very sacred area that we're heading to now. It's a power vortex for this area.* We arrive at a little open area with some low bush growth. Not sure if she's come for vegetation or what. Getting off the horses and walking further through the low brush. Oh, now we've come to the back side of a high butte. *Sit down with me.* She's taking some of the clay, kind of red clay of the area, like what the pipes are made from. *It's exactly that. It's very sacred earth. It's very powerful. It's not shared often. You should be very proud that I've been asked to take some back for this healing for Stormy.* I am. I'm so very grateful!

The scenery from off the back of this butte is just ... you can feel the energy, the power. My heart chakra is just broken wide open. It's just so beautiful and powerful! She's putting a fair amount of the red clay in a medicine bag, but a bigger medicine bag than I'm used to, that hangs around your neck. *Hold this and keep it safe. It's very valuable! It's not often given away.*

We're back on our ponies and heading down off the butte. We're headed towards the little creek that runs through this area. We're headed to a pond of sorts where it's been accumulating. The wildlife probably all water here. She's walking into the pond searching for I don't know what. *I'm searching for the exact stone that is offering itself to me to offer to you for Stormy's healing. I'm waiting to hear the voice of the stone calling to me.* She's bending down and picking up a stone. It's just a small river stone – very smooth, slate green and blue. *Put this in the pouch with the red clay.*

We're back on the ponies moving again. She stops under a tree. I don't know what type of tree. Obviously, one that grows in an arid region. It's not tall by any means, but it's definitely a tree and not a bush. *May I have a few of your leaves for this woman's horse?* It offers them freely and I can hear the tree – *I wish you and your horse well. I hope that my healing properties will be of benefit to your horse. I can feel how concerned you are, and how much you love your horse. I feel how much you love the natural world, and we're so happy that you've come on behalf of your horse.* I put the leaves in the pouch.

We're moving along faster. We've pulled up in front of something I recognize, Manzanita. I met Manzanita in Sedona. I have a Manzanita piece of art at home. She's taking a branch. *I need the bark. The healing is not within the leaves of this plant. It's in the bark. It's offering me an entire branch. I'll carry this. It's too big for the pouch.* We're still not heading back towards the . . .

We're in an area of more cactus and cacti that are blooming. She's carefully picking an absolutely beautiful variegated yellow flower off a very spiky cactus. I wouldn't even attempt to do this, but she knows exactly how to get the flower without getting injured. She's handing me the flower to put in the pouch. My pouch is getting kind of full. *That's not a problem because that's the last component.*

We're heading back to her teepee. Thanking the horses for taking us. She's taking some utensils and a jug of liquid that she's offering me to drink. *You need to drink. This liquid is very powerful and it will help you when you apply the healing to your horse. It's a special sacred solution that I make and use in my ceremonies. It's been handed down for generations upon generations. You are welcome to drink as much as you care to.* It's actually very refreshing and very tasty. Some things I've had to drink in the past have not been pleasant, but this is actually very nice.

She's taking the jug and the pouch. Now, she's beginning to strip the bark off the Manzanita and is chopping it as finely as possible. She's mashing the leaves from the tree. I don't know what kind of tree. *That's not important.* She's mashing the cactus flower and combining it with the bark. She's taking the sacred clay from the butte (slightly moist). It's almost like she's making an ointment like I used to do back in my pharmacy days. She's taking some of the liquid I drank to mix with the clay and the bark and leaves. It's thinner than an ointment but not liquid.

She wants the stone that we got from the river. *The river pond is a very powerful sacred spot as well. The stone carries immense healing power.* She's covering the stone with the creamy paste of all the other ingredients. Now she's bringing . . . *It's the hide of a wolf that gave itself to the Indians. It's a small portion to wrap Stormy's healing within the wolf hide. The wolf and the sense of family that wolf displays is important. I feel you are the mother wolf for Stormy.* I explain I'm actually grandmother wolf. She shakes her head and smiles. *The sense of family and your need to want to heal your child, your grandchild, and the love you feel for him even though he is horse and you are human is rare to find in a person. It's the same love that's throughout the wolf clan and what makes them such a strong, strong, animal.*

She hands me the packet of all the healing ingredients within the wolf hide. She's tied it with . . . *It's horsehair, because this is a healing for a horse. You need to bring this back and apply it as you've applied others in the past. Know that this condition will be healed, because these are very, very powerful healing ingredients. I've never been directed to bring all of these together in one healing before. You should feel confident that this will correct the problem, and Stormy will have the free use of his body as though he never had any type of restriction or limitation.* I'm taking it from her and thanking her with all of my heart for her help. And I do truly believe this will heal him because I've seen this with my other animals. I do believe. *Belief is absolutely key! Belief from you, not so much from Stormy. But, he will believe if you believe. Go now and apply the healing and know that he will be healed and normal with no further restrictions.*

As I turn to leave having thanked her again, Destiny is standing and waiting for me. I get on him and we slowly move through the community. On the outskirts, we break into a full gallop. He's bringing me back towards the rock formations where I first found him. I'm just so grateful to this beautiful Indian woman and to Great Spirit for sharing these healing gifts with me for Stormy.

I'm back by the big red rocks. Getting off of Destiny, and thanking him for finding a healing for Stormy. *No horse should have any restrictions. I don't know what I would do. I don't think I'd be very good if I had restrictions, but I have none. I'm sending my healing energies to your horse as well!* I didn't even know that was possible. *Don't stay away so long.* I'll try not to. I'm thanking him and hugging him.

Now I'm heading back up the water slide with my very valuable packet in my heart. I'll head over to the barn with my crystal-friend and apply this healing to Stormy to remove the limitations and restrictions he has caused by this neuromuscular syndrome called Shivers so that he can no longer have discomfort and be unsure of his hind end. I just want him to be free and flowing and jump if he desires. I don't want any restrictions for Stormy. For all of this, I am *so very* grateful.

I'm back now. Honored with the experience I've just had and so grateful for the abilities that I've uncovered that take me to these wonderful healers – these generous, generous beings. It's just a phenomenal thing to be able to do.

I head to the barn with my priceless healing gifts from "non-ordinary" reality safely in my heart. I've journeyed on a Sunday, because the barn is quietest on Sundays. I don't want to have to explain why I'm aiming my cannon-shaped quartz crystal at Stormy's hindquarters. I'm not bothered by skeptics anymore. I just don't want to be disturbed while I'm applying the healing I've acquired for Stormy. Before I begin, I communicate to Stormy what I'm doing. I explain that I've done this before with great success with both his mother and uncle. You need to believe that you can be healed, and you need to want to be healed. *I can do that.*

Chapter 45

∞

The Missing Element

L ife kept me away from the barn for three days after my journey. I was dying to see what effect the healing had had on Stormy. I was extremely pleased to see a significant improvement in his symptoms the first time I cross-tied him. Knowing that animals are creatures of habit, and especially horses, I attributed what remained to force of habit. After all, he'd been living like this for most of his nine years. I expected to see a lessening of symptoms as I continued to train Stormy.

About a week later, life unfortunately interfered again when I had to stop riding due to acute back pain from two days of weed-whacking and mowing on the Creston property. Life deteriorated even more when three days later, Collette called to tell me that she'd given the Board notice – she was leaving. This was *so much more* painful than any back pain. I was shocked, but not surprised. She'd been having a lot of trouble working with the governing board since they reopened. The Universe presented her with a viable opportunity to end her frustration, and she took it.

I wasn't just confronted with the loss of a dear friend, but her departure was the catalyst for the decision I'd been agonizing over for months: Stormy would be sold, and hopefully by the time the barn closed again for winter. I couldn't have him so far away while trying to sell him. Since I couldn't jump anymore, I needed to rely on Collette to get him back into training once we were sure his condition was truly healed. The biggest hurdle was Collette's new position at the University of South Carolina, which allowed her two stalls that would be occupied by her's and her daughter's horses. There was "no room at the inn" for Stormy. And I had thought healing Stormy was the hard part.

I ended up being unable to ride for three weeks. During that time, rather than seeing Stormy's symptoms lessen, I began to see them *increase*. Knowing that animals take on our stress and anxiety, I was concerned that I'd contributed to Stormy's decline. I lunged (working a horse from the ground in a circle around you using a lunge line attached to his bridle) Stormy for the first two days back to work. Each time, I ended up in tears knowing that I had to sell *the* most wonderful horse I'd ever had. My heart was broken all over again. I had to figure out a way to follow the animals' lesson of only living in the moment, or I would never get through the next six months – *never!*

The uncertainty of our future was impossible to live with. I was discouraged and confused by what I was seeing in Stormy. I'd *never* had healing from "non-ordinary" reality only work for a short period of time. I'd *always* achieved a permanent improvement. Of course, I wasn't the only one involved; Stormy was a major player as well. Following the old adage, "If at first you don't succeed, try, try again," that's just what I did. A month after my first shamanic quest for Stormy, I decided to journey again. After all, I did journey twice for Rainbow for his Geriatric Vestibular Syndrome when he had over-exerted himself.

I wanted Stormy to have all the facts before I entered "non-ordinary" reality on his behalf again. I had a long conversation with him about all the issues surrounding my riding career and him. I needed to remind him that I could never jump him again. I had accepted that within my heart, but I needed to be sure he understood it. I explained about our missing friend Collette.

I know you can't jump anymore. I am so sorry about that. I felt the joy it created for you. I do love to jump. The flat work is tedious and trail riding is okay, but I, like you, love to jump. I wondered where my friend went. She was always around giving me extra attention when you couldn't be here. I can feel the strife in the barn of late. It's just not the same as it used to be. My body just can't handle the requirements of jumping. My back is getting worse, which is why I couldn't ride recently. I'm sorry that your person is so old. *Don't be sorry. I love you and whatever we do is okay with me.*

There are more issues with the barn and the turn-out. With Collette leaving, it's forced me to admit that I need to find a new person for you before the barn closes again. I want you to be able to jump with your new person, so at least one of us is still feeling the joy of doing what we love. I hate the idea of parting with you, but I always knew the day would come. My heart will break, but if I know you're doing what you love with a special person, then I can feel okay about it. *Are you sure? I don't want a new person.* I'm afraid I am.

I thought the healing I had acquired for you a month ago had solved the problem in your hind legs, but the signs are returning. It is imperative that *you* believe that you can be healed. I have been successful using this technique in the past, especially with your mother and uncle. Your uncle had a fatal hoof ailment, but he was healed within a day and lived for several more years. You wouldn't even be here if I hadn't used this method to help your mother heal from her fears of not having offspring survive. The knowingness that I obtained for her allowed both you and Randy to be conceived, born, and mature into beautiful adults. It is very powerful healing, but your involvement and belief is crucial. I am going to seek some more healing for you, as long as you want me to. I *will try harder this time.*

I'm going to journey to the Upper-world for a healing for my horse, Stormy's, condition of Shivers. Once again at the third level. I'm being met by my black horse, Destiny. It's so good to see him again. I'm up on him, and we're just flying so fast over a semi-arid area. Going up a steep trail, very shale-like, and back down the other side – opening into a huge prairie between two sets of mountains. Like a valley but it's very, very wide. I think we're going to the same Indian encampment. Everybody's greeting me again. *We're so happy you've returned!* Destiny's stopped by the beautiful Indian woman who helped me before.

I've come back for more healing for Stormy. Your healing was very powerful, but I think Stormy didn't believe in his heart, because he's starting to show symptoms again. I've been injured and unable to work with him for weeks. Can I get more healing? *Of course you can. You can come anytime! I'm so glad you've come back. I won't be providing it this time. Please follow me.*

Walking through the village. Everyone seems so happy to see me. I feel so welcome. It's such a peaceful, peaceful way to live. Going to an area we didn't go to before. There's a teepee we're going to. *Someone inside will help you. He's our shaman, our medicine man. I'm his apprentice.* Walking inside, expecting to see an older man, but he's probably my age – which I guess I'm getting old.

Sit down in front of me. I know you just had a conversation with your horse, and it is key to the healing I'll send you home with. You've learned well from your previous visits to get healing that belief is the key to all healing. It doesn't matter how powerful the healing is, if the individual receiving it doesn't believe in their heart that they will heal, then they won't. It doesn't even matter . . . it's important that you believe, but if Stormy doesn't believe, what you've seen happen over the last month is what will happen. He will get initial improvement, but it won't be permanent. It is imperative that your horse believe and trust that he can be fully healed. In order to do that, come with me.

He's a very gentle being, gentle yet powerful. I don't how else to explain it. We're going out to a wide open area a little bit away from the encampment. *Use your third eye to see the healing and bring it back and help your horse see it so he will believe.* He's waved his hand in front of my third eye.

Now I'm seeing Stormy jumping. (*very* emotional) He's jumping in a horse show, and he's amazing! I don't know the person jumping him, but they're a wonderful pair. (more tears) He ends up winning the class, and I can tell it's at a really big horse show. He's doing what I always *knew* he could do, but I just couldn't do it with him. It's a gal that's showing him, and I can tell she really loves him. (crying and sighing) I'm so glad to be able to see this, because I think it will help me as well accept that Stormy has a future – it's just not with me. (*very* emotional)

Now, I'm seeing him back on a farm. He's not at the horse show anymore. He's got a wonderful pasture that he's out in. He's being cared for very well. He seems to be a favorite of everybody in the barn. It's a future that I really hope for him if he can't be with me. (more tears) The Indian has touched my arm. *Come with me.*

We're getting on horses. Oh, that was *hard* to watch, but *so* encouraging. (big sighs) *You have to show that vision to your horse without your sadness.* (more tears) *You have to help Stormy realize that this is the future you want for him as well, so you don't hold back any belief in him. It's very important that you apply this vision, you show this vision, without any sadness, but with encouragement – helping Stormy to know that this is the future you want for him.* (*very* emotional) That's going to be *really* hard to do. *You are a strong healer. I have faith in you. I know when the time comes you will be able to do it because of your love for Stormy.* (sighing)

We're heading to a different place than where I went with his apprentice. We're not climbing. We're going along the edge of the canyon wall down into a sort of huge cave, big enough that the horses are going down in it with us. We've stopped by a stream that runs underground through this cave area. *Get down. We need to gather some items here.* I'm glad we don't have to go any further into it, because I'm still not comfortable with caves. It just a beautiful high-ceiling area, obviously, with the horses in it.

We're going to the stream. He's finding several rocks, pebble-size. He's handing me about a half dozen of them. He's brought a pouch for me to put them in. When I hold them . . . it's almost like they're vibrating in my hand. It's quite interesting. *This is a very sacred site that few are allowed into. My apprentice doesn't even know about it yet. She has many more years of training before she would be given access to this area.* I'm so very grateful to be allowed in here. *You are an extremely powerful healer, and you would be able to access this site even without me. You need to begin to realize the power that you hold within you. You need to begin to unlock it more and more because there are many that are in need of your healing abilities.*

We're back on the horses leaving the cave. I'm thanking the stream for the gifts it's given me. Going *really* fast to an area where the stream comes out from under the canyon wall, which

I still don't understand how. It's green growth around here. Trees and shrubs. More forest-like than the rest of the area. Walking the horses in the woods, going along to find whatever he's looking for next. Now we've come to an incredibly high waterfall – spectacular! It was just around a bend and drops from the top of the canyon wall down into an area that's very beautiful.

Get down. We must walk under the waterfall and behind it. We're in another cavern-type area. He's picking up a feather. There's a feather on the edge . . . not on the ground. It's kind of hanging on a branch where it's fallen down. *It's an eagle's feather.* It's not a big wing-type feather. It's a smaller feather. He's handing it to me. *This was put here specifically for you and your horse. It has immense healing power. Put it in with the pebbles.* That's all we're taking from here. I'm thanking the eagle. I wish I could see him. *No one ever sees this eagle. This is a magical bird that comes and offers healing gifts from time to time. I saw it in a dream last night that you were coming, and I was to bring you here for this feather.* I'm thanking the eagle as we leave.

Now we're back on the horses, leaving the waterfall. Traveling away from the forest. Stopping at a huge cactus garden – not planted by man, that's for sure. He's gathering several different flowers from three different types of cactus. *Put these in the pouch.* He's taking a piece of one of the cactus. *The inside has great power. It will be important to use in the healing I'm making for your horse.*

Heading back towards the encampment. Stopping by a type of bush. He's gathering some of the leaves. *It's myrtle.* Okay. Going back to his teepee. He's taking an old mortar-and-pestle-type tool and putting some of the cactus, the three different blossoms, and the myrtle leaves in it. They're all being smashed up in the mortar. He's offering me something to drink. *It's similar to what my apprentice offered you, but it has many more mineral components to it. It is much more powerful!* Oh, it tastes *really* good. *Drink as much as you can to bring back the energy of it – to help instill the healing within your horse.* He's using a little of the same solution to add to the blossoms and leaves. He's forming a paste with some of the clay. *This is the same red clay earth that came from the top of the butte where you went with my apprentice. It will help to bind all of these components together.*

He's putting those within the skin of some type of animal. *I don't want you to be upset, but it is actually the hide of a horse.* I'm not upset. I understand. The horse has given itself. I have a piece of hide myself that I took from a dear friend when she transitioned. *That's because you are a knowledgeable shaman, and even though you didn't know it at the time, you recognized the power that that hide would contain.* He's wrapping it up in the horse hide and tying it with horsetail to put in the pouch with the pebbles and the eagle tuft.

He's giving me a *huge* embrace, which I've never experienced except from Dancing Hawk, and recently with Blue Rain. *I want you to know that you're a very powerful healer. There's no reason why your horse won't be completely healed. I know you can show him the vision without any attached sadness or grief. I know you'll carry these healing gifts back and apply them exactly how they need to be applied. I want you to realize that you have as much power as I have. You just haven't realized it yet. I hope this exchange of energy that I've just gifted you, will help you to reawaken all of the memories of all of the lifetimes that you have been a shaman – and a revered shaman.*

Thank you so much for all of this! Just the vision alone is going to help me get through the next few months. I'm going back and apply this healing to Stormy and show him the vision of his future, which is a wonderful future.

Destiny is back. I'm getting on him with my pouch and my vision. Heading back to the area he found me in. Thank you for always being here for me and helping me find these amazing individuals, who are *so* generous and *so* humble. *You're most welcome.*

I'll head back home and then to the barn to show Stormy this vision of the wonderful future that lays before him – that he needs to believe he can live and have. And to apply the healing through my wonderful crystal. I thank everyone!

Once again, I journeyed on Sunday so I wouldn't be disturbed while I applied my treasure from "non-ordinary" reality. The first thing I did was have another conversation with Stormy while I showed him the vision of the future he could have – if he chose it. As much as I wanted this for him, *he* was the creator of his life experiences, just like I was of mine. His thoughts would create his reality. I hoped he embraced the vision of the talented show jumper that I always knew he could be. I applied the fantastic healing that I acquired from the Indian shaman, using my love for Stormy as the impetus behind it. I wanted one of us to be able to live with passion and joy. As long as we had to part, I wanted to offer Stormy the *best* life experience possible. My Master Teacher extraordinaire deserved nothing less.

For the first time *ever*, I saw *no* appreciable change in Stormy's symptoms. I was so frustrated and confused. I hadn't checked on any past life influence before the journey, so I checked three days later. There were a few, so I cleared him again with SRT for anything contributing to his Shivers. I saw no improvement. I was so disheartened. Journeying for acceptance for me took on a whole new significance. My complete and instantaneous acceptance of never jumping again proved beyond a shadow of a doubt the efficacy of my shamanic abilities and the healings conceived in "non-ordinary" reality.

While I continued to train and trail-ride Stormy, I searched for an answer to my dilemma. Why was this happening? Having worked as a communicator and healer for hundreds of individuals, I knew that I was merely a facilitator. The actual healing was accomplished by each individual. For whatever reason, Stormy didn't want to be healed. He was not embracing the remarkable gifts from "non-ordinary" reality. Eventually my intuition delivered my answer. Stormy was blocking the healing because he thought if he couldn't jump, I couldn't find him a new person. It made perfect sense. I really wasn't sure why it had been such a mystery to me.

Never being one to give up with something as important as this, I had a *long* conversation with Stormy. I explained that it was time for me to focus on sharing all the knowledge that animals, and especially he, had taught me throughout my life. Everything I'd done up until now had been to prepare me for this. I told him that regardless of whether he could jump or not, I needed to find him a new person, so he might as well do something he loves. If he didn't accept the healing being offered to him, he'd have to trail-ride and work on the flat for the rest of his life – neither of which he loved. I could sense him taking in the entire conversation, but he really didn't respond – which was very much like his older brother, Dash, a horse of few words.

So two weeks after my second journey for Stormy, I headed on another adventure. I *so* hoped that he listened to what I had said and would make the wiser choice. But it was *his* choice, and I would have to respect whatever decision he made. I prayed that this third quest on Storm's behalf would be the charm.

I'm going to journey for a healing for my horse, Stormy, for his condition, Shivers, so that he will be able to jump in the future and do the thing that he loves to do most. I will be journeying to the Lower-world to seek a healing for Stormy. I've gone through the pond behind my old farm, down the waterslide, and come up in the middle of a beautiful, huge lake. It's very still and quiet. I'm going to swim over to the shore to see if I can find somebody to help me with a healing for Stormy's Shivers and also for his blocking of the recent healing he's been offered.

There are a couple of little kids that have come out of the woods. They're laughing and giggling. *Come with us!* They're each taking a hand and pulling me. They're very happy and giggling. A little boy and a little girl. *Follow us into the woods. We know who can help you.* It's a very, very beautiful forest. Refreshingly cool. Almost like the feeling you get after a rain when everything is cleansed and crisp-feeling. They keep pulling me and pulling me. *We're so excited that you're here!*

Going to a little cabin in the woods. Very old, very cute. Now they're behind me, pushing me forward. *Go knock on the door. Someone inside can help you.* Thank you for bringing me. I've knocked on the door. *Come in!* I'm going inside the cabin. It's not really a cabin. When I open the door and walk through I'm in another very beautiful area. It's very large and expansive. It has little waterfalls and creeks all throughout it. *Come on in. Come on in.* I'm walking in, but I'm not in a cabin. I'm in a beautiful area of creeks and waterfalls and a meadow with wildflowers. Gorgeous scene.

Now there's a man walking out from the edge of the meadow through all the wildflowers with animals around him. *Come and sit by the creek with me.* Can you help me with a healing for my horse Stormy? *Absolutely! Stormy hasn't been receptive to this, because he hasn't understood your intention. But you've now made that perfectly clear to him that he needs to find a new person because it's time for you to move on to other endeavors, which I understand breaks your heart. You will find much joy and satisfaction in the future that your soul will create for you.*

I wish I could believe that, but . . . *it's very important for you to believe, as well as Stormy. What you need to believe in, is that the future that is ahead for you will be one of joy and happiness. You have so much to share that the animals have taught you and you have learned yourself. It's imperative that you do this at this time. You need to believe in your heart that you will have a happy, joyful, satisfying future. Stormy isn't the only one who needs to believe.* I'm trying to believe that, but it's hard when you don't know what your future holds. The one thing that has always brought me joy is no longer going to be a part of my life. It's just *very* hard. (emotional) *I see you're getting emotional. Follow me. We'll find a healing for your horse.* Walking through the woods – it reminds me of . . . What's your name? *Merlin.* I smile. I've been here before. *Yes.* When Merlin channeled through my friend, Gregory, he told me that the person I met on my journey was actually his apprentice. Are you Merlin's apprentice as well? *Yes, there are several of us.*

I'm very encouraged because the other healing from Merlin, years ago, was very powerful and beneficial – as have all the healings that I've been gifted in "non-ordinary" reality. Going over to a small spring. He has a pottery vessel that he's collecting some of the water in. *This is extremely high vibrational healing liquid. It has just become liquid as it reaches the surface of the spring. It is very energetic liquid. It will be used as the basis of the solution, which will be extremely powerful, that you will bring back and apply through your heart to your horse. Carry this vessel.*

Next he's taking bark from a tree, just a little bit. He's putting that in another container. I'm thanking the tree for its offering. Walking through the forest. He's taking leaves from a fern-type plant – a low-growing fern that I've not seen before. It's very lacey and beautiful and *vibrant* green. *The color is so vibrant because it too has just come into solid form. The energy behind it is vibrationally rapid. This entire area is just on the touch of having become solid – right on the veil between energy and form. It's the place of highest healing which is what happened when you walked through the cabin door. You entered a realm where things just begin to take form. It is an incredibly powerful area.*

He's putting the fern in with the bark, and we're continuing back towards where we came from. He's finding some type of earth, but it's very light. It's rich in color but light in weight. It's *very* fluffy. *Again, it's because it's just transformed from energy to solid. It is matter at its purest form.* He's putting it in the container with the solids. I'm still carrying the vessel with the liquid.

Now we're back out in the area where the streams and creeks and waterfalls are. Just beautiful wildflowers everywhere. He's beginning to pick an assortment of wildflowers. They're flowers I don't recognize. There not the usual ones I'm aware of. *These are flowers that can't exist in the earth-realm, because the vibration of the flowers is too high. They can be in physical form here, but they can't survive outside the cabin doors, so to speak.* He's picking about six different ones.

Now we're heading to an area that's actually sort of a cave-type area. There are a lot of utensils inside and some very unique-looking instruments that I don't recognize at all. Unusual kinds of apparatus, tools unlike anything I've ever seen. *These are not of the earth-realm either, which is why you've never seen them.* He's using some of the tools to manipulate the bark and the soil and the flowers and the fern. He's combining them using . . . this is very high-tech. He's not macerating them in a mortar and pestle. He's using more like an electronic-type of instrument. *It's not electronic. It's crystalline in nature – the technology behind it. You've worked with this before in other dimensions.* I'm just not recognizing it, but.

He's joining all of these structures together using the crystal apparatus. *I need the vessel with the liquid.* He's pouring the liquid in and making kind of a syrupy solution. The more he uses the crystalline instrument, the thicker the stuff is getting. He needs more of the solution, because he doesn't want it that thick. He's got the consistency he wants. He's bringing it to another instrument. The entire container is sitting inside of it, and it's being illuminated or something. I don't want to say irradiated because that's not the right term. *It needs to remain in here for a little while.*

While we wait he tells me, *I'm so glad that you didn't give up on coming for healing. The key is helping your horse understand that you have a future ahead of you without him, and that you want to give him the best future that you can. I feel this is the key, but if your horse chooses not to accept this healing, you need to accept it as well.* That's going to be *very* hard for me to do, but I don't believe there's any more I can do to help Stormy.

No. This area we're in is the area of highest healing potential, which is why you were brought through the cabin and into this area. Healing from this area is not used on the earth plane often. It's incredibly powerful. You must be careful when you're applying it because of the strength of it. I know you have the ability and the experience in working with these energies – which is why they've allowed you to seek this for your horse.

He's taking the container out from this second instrument. It's almost like it's energized it. *That's exactly what it's done. It allowed the molecular structures of all the different ingredients to meld together so that when you apply it to your horse his body will be able to accept it and utilize it properly. If I hadn't used this instrument it would have been too strong. It could have hurt his tissues. It has been adjusted so that it can be used in the earth-realm.*

I'm thanking him so much for allowing me to come here and to obtain this type of potent healing for Stormy. I promise that I will look towards my future without horses with an open mind, allowing my soul to create joy and happiness in an area that I'm unfamiliar with. *That is the key. You must keep an open heart and an open mind and allow your soul to bring to you that which will bring you joy and happiness and to believe that you will have much of that.*

Merlin embraces me and the energy he's flowing into me is remarkable. I feel like all the resistance that I've had towards everything surrounding the horse for the past eight months is just melting. He looks me directly in the eye. *Believe in yourself. Believe in Stormy. Believe in the work you have to do for humanity.* I do, and I will. I thank you so much. *Bring this extraordinary healing back to your horse and know that rarely, rarely is this gift given. Hold it in your heart with great reverence* – and I add, with great gratitude – *and apply it to your horse, along with the belief in your future and the belief in Stormy's future that you want to give him.*

Heading out the cabin door. The two little kids are waiting on the porch for me. Just laughing and giggling. Why are you so happy? What are you laughing about? *We don't get many to come here. Entry into the cabin is very guarded, but those that enter and come out always seem changed – changed for the better and the positive. We're always happy and excited when we hear we need to bring someone to the cabin. We're so glad you came today!*

We're heading back down the path. I look around to take one more look at the cabin, but it's disappeared! All I see is woods behind me. I look at the little kids and they just giggle and laugh as they drag me towards the lake. Thanking them for helping me today. I'm going to bring this healing, this extraordinary gift that I feel so privileged to have been given, back down through the lake, which is just wonderfully refreshing. I feel my heart filled with this healing. Bringing it back through the lake, the waterslide, and the pond in the back of my old farm. Now I'm back. Feeling filled to the brim with energies. My entire body is alive with them. Fingers are tingling. Everything is *tingling!*

Heading over to the barn to offer this *exceptional* gift to Stormy and hope that he will accept it and allow his body to be healed fully of all the symptoms of Shivers. This will allow him to have no limitation or restriction in his body whatsoever, so he can once again jump and do the thing that brings him the most joy. Even though I can't do it with him, I accept that. And I fully embrace the fact that it's time for him to find a new person and for me to focus on my future – what I've been preparing to do for the first 60 years of my life. I believe it will bring me great joy and happiness and satisfaction and love.

I applied the healing from Merlin to Stormy – along with reiterating that no matter what, our time together was coming to a close, as sad as that made me. I'd been given notice by the Universe that my time was to be devoted to things other than horses. The time had arrived for me to share the knowledge I'd acquired from communicating and healing animals for nearly 20 years.

I arrived to work Stormy the next day with some trepidation. Did Stormy listen to what I had to say? Did he accept the potent healing from Merlin's hand? What would he chose to do? You can imagine my joy – yes *joy* – when I noticed a significant change in Stormy's hind legs when cross-tied. It wasn't totally normal, but vastly improved.

About a week before I met Merlin in the woods of the Lower-world, I had a semi-dangerous ride in the arena due to a flapping blue tarp that a group (that comes each year) had put in the arena. As long as the tarp lay still, Stormy was fine. The minute the breezes turned it into something that appeared alive, it became a threat and Stormy freaked. We worked through his anxiety, but not mine. I was *so* angry that we had no one to speak up for us boarders, now that Collette had left.

That same day, I had arranged for the young man who runs the Ranch to come to the local barn and float (file) Stormy's teeth. When he arrived, I was still fuming. He asked how I was. I said, "I'd be a lot better if you'd fence a small pasture for Stormy. Things have just gotten intolerable here!"

He floated Stormy's teeth while I vented. As he was leaving, he said, "Give me a call, and we'll talk."

I called that night and went to the Ranch a few days later to discuss my possible return with Stormy. The peaceful feeling at the Ranch was in stark contrast to the sense of angst that permeated the local barn. I was beginning to hate to go to the barn – worrying about what new issue I'd find waiting for me. We discussed several of the things that had prompted me to leave the Ranch in December. Being assured that they would be corrected, I decided to move back. Due to the higher temperatures at the Ranch's location, I opted to wait 'til Stormy would be moved from the main barn for the horse show three weeks later.

I continued to train and trail-ride Stormy. Since I couldn't jump any more, I wouldn't be able to assess his jumping future. I'd been preparing to work on flying lead changes, which we'd had some issues with last summer. When a horse canters, the legs on the same side move together, which is unlike when they trot. When trotting, the horse's *diagonal* legs move together. The correct lead is when the legs on the inside reach further forward than the outside legs, which results in the horse being and feeling balanced.

Horses can change leads while cantering, which is what is termed a flying lead change. It takes training and practice, so that the horse will perform the lead change on command. The timing is crucial. My amateur jumper, Jolly Man, really disliked flying changes, so we didn't work on them. Because of this, I never became proficient. Stormy needed to learn lead changes, so we persevered. During the previous summer, sometimes he'd change in front but not behind. His left-to-right change was much easier for him than his right-to-left. My plan for asking for changes just happened to coincide with this last healing journey for Storm.

The first day I set up to ask for flying changes over a pole on the ground (the step-over encourages the horse), I was astonished at the ease with which Stormy accomplished them. I asked for a left-to-right change first – his easier one. He gave it to me as slick as could be. We continued cantering, and I asked for a right-to-left change – yea, another smooth change. There was no need to ask for any more for our first day. I was so pleased and encouraged.

Knowing that I was leaving soon, I trail-rode with my gal pals more often than usual. It was a week between flying-lead-change sessions. Once again, I got two lead changes smoother and easier than *ever* before. This was a sign that Merlin's healing was having a tremendous effect. The miracle I'd been dreaming of looked to be in the works. Of course, the proof would come when Stormy returned to jumping, which depended on Collette's availability in South Carolina.

I moved Stormy to the Ranch amidst horse show preparation chaos. Due to the limited turn-out at the local barn, Stormy's time in his new two-acre pasture was restricted for the first week to prevent him from developing colic. Stormy has the appetite of a Labrador. He *never* picks his head up if there's grass underneath him. After regulating his time out, he's now in his two acres of wonderful grass overnight, and in his stall with his fan and dutch-door windows on three of four walls. Hana and Saba are thrilled to be back at the Ranch and spend most of their time running all over, especially through the creeks.

Whether Stormy ever jumps again, I still have to find a new person for him. I will wail for sure when the time comes for us to part, but I will only hand him over to someone I'm totally comfortable with. For now, we'll continue to train in the arena at the Ranch and ride the gorgeous trails woven through the 6,000-acre property. I trust that the Universe will present the perfect solution to Stormy's and my problem of a new home for him. I also have to trust that my soul will assist me in adjusting to my new life without horses. I've been riding for 52 years and have had a horse for 47 years. I simply can't imagine life without one, but I have to *trust* that all will be in *perfection!*

Chapter 46

∞

Gifts from the Universe

I began this book six months ago. Condensing years of experiences with my animals into these pages generated so much gratitude in me. I'm amazed how privileged I've been to share my life with these most generous Master Teachers. I have been truly blessed. Had Because Of Love not entered my life, I would have missed out on a truly amazing 18 years.

Obviously, there were many portions that were very difficult for me to retell to you, but the lessons cried out to be shared. Working through one's grief is always a healthy process, no matter how long after the event that created it. Just as with my first book, *Letting Go*, I have learned, grown, healed, and been transformed by writing about these remarkable creatures. I would *not* be the woman I am today – nor would I be doing the work that I do today – without having been taught by each of these special souls. The experiences we've shared have been invaluable to my life.

I would like to offer you a gift from the Universe that arrived during a session with Gregory two days before the second journey for healing for Stormy. I scheduled a session in order to get some guidance about the circumstances that were surrounding Stormy and my impending loss of riding. For the first time, I was *not* given an opportunity to ask questions. I was given the gift of *two* processes that proved to be far more significant than any answers I might have received.

The first, and longer, exercise came from Archangel Michael. He felt that it would be appropriate for me to share his process if I wanted.

The second exercise came from Master Teacher Spirit. I have worked often with both of these beings and am grateful for all the assistance I've received from them over the years.

Both exercises are centered on the energies that are at play on Earth at this time – those of releasing old patterns and embracing new patterns. The ease with which we accomplish this dictates our life experiences. Obviously, I've been *extremely* challenged by these energies. I've been ensconced in this dynamic since I moved from Fair Chance Farm seven years ago. I've found these two exercises to be very beneficial, which is why I feel compelled to share them with you. It is my hope that they will help you find your way more graciously through the maze of life. These are intended as a guided meditation, so I've created a CD of both processes to guarantee optimum results. It is available for purchase on my Website.

Allow yourself to breathe . . . imagine two doorways, and they are side-by-side. There is one dividing wall in between the two doorways on the other side of the wall. In other words, you can't see that wall, but you know it's there. One doorway goes into one room, and the second doorway into the other. Let's imagine that you're going to go into the doorway on the right and that's going to represent the old energies. These are the energies of the Earth for hundreds of thousands of years. These are tightly ingrained into thought patterns, into people's minds, into their emotional structure. And these old patterns, old energy patterns, they are causing some of this havoc.

Now having entered into that room, it feels comfortable. It feels like the Earth. It feels like the way it used to feel, but you can almost see through the wall, because it's practically transparent. And as you're looking around you, you are seeing what appears to be truth, but of course it isn't. And as you look through this almost transparent wall into the new patterns, you are seeing less and less stinginess. You are seeing greater and greater prosperity. You are seeing movement forward. You are seeing innovation, not only in terms of technology, but also in terms of systems. You are seeing things change. You are seeing a new paradigm as you describe it.

You are seeing history made.

You are seeing old forces, old structures, literally falling and allowing space for new structures, new patterns of behavior, new ways of being, new ways of doing business, new ways of doing education and government and healing, less restriction, less governmental regulation and interference, and – to put it bluntly, freedom – freedom on the part of people who have perhaps lost that feeling of freedom. Some have lost the benefit of freedom and that freedom is returning. This freedom that we speak of is a freedom of choice. It is a freedom to move forward or go backward. It is, of course, the freedom to move side to side if that is what you want to do. A lateral move, as they say, which in essence does not represent any progress at all.

So now let us imagine that – even though it is comfortable in the old room – you are going to actually exit out of the doorway back into the hall and make a bit of a U-turn, if you will, and go into the new room. In the new room it is very quiet and, oddly enough, somewhat dark. But that is only because you have not yet opened your eyes. As you open your eyes, it becomes brighter and brighter. As you open your eyes, it is almost as if you are a newborn baby opening its eyes for the first time and seeing everything around you as if it were absolutely brand new. And breathe . . .

There are flowers in beautiful vases. There are no stuck energy patterns. In other words, Nature and Mother Nature are absolutely going wild, creating new plants, creating new flowers, creating new blossoms – and there is a sense of phenomenal freedom, and breathe that freedom into you. Breathe the freedom of doing what you wish. Whether it's allowing yourself to swim, giving yourself permission to walk through the woods, or the mountains. Allowing yourself to breathe . . . giving yourself permission to connect with all of the creatures who are willing to come and share their knowledge, their knowingness, their intuition with you. And notice a great number of them waiting patiently.

And breathe . . . continue to breathe . . . imagine now that anything that is about one minute old lifting out of this scenario, becoming completely external. And breathe . . . and breathe once more. Breathe this fresh air, almost like a spring meadow into your nostrils and imagine a sort of outlet in the back of your head. As you breathe in to the center, you are breathing out all that holds you back, all that keeps you stuck. Breathe . . . breathe . . . breathe . . . breathe . . . you already know how to release the old. It is a matter of not feeling remorse. It is a matter of letting go of regret. It is a matter of not looking back. It is a matter of complete and unconditional surrender! And breathe . . .

I do not look back into my life and see what I could not, or cannot do. I do not look back in my life and see what could have been, or would have been, or should have been – if I had only done this or that or the other. I start from pretty much a clean slate, having released my thoughts, having released my feelings, and riding into my future.

As you look forward into the future, give yourself permission to widen the scope of opportunities. To stretch into the future and to allow yourself to see all the best. And breathe . . . And allow yourself to open . . . opening to greater possibilities, opening to greater probabilities, allowing yourself to release and to let go! (Breathing . . .) *Ready, prepared, capable, and willing. Ready, prepared, capable, and willing.* I am ready! I am capable and willing!

Breathe . . . see first the changes in your physical body – feeling more youthful, younger. Allow yourself to breathe . . . all of the old out of you, and all of the new into you. (Breathing . . .) *and now all of the material world around you changes completely. All that you have known reverts to ownership of another. And breathe . . . and now begin to see in the old room all of the patterns dispelled, everything unraveling, vaporizing. And breathe . . . with all of these patterns unraveled, as they disappear, what is left is space. And discover, find within you, a greater inner central peace. All is falling into place. Your own structure is shifting and changing. It is falling into place. Much more calm.*

(Breathing . . . breathing . . . breathing . . . breathing . . .

breathing . . . breathing) *And breathe finally, and exit the doorway from the future.*

The next process was offered by Master Teacher Spirit – a conglomerate of entities.

Allow yourself to breathe, and see all that you are involved in now – all the projects, circumstances, localities, all of those things. Imagine that you are literally throwing them over a kind of cliff, and you can't see the bottom of the cliff. You can't even see halfway down the ravine. It is all out of sight, so to speak. Breathe . . . Imagine that you have allowed yourself to throw them over the cliff one at a time – one situation at a time.

You cannot begin to imagine how optimistically they can turn out 'til things begin to happen. Each item unfinished or undone is thrown over this cliff and waiting down at the bottom – conflict resolution. Just let all of the pressure go, let all of that which no longer serves you go. Imagine everything rolling off and away. There is a solution to all of this, and it is indeed waiting at the bottom where you cannot see it. And these solutions will be made available to you in their time. We shall take our leave.

When I listened to the recording of these exercises in order to include them here, I found an even greater sense of reduced anxiety regarding the circumstances surrounding Stormy. The physical situation with Stormy hasn't changed. What has changed is that I have surrendered more to the future I'm heading towards, of a life without horses. My faith in a suitable resolution has been renewed – despite not having a clue as to what that might be. I can only hope that you will find assistance with your life challenges from both of these gifts from the Universe that are offered here.

My hope for this book is that its characters and their tales will cause you to view your own animals with new eyes and with a new perspective about their significance to your life. Remember, they've answered your soul's cries for help. So why not let them help? They have so much to share and to teach you.

I have been blessed to lend my voice to hundreds of special animals over the years. They've taught me much in return, which is why there will be another book, *Tales of an Animal Communicator ~ Being A Clear Voice*, dedicated to the lessons of my clients' animals. I *trust* it will be created in its perfect timing. I will end with an American Indian saying that is dear to my heart.

Mitakuye oyasin – we are all related!

∞

Appendix

A portion of the proceeds to be donated to:

Watauga Humane Society ~ www.wataugahumanesociety.org
Noah's Wish ~ www.noahswish.org
The Wild Horse Sanctuary ~ www.wildhorsesanctuary.org

Also by this author:
*Letting Go: An Ordinary Woman's Extraordinary Journey of
Healing & Transformation*

Feel free to ask questions, offer comments, and/or share stories
concerning *Master Teachers*. Nancy can be contacted at
nancy@nancykaiseranimalcommunicator.com.

To learn more about Nancy and her services at
"Just Ask" Communications, please visit her Website at
www.NancyKaiserAnimalCommunicator.com.

Keep checking Nancy's Website for updates regarding
Tales of an Animal Communicator ~ Being a Clear Voice

Front cover

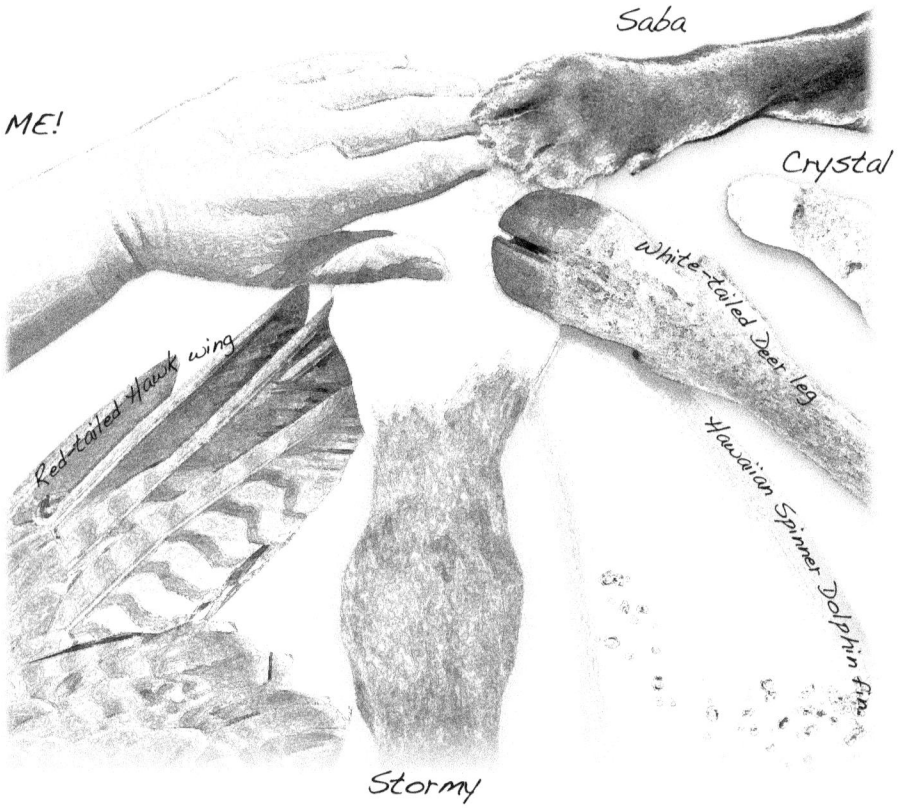

ME!

Saba

Crystal

Red-tailed Hawk wing

White-tailed Deer leg

Hawaiian Spinner Dolphin fin

Stormy

Back cover

Shadow & Licorice

Hana, Saba, & Crystal

Because Of Love

Squiggles & Dash

Stormy & Me